KOREA

NORTH

EXPORT-IMPORT, TRADE AND BUSINESS DIRECTORY

VOLUME 1
STRATEGIC INFORMATION AND CONTACTS

International Business Publications, USA
Washington DC, USA –Korea North

KOREA NORTH
EXPORT-IMPORT, TRADE AND BUSINESS DIRECTORY
VOLUME 1 STRATEGIC INFORMATION AND CONTACTS

UPDATED ANNUALLY

We express our sincere appreciation to all government agencies and international organizations which provided information and other materials for this directory

Cover Design: **International Business Publications, USA**

2016 Edition Updated Reprint International Business Publications, USA
ISBN 1-4330-2783-6

For customer service and information, please contact:
in the USA: **International Business Publications, USA**
      P.O.Box 15343, Washington, DC 20003
      Phone: (202) 546-2103, Fax: (202) 546-3275.
      E-mail: rusric@erols.com

Printed in the USA

cal, business and investment opportunities information,
ct Global Investment & Business Center, USA
3. Fax: (202) 546-3275. E-mail: rusric@erols.com

KOREA
NORTH

EXPORT-IMPORT, TRADE AND BUSINESS DIRECTORY
VOLUME 1
STRATEGIC INFORMATION AND CONTACTS

TABLE OF CONTENTS

**For additional analytical, business and investment opportunities information,
please contact Global Investment & Business Center, USA
at (202) 546-2103. Fax: (202) 546-3275. E-mail: rusric@erols.com**

**For additional analytical, business and investment opportunities information,
please contact Global Investment & Business Center, USA
at (202) 546-2103. Fax: (202) 546-3275. E-mail: rusric@erols.com**

For additional analytical, business and investment opportunities information,
please contact Global Investment & Business Center, USA
at (202) 546-2103. Fax: (202) 546-3275. E-mail: rusric@erols.com

**For additional analytical, business and investment opportunities information,
please contact Global Investment & Business Center, USA
at (202) 546-2103. Fax: (202) 546-3275. E-mail: rusric@erols.com**

**For additional analytical, business and investment opportunities information,
please contact Global Investment & Business Center, USA
at (202) 546-2103. Fax: (202) 546-3275. E-mail: rusric@erols.com**

**For additional analytical, business and investment opportunities information,
please contact Global Investment & Business Center, USA
at (202) 546-2103. Fax: (202) 546-3275. E-mail: rusric@erols.com**

- 10 -

STRATEGIC, BUSINESS AND DEVELOPMENT PROFILES

Capital (and largest city)	Pyongyang 39°2′N 125°45′E39.033°N 125.75°E
Official language(s)	Korean
Official scripts	Chosŏn'gŭl
Ethnic groups	Korean (100%)
Demonym	North Korean, Korean
Government	Juche unitary single-party state
- Eternal President	Kim Il-sung (deceased)
- Supreme Leader	**Kim Jong-un**
- NDC Chairman	**Kim Jong-un**
- Chairman of the Presidium	Kim Yong-nam
- Premier	Choe Yong-rim
Legislature	Supreme People's Assembly
Establishment	
- Independence declared	March 1, 1919
- Liberation	August 15, 1945
- Formal declaration	September 9, 1948
Area	
- Total	120,540 km^2 (98th) 46,528 sq mi
- Water (%)	4.87
Population	
- 2009 estimate	24,051,218 (51st)
- 2008 census	24,052,231
- Density	198.3/km^2 (55th) 513.8/sq mi
GDP (PPP)	2008 estimate
- Total	$40 billion (94th)
- Per capita	$1,900 (2009 est.) (154th)
GDP (nominal)	estimate
- Total	$28.2 billion (88th)
- Per capita	$1,244 (139th)
Gini (2009)	N/A (low)
Currency	North Korean won (KPW)
Time zone	Korea Standard Time (UTC+9)
Drives on the	right
ISO 3166 code	KP
Internet TLD	.kp
Calling code	850

For additional analytical, business and investment opportunities information,
please contact Global Investment & Business Center, USA
at (202) 546-2103. Fax: (202) 546-3275. E-mail: rusric@erols.com

BASIC INFORMATION

North Korea, officially the **Democratic People's Republic of Korea**, is an East Asian country occupying the northern half of the Korean Peninsula. Its government defines itself as a Communist-led democratic multi-party state of the Juche political ideology, although in practice, it is believed to function as a dictatorship. North Korea is often referred to by global media sources as a Stalinist, isolationist, and authoritarian country; it uses repressive central planning to implement its economic and social policies. Its ideological stance on issues such as the mass line, the role of intellectuals, and the source of revolutionary fervor mark North Korea's government as different from the Leninist Soviet Union or Maoist China.

North Korea has been characterized by a professor at the American Strategic Studies Institute as: "Highly repressive, heavily militarized, strongly resistant to reform, and ruled by a dynastic dictatorship that adheres to a hybrid ideology, North Korea might be 'the strangest political system in existence.' While distinctive, North Korea is an orthodox communist party-state best classified as an eroding totalitarian regime."

Its northern border is predominantly shared with the People's Republic of China. Russia shares an 18.3 kilometre (11.4 mi) border along the Tumen River in the far northeast corner of the country. To the south, it is bordered by South Korea, with which it formed a single territorial unit known as Korea until 1945.

At the end of World War II, the US and the Soviet Union agreed that US troops would accept the surrender of Japanese forces south of the 38th parallel and the Soviet Union would do so in the north. In 1948, the UN proposed nationwide elections; after P'yongyang's refusal to allow UN inspectors in the north, elections were held in the south and the Republic of Korea was established. The Democratic People's Republic of Korea was established the following month in the north. Communist North Korean forces invaded South Korea in 1950. US and other UN forces intervened to defend the South and Chinese forces intervened on behalf of the North. After a bitter three-year war, an armistice was signed in 1953, establishing a military demarcation line near the 38th parallel. The North's heavy investment in military forces has produced an army of 1 million troops equipped with thousands of tanks and artillery pieces. Despite growing economic hardships, North Korea continues to devote a significant portion of its scarce resources to the military.

GEOGRAPHY

Location: Eastern Asia, northern half of the Korean Peninsula bordering the Korea Bay and the Sea of Japan, between China and South Korea

Geographic coordinates: 40 00 N, 127 00 E

Map references: Asia

Area:
total: 120,540 sq km

land: 120,410 sq km
water: 130 sq km

Area—comparative: slightly smaller than Mississippi

Land boundaries:
total: 1,673 km
border countries: China 1,416 km, South Korea 238 km, Russia 19 km

Korean Peninsula

China

Siping
Huadian
Tumen
Vladivostok
Russia
Nakhodka
Musan
Khasan
Najin
Badaojiang
Ch'ongjin
Shenyang
Tonghua
Ji'an
Manp'o
Hyesan
Anshan
Kanggye
Kimch'aek
Dandong
Sinuiju
Kusong
North
Yongbyon
Hamhung
Sojoson-man
Tongjoson-man
Korea
Wonsan
Sea of
Japan
P'YONGYANG
Korea
Bay
Namp'o
Sariwon
P'yonggang
Demarcation
Line
Changyon
Ch'orwon
Haeju
Paengnyong-do
Kaesong
Munsan
Ch'unch'on
Kangnung
Sunwi-do
Ongjin
Ullung-do
Kyonggi-man
Inch'on
SEOUL
Wonju
South
China
Suwon
Ch'onan
Korea
Ch'ongju
Taejon
Andong
P'ohang
Yellow
Sea
Kunsan
Chonju
Taegu
Ulsan
Kwangju
Masan
Pusan
Mokp'o
Koje-do
Japan
Hiroshima
Yosu
Tsushima
Chin-do
Korea
Cheju-haehyop
Fukuoka
Kitakyushu
Cheju
Sasebo
Cheju-do

Hun He
Liao He
Huifa He
Erdao
Yalu Jiang
Yalu
Sup'ung-ho
Taedong-gang
Imjin-gang
Han-gang
Kum-gang
Naktong-gang
Tumen
Korea Strait

0   50   100 Kilometers
0   50   100 Miles
Lambert Conformal Conic Projection SP 23N/45N

Boundary representation is
not necessarily authoritative.

125   130

802191 (R00141) 7-93

For additional analytical, business and investment opportunities information,
please contact Global Investment & Business Center, USA
at (202) 546-2103. Fax: (202) 546-3275. E-mail: rusric@erols.com

The Korean Peninsula
Demilitarized Zone Area

Coastline: 2,495 km

For additional analytical, business and investment opportunities information,
please contact Global Investment & Business Center, USA
at (202) 546-2103. Fax: (202) 546-3275. E-mail: rusric@erols.com

Maritime claims:
territorial sea: 12 nm
exclusive economic zone: 200 nm
note: military boundary line 50 nm in the Sea of Japan and the exclusive economic zone limit in the Yellow Sea where all foreign vessels and aircraft without permission are banned

Climate: temperate with rainfall concentrated in summer

Terrain: mostly hills and mountains separated by deep, narrow valleys; coastal plains wide in west, discontinuous in east

Elevation extremes:
lowest point: Sea of Japan 0 m
highest point: Paektu-san 2,744 m

Natural resources: coal, lead, tungsten, zinc, graphite, magnesite, iron ore, copper, gold, pyrites, salt, fluorspar, hydropower

Land use:
arable land: 14%
permanent crops: 2%
permanent pastures: 0%
forests and woodland: 61%
other: 23%

Irrigated land: 14,600 sq km

Natural hazards: late spring droughts often followed by severe flooding; occasional typhoons during the early fall

Environment—current issues: localized air pollution attributable to inadequate industrial controls; water pollution; inadequate supplies of potable water

Environment—international agreements:
party to: Antarctic Treaty, Biodiversity, Climate Change, Environmental Modification, Ozone Layer Protection, Ship Pollution
signed, but not ratified: Antarctic-Environmental Protocol, Law of the Sea

Geography—note: strategic location bordering China, South Korea, and Russia; mountainous interior is isolated, nearly inaccessible, and sparsely populated

PEOPLE

Population: 21,386,109

Age structure:
0-14 years: 26% (male 2,800,748; female 2,666,207)

15-64 years: 68% (male 7,143,969; female 7,447,147)
65 years and over: 6% (male 412,161; female 915,877)

Population growth rate: 1.45%

Birth rate: 21.37 births/1,000 population

Death rate: 6.92 deaths/1,000 population

Net migration rate: 0 migrant(s)/1,000 population

Sex ratio:
at birth: 1.05 male(s)/female
under 15 years: 1.05 male(s)/female
15-64 years: 0.96 male(s)/female
65 years and over: 0.45 male(s)/female
total population: 0.94 male(s)/female

Infant mortality rate: 25.52 deaths/1,000 live births

Life expectancy at birth:
total population: 70.07 years
male: 67.41 years
female: 72.86 years

Total fertility rate: 2.3 children born/woman

Nationality:
noun: Korean(s)
adjective: Korean

Ethnic groups: racially homogeneous; there is a small Chinese community and a few ethnic Japanese

Religions: Buddhism and Confucianism, some Christianity and syncretic Chondogyo
note: autonomous religious activities now almost nonexistent; government-sponsored religious groups exist to provide illusion of religious freedom

Languages: Korean

Literacy:
definition: age 15 and over can read and write Korean
total population: 99%
male: 99%
female: 99%

GOVERNMENT

For additional analytical, business and investment opportunities information,
please contact Global Investment & Business Center, USA
at (202) 546-2103. Fax: (202) 546-3275. E-mail: rusric@erols.com

Country name:

conventional long form: Democratic People's Republic of Korea
conventional short form: North Korea
local long form: Choson-minjujuui-inmin-konghwaguk
local short form: Choson
abbreviation: DPRK

Government type:

Communist state one-man dictatorship

Capital:

name: Pyongyang
geographic coordinates: 39 01 N, 125 45 E
time difference: UTC+9 (14 hours ahead of Washington, DC, during Standard Time)

Administrative divisions:

9 provinces (do, singular and plural) and 2 municipalities (si, singular and plural)
provinces: Chagang-do (Chagang), Hamgyong-bukto (North Hamgyong), Hamgyong-namdo (South Hamgyong), Hwanghae-bukto (North Hwanghae), Hwanghae-namdo (South Hwanghae), Kangwon-do (Kangwon), P'yongan-bukto (North P'yongan), P'yongan-namdo (South P'yongan), Yanggang-do (Yanggang)
municipalities: Nason-si, P'yongyang-si (Pyongyang)

Independence:

15 August 1945 (from Japan)

National holiday:

Founding of the Democratic People's Republic of Korea (DPRK), 9 September (1948)

Constitution:

previous 1948, 1972 (revised several times); latest adopted 1998 (during KIM Jong Il era); revised 2009, 2012 (2012)

Legal system:

civil law system based on the Prussian model; system influenced by Japanese traditions and Communist legal theory

International law organization participation:

has not submitted an ICJ jurisdiction declaration; non-party state to the ICCt

For additional analytical, business and investment opportunities information,
please contact Global Investment & Business Center, USA
at (202) 546-2103. Fax: (202) 546-3275. E-mail: rusric@erols.com

Suffrage:

17 years of age; universal

Executive branch:

chief of state: KIM Jong Un (since 17 December 2011); note - in 2014, the rubberstamp Supreme People's Assembly (SPA) re-elected KIM Yong Nam president of its Presidium with responsibility of representing the state and receiving diplomatic credentials
head of government: Premier PAK Pong Ju (since 2 April 2013); Vice Premiers: KIM Tok Hun (since 30 April 2014), KIM Yong Jin (since 6 January 2012), RI Chol Man (since 13 April 2012), RI Mu Yong (since 31 May 2011), RO Tu Chol (since 3 September 2003)
cabinet: Naegak (cabinet) members, except for the Minister of People's Armed Forces, are appointed by SPA
elections: last election on 9 March 2014; date of next election NA
election results: KIM Jong Un elected unopposed
note: the Korean Workers' Party continues to list deceased leaders KIM Il Sung and KIM Jong Il as Eternal President and Eternal General Secretary respectively

Legislative branch:

unicameral Supreme People's Assembly or Ch'oego Inmin Hoeui (687 seats; members elected by popular vote to serve five-year terms)
elections: last held on 9 March 2014 (next to be held in March 2019)
election results: percent of vote by party - NA; seats by party - NA; ruling party approves a list of candidates who are elected without opposition; a token number of seats are reserved for minor parties

Judicial branch:

highest court(s): Supreme Court or Central Court (consists of the chief justice and two "People's Assessors" and for some cases, 3 judges)
judge selection and term of office: judges elected by the Supreme People's Assembly for 5-year terms
subordinate courts: provincial, municipal, military, special courts; people' courts (lowest level)

Political parties and leaders:

major party:
Korean Workers' Party or KWP [KIM Jong Un]
minor parties:
Chondoist Chongu Party [RYU Mi Yong] (under KWP control)
Social Democratic Party [KIM Yong Dae] (under KWP control)

Political pressure groups and leaders:

International organization participation:

ARF, FAO, G-77, ICAO, ICC (NGOs), ICRM, IFAD, IFRCS, IHO, IMO, IOC, IPU, ISO, ITSO, ITU, NAM, UN, UNCTAD, UNESCO, UNIDO, UNWTO, UPU, WFTU (NGOs), WHO, WIPO, WMO

Diplomatic representation in the US:

none; North Korea has a Permanent Mission to the UN in New York

Diplomatic representation from the US:

none; note - Swedish Embassy in Pyongyang represents the US as consular protecting power

Flag description:

three horizontal bands of blue (top), red (triple width), and blue; the red band is edged in white; on the hoist side of the red band is a white disk with a red five-pointed star; the broad red band symbolizes revolutionary traditions; the narrow white bands stands for purity, strength, and dignity; the blue bands signify sovereignty, peace, and friendship; the red star represents socialism

National symbol(s):

red star

National anthem:

name: "Aegukka" (Patriotic Song)
lyrics/music: PAK Se Yong/KIM Won Gyun
note: adopted 1947; both North Korea and South Korea's anthems share the same name and have a vaguely similar melody but have different lyrics; the North Korean anthem is also known as "Ach'imun pinnara" (Let Morning Shine)

ECONOMY

North Korea, one of the world's most centrally directed and least open economies, faces chronic economic problems. Industrial capital stock is nearly beyond repair as a result of years of underinvestment, shortages of spare parts, and poor maintenance. Large-scale military spending draws off resources needed for investment and civilian consumption. Industrial and power output have stagnated for years at a fraction of pre-1990 levels. Frequent weather-related crop failures aggravated chronic food shortages caused by on-going systemic problems, including a lack of arable land, collective farming practices, poor soil quality, insufficient fertilization, and persistent shortages of tractors and fuel. Large-scale international food aid deliveries have allowed the people of North Korea to escape widespread starvation since famine threatened in 1995, but the population continues to suffer from prolonged malnutrition and poor living conditions. Since 2002, the government has allowed private "farmers' markets" to begin selling a wider range of goods. It also permitted some private farming - on an experimental basis - in an effort to boost agricultural output. In December 2009, North Korea carried out a redenomination of its currency, capping the amount of North Korean won that could be exchanged for the new notes, and limiting the exchange to a one-week window.

A concurrent crackdown on markets and foreign currency use yielded severe shortages and inflation, forcing Pyongyang to ease the restrictions by February 2010. In response to the sinking of the South Korean warship Cheonan and the shelling of Yeonpyeong Island, South Korea's government cut off most aid, trade, and bilateral cooperation activities, with the exception of operations at the Kaesong Industrial Complex. In preparation for the 100th anniversary of KIM Il-sung's birthday in 2012, North Korea continued efforts to develop special economic zones with China and expressed willingness to permit construction of a trilateral gas pipeline that would carry Russian natural gas to South Korea. The North Korean government often highlights its goal of becoming a "strong and prosperous" nation and attracting foreign investment, a key factor for improving the overall standard of living. In this regard, in 2013 the regime rolled out 14 new Special Economic Zones set up for foreign investors, though the initiative remains in its infancy. Nevertheless, firm political control remains the government's overriding concern, which likely will inhibit changes to North Korea's current economic system.

GDP (purchasing power parity):

$40 billion
country comparison to the world: 106
$40 billion (2011 est.)
$40 billion (2010 est.)
note: data are in 2012 US dollars;
North Korea does not publish reliable National Income Accounts data; the data shown here are derived from purchasing power parity (PPP) GDP estimates for North Korea that were made by Angus MADDISON in a study conducted for the OECD; his figure for 1999 was extrapolated to 2011 using estimated real growth rates for North Korea's GDP and an inflation factor based on the US GDP deflator; the results were rounded to the nearest $10 billion.

GDP (official exchange rate):

$28 billion

GDP - real growth rate:

1.3%
country comparison to the world: 167
0.8% (2011 est.)
-0.5% (2010 est.)

GDP - per capita (PPP):

$1,800
country comparison to the world: 198
$1,800
$1,900 (2009 est.)
note: data are in 2011 US dollars

GDP - composition, by sector of origin:

agriculture: 23.4%
industry: 47.2%
services: 29.4%

Agriculture - products:

rice, corn, potatoes, soybeans, pulses; cattle, pigs, pork, eggs

Industries:

military products; machine building, electric power, chemicals; mining (coal, iron ore, limestone, magnesite, graphite, copper, zinc, lead, and precious metals), metallurgy; textiles, food processing; tourism

Industrial production growth rate:

0.5%
country comparison to the world: 157

Labor force:

12.6 million
country comparison to the world: 42
note: estimates vary widely

Labor force - by occupation:

agriculture: 35%
industry and services: 65% (2008 est.)

Budget:

revenues: $3.2 billion
expenditures: $3.3 billion (2007 est.)

Taxes and other revenues:

11.4% of GDP
country comparison to the world: 206
note: excludes earnings from state-operated enterprises (2007 est.)

Budget surplus (+) or deficit (-):

-0.4% of GDP
country comparison to the world: 55

For additional analytical, business and investment opportunities information,
please contact Global Investment & Business Center, USA
at (202) 546-2103. Fax: (202) 546-3275. E-mail: rusric@erols.com

Fiscal year:

calendar year

Inflation rate (consumer prices):

NA%

Exports:

$3.954 billion
country comparison to the world: 121
$3.703 billion (2011 est.)

Exports - commodities:

minerals, metallurgical products, manufactures (including armaments), textiles, agricultural and fishery products

Exports - partners:

China 63%, South Korea 27%

Imports:

$4.828 billion
country comparison to the world: 131
$4.367 billion

Imports - commodities:

petroleum, coking coal, machinery and equipment, textiles, grain

Imports - partners:

China 73%, South Korea 19%

Debt - external:

$3 billion
country comparison to the world: 137

Exchange rates:

North Korean won (KPW) per US dollar (market rate)
157
155.5
145 (2010 est.)
3,630 (December 2008)

For additional analytical, business and investment opportunities information,
please contact Global Investment & Business Center, USA
at (202) 546-2103. Fax: (202) 546-3275. E-mail: rusric@erols.com

140

ENERGY

Electricity - production:

21.04 billion kWh
country comparison to the world: 73

Electricity - consumption:

17.62 billion kWh
country comparison to the world: 73

Electricity - exports:

0 kWh
country comparison to the world: 154

Electricity - imports:

0 kWh
country comparison to the world: 162

Electricity - installed generating capacity:

9.5 million kW
country comparison to the world: 60

Electricity - from fossil fuels:

47.4% of total installed capacity
country comparison to the world: 160

Electricity - from nuclear fuels:

0% of total installed capacity
country comparison to the world: 118

Electricity - from hydroelectric plants:

52.6% of total installed capacity
country comparison to the world: 41

Electricity - from other renewable sources:

0% of total installed capacity
country comparison to the world: 187

For additional analytical, business and investment opportunities information,
please contact Global Investment & Business Center, USA
at (202) 546-2103. Fax: (202) 546-3275. E-mail: rusric@erols.com

Crude oil - production:

0 bbl/day
country comparison to the world: 183

Crude oil - exports:

0 bbl/day
country comparison to the world: 137

Crude oil - imports:

10,500 bbl/day
country comparison to the world: 77

Crude oil - proved reserves:

0 bbl
country comparison to the world: 149

Refined petroleum products - production:

6,965 bbl/day
country comparison to the world: 106

Refined petroleum products - consumption:

15,000 bbl/day
country comparison to the world: 143

Refined petroleum products - exports:

0 bbl/day
country comparison to the world: 189

Refined petroleum products - imports:

4,000 bbl/day
country comparison to the world: 162

Natural gas - production:

0 cu m
country comparison to the world: 148

Natural gas - consumption:

1 cu m
country comparison to the world: 114

For additional analytical, business and investment opportunities information,
please contact Global Investment & Business Center, USA
at (202) 546-2103. Fax: (202) 546-3275. E-mail: rusric@erols.com

Natural gas - exports:

0 cu m
country comparison to the world: 128

Natural gas - imports:

0 cu m
country comparison to the world: 212

Natural gas - proved reserves:

0 cu m
country comparison to the world: 154

Carbon dioxide emissions from consumption of energy:

65.96 million Mt

COMMUNICATIONS

Telephones - main lines in use:

1.18 million
country comparison to the world: 70

Telephones - mobile cellular:

1.7 million
country comparison to the world: 148

Telephone system:

general assessment: adequate system; nationwide fiber-optic network; mobile-cellular service expanding beyond Pyongyang
domestic: fiber-optic links installed down to the county level; telephone directories unavailable; GSM mobile-cellular service initiated in 2002 but suspended in 2004; Orascom Telecom Holding, an Egyptian company, launched W-CDMA mobile service on 15 December 2008 for the Pyongyang area, has expanded service to several large cities and now has a 1-million-person subscriber base
international: country code - 850; satellite earth stations - 2 (1 Intelsat - Indian Ocean, 1 Russian - Indian Ocean region); other international connections through Moscow and Beijing

Broadcast media:

no independent media; radios and TVs are pre-tuned to government stations; 4 government-owned TV stations; the Korean Workers' Party owns and operates the Korean Central Broadcasting Station, and the state-run Voice of Korea operates an external broadcast service; the government prohibits listening to and jams foreign broadcasts

For additional analytical, business and investment opportunities information,
please contact Global Investment & Business Center, USA
at (202) 546-2103. Fax: (202) 546-3275. E-mail: rusric@erols.com

Internet country code:

.kp

Internet hosts:

8
country comparison to the world: 226

TRANSPORTATION

Airports:

82
country comparison to the world: 67

Airports - with paved runways:

total: 39
over 3,047 m: 3
2,438 to 3,047 m: 22
1,524 to 2,437 m: 8
914 to 1,523 m: 2
under 914 m: 4

Airports - with unpaved runways:

total: 43
2,438 to 3,047 m: 3
1,524 to 2,437 m: 17
914 to 1,523 m: 15
under 914 m:
8 (2013)

Heliports:

23

Pipelines:

oil 6 km

Railways:

total: 5,242 km
country comparison to the world: 33
standard gauge: 5,242 km 1.435-m gauge (3,500 km electrified)

For additional analytical, business and investment opportunities information,
please contact Global Investment & Business Center, USA
at (202) 546-2103. Fax: (202) 546-3275. E-mail: rusric@erols.com

Roadways:

total: 25,554 km
country comparison to the world: 100
paved: 724 km
unpaved: 24,830 km

Waterways:

2,250 km (most navigable only by small craft)
country comparison to the world: 38

Merchant marine:

total: 158
country comparison to the world: 37
by type: bulk carrier 6, cargo 131, carrier 1, chemical tanker 1, container 4, passenger/cargo 1, petroleum tanker 12, refrigerated cargo 2
foreign-owned: 13 (Belgium 1, China 3, Nigeria 1, Singapore 1, South Korea 1, Syria 4, UAE 2)
registered in other countries: 6 (Mongolia 1, Sierra Leone 2, unknown 3) (2010)

Ports and terminals:

major seaport(s): Ch'ongjin, Haeju, Hungnam (Hamhung), Namp'o, Senbong, Songnim, Sonbong (formerly Unggi), Wonsan

MILITARY

Military branches:

North Korean People's Army: Ground Forces, Navy, Air Force; civil security forces

Military service age and obligation:

18 is presumed to be the legal minimum age for compulsory military service; 16-17 is the presumed legal minimum age for voluntary service

Manpower available for military service:

males age 16-49: 6,515,279
females age 16-49: 6,418,693

Manpower fit for military service:

males age 16-49: 4,836,567
females age 16-49: 5,230,137

Manpower reaching militarily significant age annually:

For additional analytical, business and investment opportunities information,
please contact Global Investment & Business Center, USA
at (202) 546-2103. Fax: (202) 546-3275. E-mail: rusric@erols.com

male: 207,737
female: 204,553

INTERNATIONAL ISSUES

Disputes - international:

risking arrest, imprisonment, and deportation, tens of thousands of North Koreans cross into China to escape famine, economic privation, and political oppression; North Korea and China dispute the sovereignty of certain islands in Yalu and Tumen rivers; Military Demarcation Line within the 4-km-wide Demilitarized Zone has separated North from South Korea since 1953; periodic incidents in the Yellow Sea with South Korea which claims the Northern Limiting Line as a maritime boundary; North Korea supports South Korea in rejecting Japan's claim to Liancourt Rocks (Tok-do/Take-shima)

Refugees and internally displaced persons:

IDPs: undetermined (periodic flooding and famine during mid-1990s)

Trafficking in persons:

current situation: North Korea is a source country for men, women, and children who are subjected to forced labor, forced marriage, and sex trafficking; in the recent past, many North Korean women and girls lured by promises of food, jobs, and freedom migrated to China illegally to escape poor social and economic conditions only to be forced into prostitution, marriage, or exploitative labor arrangements; North Koreans do not have a choice in the work the government assigns them and are not free to change jobs at will; many North Korean workers recruited to work abroad under bilateral contracts with foreign governments are subjected to forced labor and reportedly face government reprisals if they try to escape or complain to outsiders; thousands of North Koreans, including children, are subjected to forced labor in prison camps
tier rating: Tier 3 - North Korea does not fully comply with minimum standards for the elimination of trafficking and is not making significant efforts to do so; the government has conducted no known investigations, prosecutions, or convictions of trafficking offenders or officials complicit in forced labor or forced prostitution; the government also has reported no efforts to identify or assist trafficking victims and continues to deny human trafficking is a problem; authorities provide no discernible protection services to trafficking victims and does not permit NGOs to assist victims

Illicit drugs:

for years, from the 1970s into the 2000s, citizens of the Democratic People's Republic of (North) Korea (DPRK), many of them diplomatic employees of the government, were apprehended abroad while trafficking in narcotics, including two in Turkey in December 2004; police investigations in Taiwan and Japan in recent years have linked North Korea to large illicit shipments of heroin and methamphetamine, including an attempt by the North Korean merchant ship Pong Su to deliver 150 kg of heroin to Australia in April 2003

IMPORTANT INFORMATION FOR UNDERSTANDING NORTH KOREA

Official Name: Democratic People's Republic of Korea

The Democratic People's Republic of Korea shares borders in the north with China, in the east with the Sea of Japan, in the west with the Yellow Sea and in the south with the demilitarised zone (separating it from the Republic of Korea). Most of the land consists of hills and low mountains and only a small area is cultivable. Intensive water and soil conservation programmes, including land reclamation from the sea, are given high priority. The eastern coast is rocky and steep with mountains rising from the water and this area contains most of the river waterways.

PROFILE

Geography
Area: 122,762 sq. km. (47,918 sq. mi.), about the size of Mississippi.
Cities: *Capital*--Pyongyang. *Other cities*--Hamhung, Chongjin, Wonsan, Nampo, Sinjuiju, and Kaesong.
Terrain: About 80% of land area is moderately high mountains separated by deep, narrow valleys and small, cultivated plains. The remainder is lowland plains covering small, scattered areas.
Climate: Long, cold, dry winters; short, hot, humid, summers.

People*
Nationality: *Noun and adjective*--Korean(s).
Population: 25.5 million.
Annual population growth rate: About +0.42%.
Ethnic groups: Korean; small ethnic Chinese and Japanese populations.
Religions: Autonomous religious activities have been virtually nonexistent since 1945. Buddhism, Confucianism, Shamanism, Chongdogyo, and Christianity existed previously and have influenced the country.
Language: Korean.
Education: *Years compulsory*--11. *Attendance*--3 million (primary, 1.5 million; secondary, 1.2 million; tertiary, 0.3 million). *Literacy*--99%.
Health (1998): Medical treatment is free; one doctor for every 700 inhabitants; one hospital bed for every 350; there are severe shortages of medicines and medical equipment. *Infant mortality rate*--47/1,000 (2010 est., UN Population Fund--UNFPA). *Life expectancy*--males 65.5 yrs., females 69.7 yrs. (2010 est., UNFPA).

Government
Type: Highly centralized communist state.
Independence: August 15, 1945--Korean liberation from Japan; September 9, 1948--establishment of the Democratic People's Republic of Korea (D.P.R.K., or North Korea), marking its separation from the Republic of Korea (R.O.K., or South Korea).
Constitution: 1948; revised in 1972, 1992, 1998, and 2009.
Branches: *Executive*--President of the Presidium of the Supreme People's Assembly (chief of state); Chairman of the National Defense Commission (head of government).

Legislative--Supreme People's Assembly. *Judicial*--Central Court; provincial, city, county, and military courts.
Subdivisions: Nine provinces; two province-level municipalities (Pyongyang, Nasun, also known as Najin-Sonbong free trade zone); one special city (Nampo), 24 cities.
Political party: Korean Workers' Party (Communist).

Suffrage: Universal at 17.

HISTORICAL AND CULTURAL HIGHLIGHTS

The Korean Peninsula was first populated by peoples of a Tungusic branch of the Ural-Altaic language family, who migrated from the northwestern regions of Asia. Some of these peoples also populated parts of northeast China (Manchuria); Koreans and Manchurians still show physical similarities. Koreans are racially and linguistically homogeneous. Although there are no indigenous minorities in North Korea, there is a small Chinese community (about 50,000) and some 1,800 Japanese wives who accompanied the roughly 93,000 ethnic Koreans returning to the North from Japan between 1959 and 1962. Although dialects exist, the Korean language spoken throughout the peninsula is mutually comprehensible. In North Korea, the Korean alphabet (hangul) is used exclusively.

Korea's traditional religions are Buddhism and Shamanism. Christian missionaries arrived as early as the 16th century, but it was not until the 19th century that major missionary activity began. Pyongyang was a center of missionary activity, and there was a relatively large Christian population in the north before 1945. Although religious groups exist in North Korea today, the government severely restricts religious activity.

By the first century AD, the Korean Peninsula was divided into the kingdoms of Shilla, Koguryo, and Paekche. In 668 AD, the Shilla kingdom unified the peninsula. The Koryo dynasty--from which Portuguese missionaries in the 16th century derived the Western name "Korea"--succeeded the Shilla kingdom in 935. The Choson dynasty, ruled by members of the Yi clan, supplanted Koryo in 1392 and lasted until Japan annexed Korea in 1910.

Throughout its history, Korea has been invaded, influenced, and fought over by its larger neighbors. Korea was under Mongolian occupation from 1231 until the early 14th century. The unifier of Japan, Hideyoshi Toyotomi, launched major invasions of Korea in 1592 and 1597. When Western powers focused "gunboat" diplomacy on Korea in the mid-19th century, Korea's rulers adopted a closed-door policy, earning Korea the title of "Hermit Kingdom." Although the Choson dynasty recognized China's hegemony in East Asia, Korea was independent until the late 19th century. At that time, China sought to block growing Japanese influence on the Korean Peninsula and Russian pressure for commercial gains there. The competition produced the Sino-Japanese War of 1894-95 and the Russo-Japanese War of 1904-05. Japan emerged victorious from both wars and in 1910 annexed Korea as part of the growing Japanese empire. Japanese colonial administration was characterized by tight control from Tokyo and ruthless efforts to supplant Korean language and culture. Organized Korean resistance during the colonial era was generally unsuccessful, and Japan remained firmly in control of the Peninsula until the end of World War II in 1945. The surrender of Japan in August 1945 led to the

For additional analytical, business and investment opportunities information, please contact Global Investment & Business Center, USA at (202) 546-2103. Fax: (202) 546-3275. E-mail: rusric@erols.com

immediate division of Korea into two occupation zones, with the United States administering the area south of the 38th parallel, and the Soviet Union administering the area to the north of the 38th parallel. This division was meant to be temporary until the United States, United Kingdom, Soviet Union, and China could arrange a trusteeship administration.

In December 1945, a conference was convened in Moscow to discuss the future of Korea. A 5-year trusteeship was discussed, and a joint Soviet-American commission was established. The commission met intermittently in Seoul but deadlocked over the issue of establishing a national government. In September 1947, with no solution in sight, the United States submitted the Korean question to the UN General Assembly. Initial hopes for a unified, independent Korea quickly evaporated as the politics of the Cold War and domestic opposition to the trusteeship plan resulted in the 1948 establishment of two separate nations with diametrically opposed political, economic, and social systems. Elections were held in the South under UN observation, and on August 15, 1948, the Republic of Korea (R.O.K.) was established in the South. Syngman Rhee, a nationalist leader, became the Republic's first president. On September 9, 1948, the North established the Democratic People's Republic of Korea (D.P.R.K.) headed by then-Premier Kim Il-sung, who had been cultivated and supported by the Soviet Union.

Korean War of 1950-53
Almost immediately after the establishment of the D.P.R.K., guerrilla warfare, border clashes, and naval battles erupted between the two Koreas. North Korean forces launched a massive surprise attack and invaded South Korea on June 25, 1950. The United Nations, in accordance with the terms of its charter, engaged in its first collective action and established the UN Command (UNC), to which 16 member nations sent troops and assistance. Next to South Korea, the United States contributed the largest contingent of forces to this international effort. The battle line fluctuated north and south, and after large numbers of Chinese "People's Volunteers" intervened to assist the North, the battle line stabilized north of Seoul near the 38th parallel.

Armistice negotiations began in July 1951, but hostilities continued until July 27, 1953. On that date, at Panmunjom, the military commanders of the North Korean People's Army, the Chinese People's Volunteers, and the UNC signed an armistice agreement. Neither the United States nor South Korea is a signatory to the armistice per se, although both adhere to it through the UNC. No comprehensive peace agreement has replaced the 1953 armistice pact.

GOVERNMENT AND POLITICAL CONDITIONS

North Korea has a centralized government under the rigid control of the communist Korean Workers' Party (KWP), to which all government officials belong. A few minor political parties are allowed to exist in name only. Kim Il-sung ruled North Korea from 1948 until his death in July 1994 as Secretary General of the KWP and President of North Korea. The latter post was abolished following Kim Il-sung's death and the title of the Eternal President of the Republic was established and given to Kim Il-sung.

Little is known about the actual lines of power and authority in the North Korean Government despite the formal structure set forth in its constitution. Following the death of Kim Il-sung, his son, Kim Jong-il, inherited supreme power. Kim Jong-il was named General Secretary of the KWP in October 1997, and in September 1998, the Supreme People's Assembly (SPA) reconfirmed Kim Jong-il as Chairman of the National Defense Commission (NDC) and declared that position as the "highest office of state." However, the President of the Presidium of the SPA, Kim Yong-nam, serves as the nominal head of state. North Korea's 1972 constitution was amended in late 1992, September 1998, and April 2009.

Three key entities control the government of the D.P.R.K. The cabinet, formerly known as the State Administration Council (SAC), administers the ministries and has a significant role in implementing policy. The cabinet is headed by the premier and is the dominant administrative and executive agency. The NDC is responsible for external and internal security, and under the leadership of Kim Jong-il the NDC has assumed a significant role in influencing policy. The Politburo of the Central People's Committee is the top policymaking body of the KWP, which also plays a role as the dominant social institution in North Korea.

Officially, the D.P.R.K.'s legislature, the Supreme People's Assembly, is the highest organ of state power. Its members are elected every 4 years. Usually only two meetings are held annually, each lasting a few days. A standing committee elected by the SPA performs legislative functions when the Assembly is not in session. In reality, the SPA serves only to ratify decisions made by the ruling KWP.

North Korea's judiciary is "accountable" to the SPA and the president. The SPA's standing committee also appoints judges to the highest court for 4-year terms that are concurrent with those of the Assembly.

Administratively, North Korea is divided into nine provinces and two provincial-level municipalities--Pyongyang and Nasun (also known as Najin-Sonbong). It also appears to be divided into nine military districts.

Principal Party and Government Officials
Kim Jong-un--General Secretary of the KWP; Supreme Commander of the People's Armed Forces; Chairman of the NDC; son of North Korea's founder Kim Il-sung
Kim Yong-nam--President of the Presidium of the Supreme People's Assembly; titular head of state
Han Song-ryol--Ambassador to the D.P.R.K. Permanent Mission to the UN
Pak Ui-chun--Minister of Foreign Affairs
Kim Jong-un--General of the People's Armed Forces, Vice-Chairman Central Military Commission; son of Kim Jong-Il

Human Rights
Due to its isolationist nature, North Korea's human rights record is difficult to evaluate. However, non-governmental organizations (NGOs), think tanks, and defectors continue to report that North Korea maintains a record of consistent, severe human rights violations, stemming from the government's total control over all activity. Reported human rights abuses include arbitrary and lengthy imprisonment, torture and degrading treatment, poor prison conditions (including cases of starvation), forced labor, public executions, prohibitions or severe restrictions on freedom of speech, the press,

movement, assembly, religion, and privacy, denial of the right of citizens to change their government, and suppression of workers' rights. Cases of starvation have been repeatedly documented. All sources of media, such as radio, television, and news organizations, are controlled by the government and heavily censored. Correspondence is strictly monitored and Internet use is limited to the political elite. Cellular phone access is limited to an internal network; international calls are deemed illegal except for the political elite. North Korea is ranked second to last on the World Press Freedom Index.

ECONOMY

Currency	North Korean won
Fiscal year	Calendar year
Statistics	
GDP	~$40 billion
GDP rank	125th (nominal) / 96th (PPP)
GDP growth	1.1%
GDP per capita	$1,800
GDP by sector	mining and industry 36.5%, services 30.0%, agriculture and fisheries 22.4%, construction 7.8%, utilities 4.1%. (2013 est.)
Main industries	Military products, mining (coal, iron ore, limestone, magnesite, graphite, copper, zinc, lead, and precious metals), metallurgy, textiles, food processing.
External	
Exports	$4.707 billion
Export goods	Minerals, metallurgical products, manufactures (including armaments), textiles, agricultural and fishery products, coal, iron ore, limestone, graphite, copper, zinc, and lead.
Main export partners	China 63% South Korea 27%
Imports	$4.33 billion
Import goods	Petroleum, coking coal, machinery and equipment, textiles, and grain
Main import partners	China 61.6% South Korea 20.0% European Union 4.0%
Gross external debt	$3 billion
Public finances	
Revenues	$2.88 billion
Expenses	$2.98 billion

North Korea's economy is a centrally planned system, yet the role of market allocation schemes is limited. Although there have been scattered and limited attempts at decentralization, as of 2015, Pyongyang's basic adherence to a rigid centrally planned economy continues, as does its reliance on fundamentally non-pecuniary incentives. There have been reports of economic liberalisation, particularly after Kim Jong-un assumed the leadership in 2012, but recent reports conflict over what is happening.

The collapse of communist governments around the world in 1991, particularly North Korea's principal source of support, the Soviet Union, forced the North Korean economy to realign its foreign economic relations, including increased economic exchanges with South Korea.

North Korea had a similar GDP per capita to its neighbor South Korea from the aftermath of the Korean War until the mid-1970s, but with a GDP per capita of less than $2,000 in the late 1990s and early 21st century, North Korea remains as one of the world's poorest and least developed countries, in sharp contrast to South Korea, which has one of the largest and most diversified economies in the world.

Estimating gross national product in North Korea is a difficult task because of dearth of economic data and the problem of choosing an appropriate rate of exchange for the North Korean won, the nonconvertible North Korean currency. The South Korean government's estimate placed North Korea's GNP in 1991 at US$22.9 billion, or US$1,038 per capita. In contrast, South Korea posted US$237.9 billion of GNP and a per capita income of US$5,569 in 1991. North Korea's GNP in 1991 showed a 5.2% decline from 1989, and preliminary indications were that the decline would continue. South Korea's GNP, by contrast, expanded by 9.3% and 8.4%, respectively, in 1990 and 1991. It is estimated that North Korea's GNP nearly halved between 1990 and 1999.

In 2014, the Bank of Korea estimated that the real GDP of North Korea in 2013 was 30,839 billion South Korean won. The same year, it published the following estimates of North Korea's GDP growth

DEFENSE AND MILITARY ISSUES

North Korea has one of the largest armies in the world. It has an estimated active duty military force of up to 1.2 million personnel, compared to about 680,000 in the South. Military spending is estimated at as much as a quarter of GNP, with up to 20% of men ages 17-54 in the regular armed forces. North Korean forces have a substantial numerical advantage over the South (around 2 to 1) in several key categories of offensive weapons--tanks, long-range artillery, and armored personnel carriers. The North has one of the world's largest special operations forces, designed for insertion behind the lines in wartime.

North Korea's navy is primarily a coastal navy, with antiquated surface and submarine fleets. Its air force has twice the number of aircraft as the South, but, except for a few advanced fighters, the North's air force is obsolete.

The North deploys the bulk of its forces well forward, along the demilitarized zone (DMZ). Several North Korean military tunnels under the DMZ were discovered in the period from the 1970s to the present day. Over the course of several years, North Korea realigned its forces and moved some rear-echelon troops to hardened bunkers closer to the DMZ. Given the proximity of Seoul to the DMZ (some 25 miles), South Korean and U.S. forces are likely to have little warning of attack. The United States and South Korea continue to believe that the U.S. troop presence in South Korea remains an effective deterrent. North Korea's attempts to develop a nuclear weapons program has also been a source of international tension (see below, Reunification Efforts Since 1971; Denuclearization of the Korean Peninsula).

In 1953, the Military Armistice Commission (MAC) was created to oversee and enforce the terms of the armistice. North Korea has sought to dismantle the MAC in a push for a new "peace mechanism" on the peninsula. In April 1994, it declared the MAC void and withdrew its representatives.

FOREIGN RELATIONS

North Korea's relationship with the South has determined much of its post-World War II history and still undergirds much of its foreign policy. North and South Korea have had a difficult and acrimonious relationship since the Korean War. In recent years, North Korea has pursued a mixed policy--seeking to develop economic relations with South Korea and to win the support of the South Korean public for greater North-South engagement while at the same time continuing to denounce the R.O.K.'s security relationship with the United States and maintaining a threatening conventional force posture on the DMZ and in adjacent waters.

The military demarcation line (MDL) of separation between the belligerent sides at the close of the Korean War divides North Korea from South Korea. A demilitarized zone (DMZ) extends for 2,000 meters (just over 1 mile) on either side of the MDL. Both the North and South Korean governments hold that the MDL is only a temporary administrative line, not a permanent border.

During the postwar period, both Korean governments have repeatedly affirmed their desire to reunify the Korean Peninsula, but until 1971 the two governments had no direct, official communications or other contact.

Reunification Efforts Since 1971

In August 1971, North and South Korea held talks through their respective Red Cross societies with the aim of reuniting the many Korean families separated following the division of Korea and the Korean War. In July 1972, the two sides agreed to work toward peaceful reunification and an end to the hostile atmosphere prevailing on the peninsula. Officials exchanged visits, and regular communications were established through a North-South coordinating committee and the Red Cross. These initial contacts broke down in 1973 following South Korean President Park Chung-hee's announcement that the South would seek separate entry into the United Nations, and after the kidnapping of South Korean opposition leader Kim Dae-jung--perceived as friendly to unified entry into the UN--by South Korean intelligence services. There was no other significant contact between North and South Korea until 1984.

Dialogue was renewed in September 1984, when South Korea accepted the North's offer to provide relief goods to victims of severe flooding in South Korea. Red Cross talks to address the plight of separated families resumed, as did talks on economic and trade issues and parliamentary-level discussions. However, the North then unilaterally suspended all talks in January 1986, arguing that the annual U.S.-R.O.K. "Team Spirit" military exercises were inconsistent with dialogue. There was a brief flurry of negotiations that year on co-hosting the upcoming 1988 Seoul Olympics, which ended in failure and was followed by the 1987 bombing of a South Korean commercial aircraft (Korean Airlines flight 858) by North Korean agents.

In July 1988, South Korean President Roh Tae-woo called for new efforts to promote North-South exchanges, family reunification, inter-Korean trade, and contact in international forums. Roh followed up this initiative in a UN General Assembly speech in which South Korea offered for the first time to discuss security matters with the North. Initial meetings that grew out of Roh's proposals started in September 1989. In September 1990, the first of eight prime minister-level meetings between North Korean and South Korean officials took place in Seoul. The prime ministerial talks resulted in two major agreements: the Agreement on Reconciliation, Nonaggression, Exchanges, and Cooperation (the "Basic Agreement") and the Declaration on the Denuclearization of the Korean Peninsula (the "Joint Declaration").

The Basic Agreement, signed on December 13, 1991, called for reconciliation and nonaggression and established four joint commissions. These commissions--on South-North reconciliation, South-North military affairs, South-North economic exchanges and cooperation, and South-North social and cultural exchange--were to work out the specifics for implementing the Basic Agreement. Subcommittees to examine specific issues were created, and liaison offices were established in Panmunjom. However, in the fall of 1992 the process came to a halt because of rising tension over North Korea's nuclear program.

The Joint Declaration on denuclearization was initialed on December 31, 1991. It forbade both sides from testing, manufacturing, producing, receiving, possessing, storing, deploying, or using nuclear weapons and forbade the possession of nuclear reprocessing and uranium enrichment facilities. A procedure for inter-Korean inspection was to be organized, and a North-South Joint Nuclear Control Commission (JNCC) was mandated to verify the denuclearization of the peninsula.

On January 30, 1992, the D.P.R.K. finally signed a nuclear safeguards agreement with the International Atomic Energy Agency (IAEA), as it had pledged to do in 1985 when it acceded to the Nuclear Non-Proliferation Treaty (NPT). This safeguards agreement allowed IAEA inspections to begin in June 1992. In March 1992, the JNCC was established in accordance with the Joint Declaration, but subsequent meetings failed to reach agreement on the main issue of establishing a bilateral inspection regime.

As the 1990s progressed, concern over the North's attempts to develop a nuclear program became a major issue in North-South relations and between North Korea and the United States. The lack of progress on implementation of the Joint Declaration's provision for an inter-Korean nuclear inspection regime led to reinstatement of the U.S.-R.O.K. Team Spirit military exercises for 1993. The situation worsened rapidly when North Korea, in January 1993, refused IAEA access to two suspected nuclear waste sites and then announced in March 1993 its intent to withdraw from the NPT. During the next 2 years, the United States held direct talks with the D.P.R.K. that resulted in a series of agreements on nuclear matters, including the 1994 Agreed Framework (which broke down in 2002 when North Korea was discovered to be pursuing a uranium enrichment program for nuclear weapons--see below, Denuclearization of the Korean Peninsula).

At his inauguration in February 1998, R.O.K. President Kim Dae-jung enunciated a new policy of engagement with the D.P.R.K., named "the Sunshine Policy." The policy had three fundamental principles: no tolerance of provocations from the North, no intention to absorb the North, and the separation of political cooperation from economic cooperation.

For additional analytical, business and investment opportunities information,
please contact Global Investment & Business Center, USA
at (202) 546-2103. Fax: (202) 546-3275. E-mail: rusric@erols.com

Private sector overtures would be based on commercial and humanitarian considerations. The use of government resources would entail reciprocity. This policy set the stage for the first inter-Korean summit, held in Pyongyang on June 13-15, 2000.

Following his inauguration in February 2003, R.O.K. President Roh Moo-hyun, continued his predecessor's policy of engagement with the North, although he abandoned the name "Sunshine Policy." The R.O.K. and D.P.R.K. held a second inter-Korean summit on October 2-4, 2007 in Pyongyang. Following the inauguration of R.O.K. President Lee Myung-bak in February 2008, inter-Korean relations have declined as the D.P.R.K. criticized Lee's policy of seeking greater reciprocity in inter-Korean relations. In the fall of 2009, inter-Korean relations showed some signs of potential improvement following a reunion of separated families and several meetings to discuss joint economic projects and other issues. However, no progress was made.

Inter-Korean relations further deteriorated following the D.P.R.K.'s sinking of the R.O.K. warship *Cheonan* on March 26, 2010, which killed 46 R.O.K. sailors. Although the D.P.R.K. has continued to deny responsibility for the attack, an objective and scientific investigation found overwhelming evidence that the warship was sunk by a North Korean torpedo fired from a North Korean submarine. On July 9, 2010, the UN Security Council unanimously adopted a Presidential Statement that condemned the attack on the *Cheonan*. On November 23, 2010, the D.P.R.K. launched an unprovoked attack against Yeonpyong Island, killing two R.O.K. soldiers and two civilians. The D.P.R.K.'s attack on Yeonpyong Island was a clear violation of the armistice agreement.

The United States supports engagement and North-South dialogue and cooperation. Major joint economic projects have included a tourism development in Mt. Kumgang, the re-establishment of road and rail links across the DMZ, and a joint North-South industrial park near the North Korean city of Kaesong (see further information below in the section on the Economy). Following the sinking of the *Cheonan*, the R.O.K. severed nearly all economic links with the D.P.R.K., with the exception of the Kaesong Industrial Complex (KIC).

Relations Outside the Peninsula
Throughout the Cold War, North Korea balanced its relations with China and the Soviet Union to extract the maximum benefit from the relationships at minimum political cost. In the 1970s and early 1980s, the establishment of diplomatic relations between the United States and China, the Soviet-backed Vietnamese occupation of Cambodia, and the Soviet occupation of Afghanistan created strains between China and the Soviet Union and, in turn, in North Korea's relations with its two major communist allies. North Korea tried to avoid becoming embroiled in the Sino-Soviet split, obtaining aid from both the Soviet Union and China and trying to avoid dependence on either. Following Kim Il-sung's 1984 visit to Moscow, there was an improvement in Soviet-D.P.R.K. relations, resulting in renewed deliveries of Soviet weaponry to North Korea and increases in economic aid.

The establishment of diplomatic relations by South Korea with the Soviet Union in 1990 and with China in 1992 seriously strained relations between North Korea and its traditional allies. Moreover, the fall of communism in eastern Europe in 1989 and the disintegration of the Soviet Union in 1991 resulted in a significant drop in communist aid to North Korea. Despite these changes and its past reliance on this military and economic assistance, North Korea continued to proclaim a militantly independent stance in its foreign policy in accordance with its official ideology of "Juche," or self-reliance.

Both North and South Korea became parties to the Biological Weapons Convention in 1987. North Korea is not a member of the Chemical Weapons Convention, nor is it a member of the Missile Technology Control Regime (MTCR).

North Korea has maintained membership in several multilateral organizations. It became a member of the UN in September 1991. North Korea also belongs to the Food and Agriculture Organization (FAO); the International Civil Aviation Organization; the International Postal Union; the UN Conference on Trade and Development; the International Telecommunications Union; the UN Development Program (UNDP); the UN Educational, Scientific, and Cultural Organization; the World Health Organization; the World Intellectual Property Organization; the World Meteorological Organization; the International Maritime Organization; the International Committee of the Red Cross; and the Nonaligned Movement. The UN country team (a group of the 5 UN agencies with a permanent presence in the D.P.R.K.) consists of the UNDP, the World Food Program, the UN Population Fund (UNFPA), the UN Children's Fund (UNICEF), the World Health Organization (WHO), and the FAO. The D.P.R.K. is also a member of the ASEAN Regional Forum.

The D.P.R.K. was forced to abandon some of the more extreme manifestations of its "self-reliance" ideology in the mid-1990s following the death of Kim Il-sung and the deterioration of its economy. In subsequent years, the D.P.R.K. has continued to pursue a tightly restricted economic policy while continuing to search for economic aid and development assistance. These efforts have been matched by an increased determination to counter perceived external and internal threats by a self-proclaimed "Songun," or military first, policy.

At times, North Korea has sought to broaden its formal diplomatic relationships in a limited and cautious manner. In July 2000, North Korea began participating in the ASEAN Regional Forum (ARF), with Foreign Minister Paek Nam-sun attending the ARF ministerial meeting in Bangkok. The D.P.R.K. also expanded its bilateral diplomatic ties in 2000 by establishing diplomatic relations with Italy, the Philippines, Australia, Canada, the U.K., Germany, and many other European countries.

In the September 19, 2005 Joint Statement issued at the end of the fourth round of Six-Party Talks, the United States and the D.P.R.K. committed to undertake steps to normalize relations. The D.P.R.K. and Japan also agreed to take steps to normalize relations and to discuss outstanding issues of concern, such as the North Korean Government's abductions of Japanese citizens. The February 13, 2007 Initial Actions agreement established U.S.-D.P.R.K. and Japan-D.P.R.K. bilateral working groups on normalization of relations, both of which met several times before the D.P.R.K.'s withdrawal from the Six-Party Talks (see below, Denuclearization of the Korean Peninsula).

Since 2006, China has implemented UN sanctions against North Korea while simultaneously providing economic support to maintain North Korea's stability. The

For additional analytical, business and investment opportunities information, please contact Global Investment & Business Center, USA at (202) 546-2103. Fax: (202) 546-3275. E-mail: rusric@erols.com

traditional China-D.P.R.K. friendship dating back to before the Korean War was described in November 2009 by Kim Jong-il as "unbreakable."

Terrorism

The D.P.R.K. is not known to have sponsored terrorist acts since the 1987 bombing of Korean Airlines flight 858. Pyongyang continues to provide sanctuary to members of the Japanese Communist League-Red Army Faction (JRA) who participated in the hijacking of a Japan Airlines flight to North Korea in 1970.

The D.P.R.K. has made several statements condemning terrorism. In October 2000, the United States and the D.P.R.K. issued a joint statement on terrorism in which "the two sides agreed that international terrorism poses an unacceptable threat to global security and peace, and that terrorism should be opposed in all its forms." The United States and the D.P.R.K. agreed to support the international legal regime combating international terrorism and to cooperate with each other to fight terrorism. The D.P.R.K. became a signatory to the Convention for the Suppression of Financing of Terrorism and a party to the Convention Against the Taking of Hostages in November 2001. In June 2008, the D.P.R.K. Foreign Ministry issued an authoritative statement providing assurances that the D.P.R.K. supports international efforts to combat terrorism and opposes all forms of terrorism.

In the February 13, 2007 Initial Actions agreement, the United States agreed to begin the process of removing the designation of the D.P.R.K. as a state sponsor of terrorism. On June 26, 2008, following the D.P.R.K.'s submission of its nuclear declaration and progress on disablement, President George W. Bush announced that the United States would no longer apply the Trading with the Enemy Act to North Korea. Additionally, on October 11, the Secretary of State rescinded the United States' designation of North Korea as a state sponsor of terrorism.

In May 2010, the United States re-certified North Korea as "not cooperating fully" with U.S. counterterrorism efforts under Section 40A of the Arms Export and Control Act, as amended. Pursuant to this certification, defense articles and services could not be sold or licensed for export to North Korea from October 1, 2009 to September 30, 2010.

Abductions

In the past, the D.P.R.K. has also been involved in the abduction of foreign citizens. In 2002, Kim Jong-il acknowledged to Japanese Prime Minister Junichiro Koizumi the involvement of D.P.R.K. "special institutions" in the kidnapping of Japanese citizens between 1977 and 1983 and said that those responsible had been punished. While five surviving victims and their families were allowed to leave the D.P.R.K. and resettle in Japan in October 2002, 12 other cases remain unresolved and continue to be a major issue in Japan-D.P.R.K. relations. The R.O.K. Government estimated that approximately 480 of its civilians, abducted or detained by the D.P.R.K. following the end of the Korean War, remained in the D.P.R.K. The R.O.K. Government also estimated that 560 soldier and prisoners of war missing in action also remained alive in the D.P.R.K. In October 2005, the D.P.R.K. acknowledged for the first time having kidnapped R.O.K. citizens in previous decades, claiming that several abductees, as well as several POWs from the Korean War, were still alive. In June 2006, North Korea allowed Kim Young-nam, a South Korean abducted by the North in 1978, to participate in a family reunion. In June

2008, the D.P.R.K. agreed to reopen the investigation into the abduction issue. In August 2008, the D.P.R.K. and Japan agreed to a plan for proceeding with the abductions investigation. However, the D.P.R.K. has not yet begun the investigation. The United States has continued to press the D.P.R.K. to address the concerns of Japan and the R.O.K. about the abductions issue.

U.S. POLICY TOWARD NORTH KOREA

U.S. Support for North-South Dialogue and Reunification
The United States supports the peaceful reunification of Korea on terms acceptable to the Korean people and recognizes that the future of the Korean Peninsula is primarily a matter for them to decide. The United States believes that a constructive and serious dialogue between the authorities of North and South Korea is necessary to resolve outstanding problems, including the North's attempts to develop a nuclear program and human rights abuses, and to encourage the North's integration with the rest of the international community.

Denuclearization of the Korean Peninsula
North Korea joined the Nuclear Non-Proliferation Treaty (NPT) as a non-nuclear weapons state in 1985. North and South Korean talks begun in 1990 resulted in the 1992 Joint Declaration for a Non-Nuclear Korean Peninsula (see Foreign Relations: Reunification Efforts Since 1971). However, the international standoff over the D.P.R.K.'s failure to implement an agreement with the IAEA for the inspection of the North's nuclear facilities led Pyongyang to announce in March 1993 its intention to withdraw from the NPT. UN Security Council Resolution (UNSCR) 825 in May 1993 urged the D.P.R.K. to cooperate with the IAEA and to implement the 1992 North-South Denuclearization Statement. It also urged all UN member states to encourage the D.P.R.K. to respond positively to this resolution and to facilitate a solution to the nuclear issue.

The United States opened talks with the D.P.R.K. in June 1993 and eventually reached agreement in October 1994 on a diplomatic roadmap, known as the Agreed Framework, for the denuclearization of the Korean Peninsula. The Agreed Framework called for the following steps:

- North Korea agreed to freeze its existing nuclear program and allow monitoring by the IAEA.
- Both sides agreed to cooperate to replace the D.P.R.K.'s graphite-moderated reactors with light water reactor (LWR) power plants, by a target date of 2003, to be financed and supplied by an international consortium (later identified as the Korean Peninsula Energy Development Organization or KEDO).
- As an interim measure, the United States agreed to provide North Korea with 500,000 tons of heavy fuel oil annually until the first reactor was built.
- The United States and D.P.R.K. agreed to work together to store safely the spent fuel from the five-megawatt reactor and dispose of it in a safe manner that did not involve reprocessing in the D.P.R.K.
- The two sides agreed to move toward full normalization of political and economic relations.
- The two sides agreed to work together for peace and security on a nuclear-free Korean Peninsula.

- The two sides agreed to work together to strengthen the international nuclear non-proliferation regime.

In accordance with the terms of the Agreed Framework, in January 1995 the U.S. Government eased economic sanctions against North Korea in response to North Korea's freezing its graphite-moderated nuclear program under United States and IAEA verification. North Korea agreed to accept the decisions of KEDO, the financier and supplier of the light water reactors, with respect to provision of the reactors. KEDO subsequently identified Sinpo as the LWR project site and held a groundbreaking ceremony in August 1997. In December 1999, KEDO and the (South) Korea Electric Power Corporation (KEPCO) signed the Turnkey Contract (TKC), permitting full-scale construction of the LWRs.

In January 1995, as called for in the 1994 Agreed Framework, the United States and D.P.R.K. negotiated a method to store the spent fuel from the D.P.R.K.'s five-megawatt nuclear reactor. Under this method, United States and D.P.R.K. operators worked together to can the spent fuel and store the canisters in a spent fuel pond; canning began in 1995. In April 2000, canning of all accessible spent fuel rods and rod fragments was completed.

In 1998, the United States identified an underground site in Kumchang-ni, North Korea, which it suspected of being nuclear-related. In March 1999, after several rounds of negotiations, the United States and D.P.R.K. agreed that the United States would be granted "satisfactory access" to the underground site at Kumchang-ni. In October 2000, during D.P.R.K. Special Envoy Marshal Jo Myong-rok's visit to Washington, and after two visits to the site by teams of U.S. experts, the United States announced in a Joint Communiqué with the D.P.R.K. that U.S. concerns about the site had been resolved.

In 1999, the D.P.R.K. announced a voluntary moratorium on testing of long-range missiles. The D.P.R.K. subsequently reaffirmed this moratorium in June 2000 and on October 12, 2000. The moratorium continued until 2005, when the D.P.R.K. announced its termination as a result of what the D.P.R.K. claimed was "U.S. hostility."

The United States and the D.P.R.K. launched Agreed Framework Implementation Talks in May 2000. The United States and the D.P.R.K. also began negotiations for a comprehensive missile agreement. In January 2001, the Bush administration discontinued nuclear and missile talks, specifying that it intended to review the U.S. policy on North Korea. The administration announced on June 6, 2001 that it was prepared to resume dialogue with North Korea on a broader agenda of issues--including North Korea's conventional force posture, missile development and export programs, human rights practices, and humanitarian issues.

In October 2002, a U.S. delegation headed by then-Assistant Secretary of State for East Asian and Pacific Affairs James A. Kelly confronted North Korea with the assessment that the D.P.R.K. was pursuing an undeclared uranium enrichment program, in violation of North Korea's IAEA safeguards obligation and its commitments in the 1992 North-South Joint Declaration on Denuclearization of the Korean Peninsula and the Agreed Framework. North Korean officials asserted to the U.S. delegation the D.P.R.K.'s "right" to a uranium enrichment program and indicated that that it had such a program. The

For additional analytical, business and investment opportunities information,
please contact Global Investment & Business Center, USA
at (202) 546-2103. Fax: (202) 546-3275. E-mail: rusric@erols.com

U.S. side stated that North Korea would have to terminate the program before any further progress could be made in U.S.-D.P.R.K. relations. The United States also made clear that if this program were verifiably eliminated, it would be prepared to work with North Korea on the development of a fundamentally new relationship. After denying a highly enriched uranium program since 2003, North Korea announced in April 2009 that it was developing uranium enrichment capability to produce fuel for a planned light water reactor; in September it claimed its enrichment research had "entered into completion phase." In November 2002, the member countries of KEDO's Executive Board agreed to suspend heavy fuel oil shipments to North Korea pending a resolution of the nuclear dispute.

In late 2002 and early 2003, North Korea terminated the freeze on its existing plutonium-based nuclear facilities at Yongbyon, expelled IAEA inspectors, removed seals and monitoring equipment at Yongbyon, announced its withdrawal from the NPT, and resumed reprocessing of spent nuclear fuel to extract plutonium for weapons purposes. North Korea announced that it was taking these steps to provide itself with a deterrent force in the face of U.S. threats and U.S. "hostile policy." Beginning in mid-2003, the North repeatedly claimed to have completed reprocessing of the spent fuel rods previously frozen at Yongbyon and publicly said that the resulting fissile material would be used to bolster its "nuclear deterrent force." There is no independent confirmation of North Korea's claims. The KEDO Executive Board suspended work on the LWR Project beginning December 1, 2003.

In early 2003, the United States proposed multilateral talks on the North Korean nuclear issue. North Korea initially opposed such a process, maintaining that the nuclear dispute was purely a bilateral matter between the United States and the D.P.R.K. However, under pressure from its neighbors and with the active involvement of China, North Korea agreed to three-party talks with China and the United States in Beijing in April 2003 and to Six-Party Talks with the United States, China, R.O.K., Japan, and Russia in August 2003, also in Beijing. During the August 2003 round of Six-Party Talks, North Korea agreed to the eventual elimination of its nuclear programs if the United States were first willing to sign a bilateral "non-aggression treaty" and meet various other conditions, including the provision of substantial amounts of aid and normalization of relations. The North Korean proposal was unacceptable to the United States, which insisted on a multilateral resolution to the issue and opposed provision of benefits before the D.P.R.K.'s complete denuclearization. In October 2003, President Bush said he would consider a multilateral written security guarantee in the context of North Korea's complete, verifiable, and irreversible elimination of its nuclear weapons program.

China hosted a second round of Six-Party Talks in Beijing in February 2004. The United States saw the results as positive, including the announced intention of all parties to hold a third round by the end of June and to form a working group to maintain momentum between plenary sessions.

At the third round of Six-Party Talks in Beijing, in June 2004, the United States tabled a comprehensive and substantive proposal aimed at resolving the nuclear issue. All parties agreed to hold a fourth round of talks by the end of September 2004. Despite its commitment, the D.P.R.K. refused to return to the table, and in the months that followed issued a series of provocative statements. In a February 10, 2005, Foreign Ministry

For additional analytical, business and investment opportunities information,
please contact Global Investment & Business Center, USA
at (202) 546-2103. Fax: (202) 546-3275. E-mail: rusric@erols.com

statement, the D.P.R.K. declared that it had "manufactured nuclear weapons" and was "indefinitely suspending" its participation in the Six-Party Talks. In Foreign Ministry statements in March, the D.P.R.K. said it would no longer be bound by its voluntary moratorium on ballistic missile launches, and declared itself a nuclear weapons state.

Following intense diplomatic efforts by the United States and other parties, the fourth round of Six-Party Talks were held in Beijing over a period of 20 days from July-September 2005, with a recess period in August. Discussions resulted in the September 19, 2005 Joint Statement, in which the six parties unanimously reaffirmed the goal of verifiable denuclearization of the Korean Peninsula in a peaceful manner. The D.P.R.K. for the first time committed to abandon all nuclear weapons and existing nuclear programs and to return, at an early date, to the NPT and to IAEA safeguards. The other parties agreed to provide economic cooperation and energy assistance. The United States and the D.P.R.K. agreed to take steps to normalize relations subject to bilateral policies, which for the United States includes concerns over North Korea's ballistic missile programs and human rights conditions. While the Joint Statement provides a vision of the end-point of the Six-Party process, much work lies ahead to implement the elements of the agreement.

A fifth round of talks began in November 2005, but ended inconclusively as the D.P.R.K. began a boycott of the Six-Party Talks, citing the "U.S. hostile policy" and specifically U.S. law enforcement action that had led in September to a freeze of North Korean accounts in Macau's Banco Delta Asia (BDA). The United States held discussions in Kuala Lumpur (July 2006) and New York (September 2006) with other Six-Party partners, except North Korea, along with representatives from other regional powers in the Asia-Pacific region, to discuss Northeast Asian security issues, including North Korea. On July 4-5, 2006 (local Korea time), the D.P.R.K. launched seven ballistic missiles, including six short- and medium-range missiles and one of possible intercontinental range. In response, the UN Security Council unanimously adopted Resolution 1695 on July 15, which demanded that the D.P.R.K. suspend all activities related to its ballistic missile program and reestablish existing commitments to a moratorium on missile launching. The resolution also required all UN member states, in accordance with their national legal authorities and consistent with international law, to exercise vigilance and prevent missile and missile-related items, materials, goods and technology from being transferred to the D.P.R.K.'s missile or weapons of mass destruction (WMD) programs, prevent the procurement of missiles or related items, materials, goods and services from the D.P.R.K., and the transfer of any financial resources in relation to the D.P.R.K.'s missile or WMD programs. The D.P.R.K. immediately rejected the resolution.

On October 9, 2006, North Korea announced the successful test of a nuclear explosive device, verified by the United States on October 11. In response, the United Nations Security Council, citing Chapter VII of the UN Charter, unanimously passed Resolution 1718, condemning North Korea and imposing sanctions on certain luxury goods and trade of military units, WMD and missile-related parts, and technology transfers.

The Six-Party Talks resumed in December 2006 after a 13-month hiatus. Following a bilateral meeting between the United States and D.P.R.K. in Berlin in January 2007, another round of Six-Party Talks was held in February 2007. On February 13, 2007, the parties reached an agreement on "Initial Actions for the Implementation of the Joint Statement" in which North Korea agreed to shut down and seal its Yongbyon nuclear facility and to invite back IAEA personnel to conduct all necessary monitoring and verification of these actions as agreed between the IAEA and the D.P.R.K. The other five parties agreed to provide emergency energy assistance to North Korea in the amount of 50,000 tons of heavy fuel oil (HFO) in the initial phase and the equivalent of 950,000 tons of HFO in the next phase of North Korea's denuclearization. The six parties also established five working groups to form specific plans for implementing the Joint Statement in the following areas: denuclearization of the Korean Peninsula, normalization of U.S.-D.P.R.K. relations, normalization of Japan-D.P.R.K. relations, economic and energy cooperation, and a Northeast Asia peace and security mechanism. All parties agreed that the working groups would meet within 30 days of the agreement, which they did. The agreement also envisions the directly-related parties negotiating a permanent peace regime on the Korean Peninsula at an appropriate separate forum.

The sixth round of Six-Party Talks took place on March 19-23, 2007. The parties reported on the first meetings of the five working groups. At the invitation of the .D.P.R.K., Assistant Secretary of State Christopher Hill visited Pyongyang in June 2007 as part of ongoing consultations with the six parties on implementation of the Initial Actions agreement. In July 2007, the D.P.R.K. shut down the Yongbyon nuclear facility, as well as an uncompleted reactor at Taechon, and IAEA personnel returned to the D.P.R.K. to monitor and verify the shut-down and to seal the facility. Concurrently, the R.O.K. delivered 50,000 metric tons of HFO in August 2007. All five working groups met in August and September to discuss detailed plans for implementation of the next phase of the Initial Actions agreement, and the D.P.R.K. invited a team of experts from the United States, China, and Russia to visit the Yongbyon nuclear facility in September 2007 to discuss specific steps that could be taken to disable the facility.

The subsequent September 27-30 Six-Party plenary meeting resulted in the October 3, 2007 agreement on "Second-Phase Actions for the Implementation of the Joint Statement." Under the terms of the October 3 agreement, the D.P.R.K. agreed to disable all existing nuclear facilities subject to abandonment under the September 2005 Joint Statement and the February 13 agreement. The Parties agreed to complete by December 31, 2007 a set of disabling actions for the three core facilities at Yongbyon-- the five-megawatt Experimental Reactor, the Radiochemical Laboratory (Reprocessing Plant), and the Fresh Fuel Fabrication Plant--with oversight from a team of U.S. experts, The D.P.R.K. also agreed to provide a complete and correct declaration of all its nuclear programs in accordance with the February 13 agreement by December 31, 2007 and reaffirmed its commitment not to transfer nuclear materials, technology, or know-how. The United States, R.O.K., China, and Russia continued to provide HFO and HFO-equivalent energy assistance to the D.P.R.K., to fulfill the commitment of one million tons in the initial and second phases, in parallel with the D.P.R.K.'s actions on disablement and declaration.

In November 2007, the D.P.R.K. began to disable the three core facilities at Yongbyon, and U.S. experts were present at the site to oversee the disabling actions. Assistant Secretary of State Christopher Hill visited Pyongyang again in December 2007 as part of ongoing consultations on the implementation of Second-Phase Actions and carried with him a letter from President George W. Bush to Kim Jong-il. While the D.P.R.K. missed the December 31 deadline to provide a complete and correct declaration, it provided its declaration to the Chinese, chair of the Six-Party Talks, on June 26, 2008. The D.P.R.K. also imploded the cooling tower at the Yongbyon facility in late June 2008 before international media. Following the D.P.R.K.'s progress on disablement and its provision of a declaration, President Bush announced the lifting of the application of the Trading with the Enemy Act (TWEA) with respect to the D.P.R.K. On October 1-3, 2008, a U.S. team traveled to the D.P.R.K. and reached agreement with the D.P.R.K. on a series of verification measures related to the D.P.R.K.'s nuclear declaration. Following this progress on verification, on October 11, 2008, the Secretary of State rescinded the United States' designation of North Korea as a state sponsor of terrorism. On December 8-11, 2008, the Six-Party heads of delegation met to discuss the issue of verification of the D.P.R.K.'s nuclear declaration and completion of Second-Phase energy assistance and disabling actions, but the meeting ended without agreement.

Sung Kim was appointed the Special Envoy for the Six-Party Talks in July 2008 and was accorded the rank of Ambassador following confirmation by the United States Senate. In February 2009, the Secretary of State appointed Ambassador Stephen Bosworth as Special Representative for North Korea Policy, making him the senior official overseeing U.S. efforts in the Six-Party Talks to achieve the verifiable denuclearization of the Korean Peninsula in a peaceful manner.

On April 5, 2009, the D.P.R.K. launched a Taepo Dong-2 missile over the Sea of Japan, in violation of UN Security Council Resolution 1718. This action prompted the UN Security Council (UNSC) to issue a unanimous Presidential Statement condemning the launch as a violation of UNSCR 1718, demanding that the D.P.R.K. refrain from further launches, and calling upon the D.P.R.K. and all member states to fully implement their obligations under UNSCR 1718. On April 14, the D.P.R.K. condemned the UNSC statement and withdrew its active participation in the Six-Party Talks. At the same time, the D.P.R.K. demanded the expulsion of IAEA inspectors and U.S. technical experts who had been monitoring the Yongbyon nuclear site. The D.P.R.K. also disclosed its intent to reactivate its nuclear facilities.

On May 25, 2009, the D.P.R.K. announced that it had conducted a second test of a nuclear explosive device. On June 12, 2009, the UN Security Council unanimously adopted Resolution 1874, which expanded on the provisions of UNSCR 1718 to include a ban on all arms transfers to and from the D.P.R.K. (with the exception of the D.P.R.K.'s import of small arms and light weapons, which require UN notification); provisions calling on states to inspect vessels in their territory when there are "reasonable grounds" that banned cargo is on a ship, and obligations to report on their inspections and when other states deny permission to inspect ships, as well as obligations for states to seize and dispose of any banned cargo; and broadened financial measures including a call on states not to provide grants, assistance, loans or public financial support for trade if such support could contribute to the D.P.R.K.'s proliferation efforts, and a call on states to deny financial services, including by freezing assets, where such assets could contribute to prohibited D.P.R.K. programs. In early 2009 the United States appointed Ambassador Philip Goldberg as the U.S. Coordinator for Implementation of UNSCR 1874. In June, July, and August 2009, Ambassador Goldberg led delegations to China, South Korea, Japan, Singapore, Malaysia, Thailand, Russia, the U.A.E., and Egypt to encourage these member states to implement sanctions in a full and transparent manner and to take actions that would shed light on North Korean proliferation-related activities. He also traveled to the United Nations, where he consulted with the UN's D.P.R.K. (1718) Sanctions Committee. Since the adoption of UNSCR 1874, several states, including the U.A.E., South Korea, Austria, Thailand, and South Africa had reported potential violations of UNSCRs 1718 and 1874 to the UN's D.P.R.K. Sanctions Committee.

On July 3-4, 2009, the D.P.R.K. fired a series of short-range ballistic missiles into the Sea of Japan. In a September 2009 letter to the UN Security Council President, the D.P.R.K. announced that "experimental uranium enrichment has been successfully conducted to enter into completion phase." On October 12, 2009, the D.P.R.K. launched additional multiple short-range ballistic missiles.

In November 2009, the D.P.R.K. declared that it had completed reprocessing 8,000 spent nuclear fuel rods in August. In December 2009, Special Representative for North Korea Policy Stephen Bosworth led an interagency delegation to Pyongyang for extensive talks that took place within the context of the Six-Party Talks and focused on the way to achieve the verifiable denuclearization of the Korean Peninsula. The United States and North Korea agreed on the importance of the Six-Party Talks and the need to implement the 2005 Joint Statement, but did not agree on when and how the D.P.R.K. would return to denuclearization talks. As of April 2011, the Six-Party Talks had not resumed.

The D.P.R.K.'s sinking of the R.O.K. naval vessel *Cheonan* on March 26, 2010 and its shelling of Yeonpyong Island on November 23, 2010 have diminished the prospects for talks to resolve the issues surrounding the D.P.R.K.'s nuclear program. The D.P.R.K.'s revelation of a uranium enrichment program in November 2010 is in violation of its own commitments under the 2005 Joint Statement and its obligations under UN Security Council Resolutions 1718 and 1874. UNSCRs 1718 and 1874 require the D.P.R.K. to abandon all nuclear weapons and existing nuclear programs in a complete, verifiable, and irreversible manner. UNSCR 1874 also requires the D.P.R.K. to immediately cease all related activities; the construction of uranium enrichment facilities is unacceptable and inconsistent with the objective of the verifiable denuclearization of the Korean Peninsula.

Peaceful resolution of the issues on the Korean Peninsula will only be possible if North Korea fundamentally changes its behavior. Secretary of State Hillary Clinton has called on North Korea to take concrete, irreversible denuclearization steps toward fulfillment of the 2005 Joint Statement, comply with international law including UNSCRs 1718 and 1874, cease provocative behaviors, and take steps to improve relations with its neighbors.

ECONOMY
North Korea's economy declined sharply in the 1990s with the end of communism in Eastern Europe, the disintegration of the Soviet Union, and the dissolution of bloc-trading countries of the former socialist bloc. Gross national income per capita is estimated to have fallen by about one-third between 1990 and 2002. The economy has since stabilized and shown some modest growth in recent years, which may be reflective

of increased inter-Korean economic cooperation. Output and living standards, however, remain far below 1990 levels. Other centrally-planned economies in similar situations opted for domestic economic reform and liberalization of trade and investment. To date, North Korea has not done so. However, North Korea did formalize some modest wage and price reforms in 2002, and North Korea has been forced to tolerate markets and a small private sector as the state-run distribution system continues to deteriorate. An increasing number of North Koreans work in the informal, private sector to cope with growing hardship and reduced government support. The government, however, seems determined to maintain control. In October 2005, emboldened by an improved harvest and increased food donations from South Korea, the North Korean Government banned private grain sales and announced a return to centralized food rationing. Reports indicate this effort to reassert state control and to control inflation has been largely ineffective. Another factor contributing to the economy's poor performance is the disproportionately large share of GDP (thought to be about one-fourth) that North Korea devotes to its military.

In late November 2009, North Korea redenominated its currency at a rate of 100 to 1. New laws were implemented, including regulations on consumption, tightened state control of the market, and a ban on the possession or use of foreign currencies. The redenomination appears to have resulted in increased inflation and confiscation of operational capital and savings earned by private traders and others working outside state-controlled sectors of the economy.

North Korean industry is operating at only a small fraction of capacity due to lack of fuel, spare parts, and other inputs. Agriculture was 20.9% of GDP as of 2009, although agricultural output has not recovered to early 1990 levels. The infrastructure is generally poor and outdated, and the energy sector has collapsed.

North Korea experienced a severe famine following record floods in the summer of 1995 and continues to suffer from chronic food shortages and malnutrition. The United Nations World Food Program (WFP) provided substantial emergency food assistance beginning in 1995 (two million tons of which came from the United States), but the North Korean Government suspended the WFP emergency program at the end of 2005 and permitted only a greatly reduced WFP program through a protracted relief and recovery operation. However, in April 2011 the WFP announced that it was launching an emergency operation to feed 3.5 million North Koreans. While China and the R.O.K. had provided most of the D.P.R.K.'s food aid in the past, the D.P.R.K. refused to accept food aid from the R.O.K. between Lee Myung-bak's inauguration in February 2008 and January 2010, when the D.P.R.K. accepted the R.O.K.'s offer to provide 10,000 tons of corn. The United States resumed the provision of food assistance to the D.P.R.K. in June 2008 after establishing a strong framework to ensure that the food will reach those most in need. The United States committed to providing up to 400,000 tons of food through WFP and 100,000 tons through U.S. NGOs. From May 2008 to March 2009, the United States provided approximately 170,000 metric tons of U.S. food to the D.P.R.K. In March 2009, the D.P.R.K. stated that it no longer wished to receive U.S. food assistance and requested that personnel monitoring U.S. food distributions depart the D.P.R.K., halting the U.S. food assistance program.

The United States also assisted U.S. NGOs in providing aid to fight the outbreak of infectious diseases following August 2007 floods, and worked with U.S. NGOs to improve the supply of electricity at provincial hospitals in North Korea. Following July 2010 floods, the United States Government supplied medical and other relief supplies to U.S. NGOs for emergency humanitarian assistance for flood relief.

In 1991, following the collapse of the Soviet Union and termination of subsidized trade arrangements with Russia, other former Communist states, and China, North Korea announced the creation of a Special Economic Zone (SEZ) in the northeast regions of Najin (sometimes rendered "Rajin"), Chongjin, and Sonbong. Problems with infrastructure, bureaucracy, and uncertainties about investment security and viability have hindered growth and development of this SEZ. The government announced in 2002 plans to establish a Special Administrative Region (SAR) in Sinuiju, at the western end of the North Korea-China border. However, the government has taken few concrete steps to establish the Sinuiju SAR, and its future is uncertain.

North-South Economic Ties
Two-way trade between North and South Korea, legalized in 1988, had risen to more than $1.68 billion by 2009, much of it related to out-processing or assembly work undertaken by South Korean firms in the Kaesong Industrial Complex (KIC). Ground was broken on the KIC in June 2003, and the first products were shipped from the KIC in December 2004. Plans envision 2,000 firms employing 350,000 workers by 2012. About 122 South Korean small and medium sized companies operate in the KIC, manufacturing mostly garments and footwear and employing more than 46,000 North Korean workers. Until 2007, a significant portion of total two-way trade had included donated goods provided to the North as humanitarian assistance or as part of inter-Korean cooperation projects. However, beginning in 2008, commercial transactions such as general trading and processing-on-commission have accounted for larger portion in overall inter-Korean trade. Most of the goods exported from KIC are sold in South Korea; a small quantity, about 18% of the KIC products, is exported to foreign markets.

Regarding inter-Korean transportation links, as of March 2011, after the *Cheonan* sinking incident, South Korea suspended all inter-Korean trade with the exception of the KIC. Since the June 2000 North-South summit, North and South Korea have reconnected their east and west coast railroads and roads where these links cross the DMZ and are working to improve these transportation routes. North and South Korea conducted tests of the east and west coast railroads on May 17, 2007 and began cross-border freight service between Kaesong in the D.P.R.K. and Munsan in the R.O.K. in December 2007. Much of the work done in North Korea has been funded by South Korea. The west coast rail and road are complete as far north as the KIC (six miles north of the DMZ), but little work is being done north of Kaesong. On the east coast, the road and the rail line are complete but the rail line is not operational.

R.O.K.-organized tours to Mt. Kumgang in North Korea began in 1998. Since then, more than a million visitors have traveled to Mt. Kumgang. However, the R.O.K. suspended tours to Mt. Kumgang in July 2008 following the shooting death of a South Korean tourist at the resort by a D.P.R.K. soldier. In April 2011 the D.P.R.K. announced that it was terminating its exclusive contract with Hyundai Asan for operating the Mt. Kumgang tours.

In August 2009, Hyundai Group Chairwoman Hyun Jung-eun met with Kim Jong-il and obtained the release of a South Korean worker who had been detained in the D.P.R.K. since March. As part of those discussions, the D.P.R.K. expressed a willingness to resume tourism links and continue talks regarding the KIC. The D.P.R.K. resumed normal cross-border passage to the KIC on September 1, 2009, and D.P.R.K. and R.O.K. officials conducted a joint visit to international industrial zones in China and Vietnam in December 2009. Between September 2009 and February 2010, D.P.R.K. and R.O.K. officials had several meetings to discuss joint tourism projects, the KIC, and other issues. However, the talks resulted in no progress.

Economic Interaction with the United States

The United States imposed a near total economic embargo on North Korea in June 1950 when North Korea attacked the South. U.S. sanctions were eased in stages beginning in 1989 and following the Agreed Framework on North Korea's nuclear programs in 1994. U.S. economic interaction with North Korea remains minimal, and North Korean assets frozen since 1950 remained frozen. In January 2007, pursuant to UN Security Council Resolution 1718, the U.S. Department of Commerce issued new regulations prohibiting the export of luxury goods to North Korea. Many statutory sanctions on North Korea, including those affecting trade in military, dual-use, and missile-related items and those based on multilateral arrangements, remain in place. Most forms of U.S. economic assistance, other than purely humanitarian assistance, are prohibited. North Korea does not enjoy "Normal Trade Relations" with the United States, so any goods manufactured in North Korea are subject to a higher tariff upon entry to the United States. At this time, goods of North Korean origin may not be imported into the United States either directly or through third countries, without prior notification to and approval from the Office of Foreign Assets Control.

On June 26, 2008, President Bush announced the termination of the application of the Trading with the Enemy Act (TWEA) with respect to the D.P.R.K., though some TWEA-based restrictions remain in place. The United States has issued sanctions targeting the D.P.R.K.'s weapons proliferation and illicit activities under Executive Orders 13382 and 13551. The Executive Orders are directed at those involved in proliferation or other illicit activities and their supporters.

Following the D.P.R.K.'s May 25, 2009 nuclear test, the UN Security Council passed Resolution 1874 on June 12, 2009. Resolution 1874 condemned North Korea's second nuclear test, demanded that the D.P.R.K. not conduct additional nuclear tests or ballistic missile launches, and called on the D.P.R.K. to return to the Non-Proliferation Treaty (NPT) and Six-Party Talks without preconditions.

In addition, the Financial Crimes Enforcement Network (FinCEN) issued an initial advisory June 18, 2009 (amended on December 18, 2009) on North Korean Government agencies' and front companies' involvement in illicit financial activities. In light of the financial measures in UNSCRs 1718 and 1874, and the use of deceptive financial practices by North Korea and North Korean entities, as well as individuals acting on their behalf, to hide illicit conduct, FinCEN advised all U.S. financial institutions to take commensurate risk mitigation measures.

Points of contact for U.S. regulations concerning economic activity with North Korea:

For additional analytical, business and investment opportunities information,
please contact Global Investment & Business Center, USA
at (202) 546-2103. Fax: (202) 546-3275. E-mail: rusric@erols.com

- Treasury--Office of Foreign Assets Control, Tel. (202) 622-2490, **http://www.treas.gov/offices/enforcement/ofac/**;
- Commerce--Foreign Policy Controls Division, Bureau of Industry and Security, Tel. (202) 482-4252;
- Transportation--Office of the Assistant General Counsel for International Law, Tel. (202) 366-2972.

TRAVEL AND BUSINESS INFORMATION

Travel Alerts, Travel Warnings, Trip Registration

The U.S. Department of State's Consular Information Program advises Americans traveling and residing abroad through Country Specific Information, Travel Alerts, and Travel Warnings. **Country Specific Information** exists for all countries and includes information on entry and exit requirements, currency regulations, health conditions, safety and security, crime, political disturbances, and the addresses of the U.S. embassies and consulates abroad. **Travel Alerts** are issued to disseminate information quickly about terrorist threats and other relatively short-term conditions overseas that pose significant risks to the security of American travelers. **Travel Warnings** are issued when the State Department recommends that Americans avoid travel to a certain country because the situation is dangerous or unstable.

For the latest security information, Americans living and traveling abroad should regularly monitor the Department's Bureau of Consular Affairs Internet web site at http://travel.state.gov, where current Worldwide Caution, Travel Alerts, and Travel Warnings can be found. The travel.state.gov website also includes information about passports, tips for planning a safe trip abroad and more. More travel-related information also is available at http://www.usa.gov/Citizen/Topics/Travel/International.shtml.

The Department's Smart Traveler app for U.S. travelers going abroad provides easy access to the frequently updated official country information, travel alerts, travel warnings, maps, U.S. embassy locations, and more that appear on the travel.state.gov site. Travelers can also set up e-tineraries to keep track of arrival and departure dates and make notes about upcoming trips. The app is compatible with iPhone, iPod touch, and iPad (requires iOS 4.0 or later).

The Department of State encourages all U.S. citizens traveling or residing abroad to register via the State Department's travel registration website or at the nearest U.S. embassy or consulate abroad (a link to the registration page is also available through the Smart Traveler app). Registration will make your presence and whereabouts known in case it is necessary to contact you in an emergency and will enable you to receive up-to-date information on security conditions.

Emergency information concerning Americans traveling abroad may be obtained by calling 1-888-407-4747 toll free in the U.S. and Canada or the regular toll line 1-202-501-4444 for callers

For additional analytical, business and investment opportunities information, please contact Global Investment & Business Center, USA at (202) 546-2103. Fax: (202) 546-3275. E-mail: rusric@erols.com

STRATEGIC INFORMATION AND CONTACTS FOR EXPORT IMPORT

BASIC INFORMATION

North Korea imported $4.34B, making it the 147th largest importer in the world. During the last five years the imports of North Korea have increased at an annualized rate of 0.5%, from $4.24B in 2008 to $4.34B in 2013. The most recent imports are led by Crude Petroleum which represent 13.8% of the total imports of North Korea, followed by Refined Petroleum, which account for 4.65%.

North Korea had a negative trade balance of $1.06B in net imports. As compared to their trade balance in 1995 when they still had a negative trade balance of $297M in net imports.

The top export destinations of North Korea are China ($2.72B), the Netherlands ($120M), Brazil ($68.2M), Pakistan ($41.4M) and India ($31.6M).

STRATEGIC EXPORT

KOREAN SPECIALTIES

Korea has diverse natural environment with both continental and oceanic features as it is located in the east of Asian continent facing the Pacific Ocean.

Thanks to these favorable natural and geographical advantages, our country has a large stock of specialties which enjoy growing demand on the world market.

Kaesong Koryo insam (ginseng) is the best of Korean specialities.

Koryo insam cultivated in Kaesong endowed with favourable soil, water and climatic conditions for insam cultivation has been exported to neighbouring countries from thousands of years ago.

Kaesong Koryo insam contains over 10 kinds of glucosides such as ginsenoside, fat, amino acid and vitamins, and a large amount of monosaccharides and polysaccharides, inorganic substance and amylase.

So, it has remarkable effects on physical and mental fatigue, ulcer, allergic disease, liver trouble, diarrhea, inflammation, radiation sickness and cancer. It is also highly efficacious for enhancing biological synthesis of nucleic acid, protein and aliphatic acid, and stimulating genital gland and central nervous system.

Over six-year-old Kaesong Koryo insam and various tonics prepared with its effective ingredients as the base including Sipjondae-bogo, Kyongokgo, Insam Extract, Insam Syrup, Insam Liquor, Insam Injection and Insam Tea find a large market in foreign countries.

Wild insam, rhubarb and white platycodon which are growing in the forests and deep valleys, and Fructus Lycii, Fructus Schizandrae, Flos Lonicerae and other highly effective medicinal herbs are also among Korean specialities.

As health foods, fresh, dried and frozen Armillaria edodes and Lentinus edodes are winning great favour among clients. Armillaria edodes is exported divided into 1st, 2nd and H grades. Lentinus edodes contains 18.32% of crude protein, 4.90% of crude fat and 7.11% of crude fibre.

Edible mountain herbs including bracken, osmund, aralia shoots, anise and platycodon are so tasty and nutritive that they have a good sale in the world market.

Hop cultivated in the northern alpine region of our country attracts a great attention of the world's beer brewers.

Mulberry cocoon, raw silk and silk fabrics also enjoy an enormous popularity in many countries.

Silk fabrics of more than 30 kinds are excellent in warmth-keeping, absorptive property and drooping, and soft to the touch, lustrous, delicate, beautiful and durable. Tasaekdan (polychromatic silk) and velvet have been awarded gold medals on several occasions at international sample fairs.

Our country surrounded by sea on three sides is abundant in marine products such as squid, octopus, lobster, oyster, clam, ear shell, trepang, hairy crab, king crab, blue crab, sea tangle and agar-agar. The export of marine products is increasing daily.

A rich selection of ceramics, craftworks and embroideries which have been awarded special prizes and gold medals at international fairs and exhibitions hold a large proportion in export items.

We will further promote economic and trade relations with different countries around the world by raising the export of Korean specialities.

Prospects of Kaesong Industrial Zone

The Kaesong Industrial Zone is to be built into an international hub of industry, commerce, finance, trade and tourism, where developers lease land, rearrange sites, construct infrastructures and invite investment in accordance with the DPRK law.

The DPRK government adopted and promulgated the law on the Kaesong Industrial Zone as a decree of the Presidium of the DPRK Supreme People's Assembly in November Juche 91 (2002), followed by regulations on the development of the industrial zone and on the establishment and management of mechanism of the industrial zone and agreements for smooth progress of telecommunications and quarantine. As a result, the legal guarantees have been provided to push forward the project.

The zone is to be divided into industrial, commercial, residential and tourist districts. Any south and overseas Koreans, foreign corporate bodies, individuals and economic organs are encouraged to invest in the zone, and they will receive preferential treatment in the employment of labor force, land use and tax payment.

The central industrial zone guidance office will direct the development of the zone in a unified way.

The legal rights and interests of foreign investors shall be protected and the inheritance to invested projects ensured in the industrial zone.

The term of land lease fixed for development of the industrial zone is 50 years, which can be extended subject to an approval by the lessor authority even after the expiry of the lease.

Infrastructure construction in the industrial zone shall fall to developers. They may build, if necessary, such infrastructures as power, telecommunications and water supplies under joint contract with other investors or by the methods of transfer and consignment.

Developers should distribute investment enterprises upon the completion of construction of infrastructures in accordance with the zone's general development program. In this case they may transfer or sublease the land use title and buildings to a third party.

Developers are permitted to carry on such business activities as housing construction, tourism, amusement and advertisement business in the zone.

The ground-breaking ceremony for the construction of the Kaesong Industrial Zone, which marks a historic event in the inter-Korean economic cooperation, took place on June 30, Juche 92 (2003).

According to the developers, the zone will cover a total area of 20 million *phyong* (1 *phyong* is 3.3 m^2) and it will be completed by 2010. The project will proceed by stages and the first stage development will cover an area of a million *phyong*.

The central industrial zone guidance office and other organs concerned have already carried out geological survey and prospecting of a million *phyong* so as to complete the zone's general development program.

Light industry will be the primary factor in the construction of the Kaesong Industrial Zone and, if necessary, electronics and machine-building industries may also be given due consideration.

It is envisaged that the zone will, in future, require a labor force of 300,000 persons and produce 15 billion euro's worth of internationally competitive goods to be exported by railways and roads linking northeast Asia and Europe.

The construction of the Kaesong Industrial Zone is a part of patriotism-inspired work for achieving coordinated progress of the national economy and promoting co-prosperity and public interest of the north and the south by the concerted efforts of the Korean nation itself.

The project which is of common concern at home and abroad will be further pushed forward by the positive efforts of businessmen and developers in the north and the south, under the banner of the historic June 15 North-South Joint Declaration.

EXPORT POTENTIAL

The creation of reliable export bases is prerequisite to further promotion of economic and technical cooperation and exchange between countries on the principle of reciprocity.

The great leader President Kim Il Sung said:

"We have already laid the solid foundation of an independent national economy, and this has enabled us to develop trade relations with other countries on an extensive scale."

Today, the export-oriented production bases established throughout the country constitute a sure guarantee for extensively carrying on trade transactions with other countries.

A large number of machine tool factories have been provided with the latest production processes ranging from ingot-making to final machining.

Machine tools of different kinds such as CNC lathes "Kusong-6", "Kusong-10" and "NCS-400", universal milling machine "F1-250", vertical milling machine "F2-250" and NC milling machine enjoy a good reputation in the world market.

Heavy machines and equipment including thermal and hydraulic generators, rotary kilns, high-pressure synthesizing towers, rollers, gears, transformers and motors in great demand abroad are turned out at the giant export-oriented enterprises.

There is also a rapid increase in the production of varieties of small-sized motors, transformers, pumps, cutting tools, batteries for lorries, bearings, wires, as well as all-steel rolled wheels, freight wagons, fishing boats and cargo ships.

The production bases for programs, semiconductors, integrated circuits and high-performance electronic apparatuses have been set up at factories, enterprises and scientific research institutes in the field of electronics industry.

For additional analytical, business and investment opportunities information, please contact Global Investment & Business Center, USA at (202) 546-2103. Fax: (202) 546-3275. E-mail: rusric@erols.com

Iron and steel, electrolytic lead, electrolytic zinc, cadmium, bismuth, tellurium and hard alloy have been mass-produced at the export-oriented bases of ferrous and non-ferrous metal industries.

The Tanchon Magnesia Clinker Factory and other enterprises are now in a position to produce millions of tons of magnesia clinker a year, and its export is on the steady increase.

The establishment of export bases in the fields of construction and building materials, textile and clothing industries, together with handicrafts and fishery has made it possible to promote trade dealings with other countries.

The DPRK government promulgated the regulations on creating export bases in October Juche 88 (1999) in conformity with the actual requirements of the developing foreign trade and took a series of measures to build them with a full support of the state. This has resulted in establishing numerous export bases at the institutions, enterprises and organizations registered as corporate bodies of the DPRK, as well as joint venture enterprises in the Republic, its economic and trade zone and in foreign countries.

The government is paying best endeavours for systematically increasing its investment in expanding the existing export-oriented bases and establishing new ones in the high-tech field including nano technology, bioengineering and gene engineering commensurate with IT era.

It will continue to promote trade transactions with other countries by creating the export bases on an extensive scale.

LARGEST EXPORT -IMPORT COMPANIES IN NORTH KOREA

1. KOREA FERROUS METALS EXPORT & IMPORT CORPORATION

Address: Pothonggang-dong No.1, Pothonggang District, Pyongyang, DPRK

Tel: 850-2-18111-381-8078

Fax: 850-2-381-4581

E-mail:

Export: Steel plates, steel billets, hot-rolled steel sheets, pig iron for steel manufacture, square steel, thick metal plates, round steel, seamless steel pipes, wire ropes, magnetic iron concentrate, ferrosilicon, steel scraps, iron scraps, iron chips

Import: Coking coal, coke, diesel oil, gasoline, machine oil, high-carbon ferromanganese, low-carbon ferromanganese, bearings, artificial graphite electrodes

2. KOREA GENERAL ZINC INDUSTRY GROUP

Address: Tongsong-dong, Central District, Pyongyang, DPRK

    Tel: 850-2-18111-381-8166

    Fax: 850-2-381-4034

E-mail:

Export: Zinc, lead, base bullion, lead and zinc concentrates, cadmium, arsenic, zinc residues, copper concentrate

Import: Equipment and accessories for mines and refineries, steel, reagents, electric equipment and machines, vehicle parts, insulating materials, fibre goods, synthetic resin goods, rubber and its products, nonferrous metals, animal feed

3. KOREA GENERAL CHEMICALS TRADING CORPORATION

Address: Sinri-dong, Tongdaewon District, Pyongyang, DPRK

    Tel: 850-2-18111-381-8974

    Fax: 850-2-381-4623

E-mail:

Export: Liquefied gas, urea fertilizer, ammonium nitrate fertilizer, explosives, blasting fuse, percussion caps, sodium nitrate, potassium nitrate, sodium nitrite, conveyor belts, rubber asbestos packing, aluminium silicon, aluminium hydroxide, chrome yellow, potash alum

Import: Caustic soda, potassium carbonate, normal hexane, accelerating agents (M, D, DM), plasticizer, chromic anhydride, zinc dusting powder, titanium white, glycerine, seamless steel pipes, steel plates, V-belts, PP bags, high alumina cement, electrolytic nickel, silver foil

4. KOREA GENERAL MACHINERY TRADING CORPORATION

Address: Tongsin-dong No. 3, Tongdaewon District, Pyongyang, DPRK

    Tel: 850-2-18111-381-8102

    Fax: 850-2-381-4495

E-mail:

Export: Various machine tools, metal processing and mining equipment, large-size gears, compressors, transformers, generators, motors, insulators, pumps, valves, rolling stocks and parts

Import: Steel, chemical materials, machine accessories

5. KOREA KWANGMYONG TRADING GROUP

Address: Jungsong-dong, Central District, Pyongyang, DPRK

    Tel: 850-2-18111-381-8111

Fax: 850-2-381-4494

E-mail:

Export: Agricultural produce, marine products, nonmetallic minerals, clothes, essential oil, processed jewels

Import: Fibre goods, vessel equipment and materials

6. KOREA PONGHWA GENERAL CORPORATION

Address: Jungsong-dong, Central District, Pyongyang, DPRK

Tel: 850-2-18111-381-8023

Fax: 850-2-381-4444

E-mail:

Export: Clothes, shoes, bags, knitwear, agricultural produce, marine products

Import: Materials for clothes and shoes, packing materials, fishing tackles, high-pressure polyethylene, sugar

7. KOREA UNHA GENERAL TRADING CORPORATION

Address: Rungra-dong No. 1, Taedonggang District, Pyongyang, DPRK

Tel: 850-2-18111-381-8236, 8642

Fax: 850-2-381-4506

E-mail:

Export: Clothes, spring water

Import: Materials and facilities for manufacturing clothes and shoes, grain, gasoline, diesel oil

8. KOREA GENERAL PETROLEUM UNITED CORPORATION

Address: Raknang-dong No. 3, Raknang District, Pyongyang, DPRK

Tel: 850-2-18111-381-8463, 8019

Fax: 850-2-381-4025

E-mail: kpic@silibank.com

Export: Processed crude oil, zinc powder, marine products, agricultural produce, processed stones, paints

Import: Crude oil, oil feeder and accessories, tank cars, building materials, vehicle parts

9. KOREA HWANGGUMSAN TRADING CORPORATION

Address: Jungsong-dong, Central District, Pyongyang, DPRK

    Tel: 850-2-18111-381-8278

    Fax: 850-2-381-3451

E-mail:

Export: Agriculture produce

Import: Fertilizers, agricultural chemicals, vinyl sheets, herbicides, farming materials

10. KOREA MINYE GENERAL CORPORATION

Address: Oesong-dong, Central District, Pyongyang, DPRK

    Tel: 850-2-18111-381-8178

    Fax: 850-2-381-8088

E-mail:

Export: Art pieces (oil paintings, Korean paintings, woodcut prints, calligraphic works), industrial craftworks, national musical instruments, clothes

Import: Piano strings, caustic soda, glycerine, stearic acid, sodium carbonate, photographic chemicals, oil colours, lacquer, carton paper

11. KOREA MANNYON GENERAL HEALTH CORPORATION

Address: Chongryu-dong No.2, Taedonggang District, Pyongyang, DPRK

    Tel: 850-2-18111-381-8905

    Fax: 850-2-381-4546

E-mail:

Export: Koryo Insam products, health food, natural medicinal herbs, medical instruments and equipment

Import: Medicines, pharmaceutical materials, packing materials, medical instruments and equipment

12. KOREA SONBONG GENERAL TRADING CORPORATION

Address: Kinmaul-dong No.1, Moranbong District, Pyongyang, DPRK

    Tel: 850-2-18111-381-8136

    Fax: 850-2-381-4416

E-mail:

Export: Clothes, medicinal honey, marine products, synthetic waddings, drawing dice, cutting bites

Import: Goods for sale at shops (cloths, sundry goods, household articles, electric appliances, furniture)

13. KOREA TAEHUNG TRADING CORPORATION

Address: Ansan-dong No.1, Phyongchon District, Pyongyang, DPRK

   Tel: 850-2-18111-381-8307, 8045, 8695

   Fax: 850-2-381-4508, 4001

E-mail:

Export: Furs, essential oil, Armillaria edodes, marine products, nonmetallic minerals, hemp cloth

Import: Diesel oil, gasoline, machine oil, rubber goods, chemical goods, grain, packing materials, ship accessories, fishing tackles, farming materials, cloths, paints, vessel parts

14. KOREA RUNGRADO GENERAL TRADING CORPORATION

Address: Segori-dong, Pothonggang District, Pyongyang, DPRK

   Tel: 850-2-18111-381-8022

   Fax: 850-2-381-4507

E-mail:

Export: Sindok Spring Water, marine products, knitwear, clothes, metallic and nonmetallic minerals, natural shell buttons

Import: Light industrial goods

15. KOREA ORYUN GENERAL TRADING CORPORATION

Address: Sohung-dong, Moranbong District, Pyongyang, DPRK

   Tel: 850-2-18111-381-8507

   Fax: 850-2-381-4529

E-mail:

Export: Footballs, basketballs, sporting goods, sportswear, marine products, sponge goods

Import: Raw materials for sporting goods, chemical materials, building parts

16. KOREA SINGWANG CORPORATION

Address: Rungra-dong No.1, Taedonggang District, Pyongyang, DPRK

   Tel: 850-2-18111-381-8266

   Fax: 850-2-381-4410

E-mail:

Export: Bivalve iems, plastic compound, marine products, agricultural produce, daily

For additional analytical, business and investment opportunities information,
please contact Global Investment & Business Center, USA
at (202) 546-2103. Fax: (202) 546-3275. E-mail: rusric@erols.com

necessities, nonmetallic minerals

Import: Used tyres, scrap plastics, scrap glass, used gypsum

17. KOREA AGRICULTURAL COOPERATION COMPANY

Address: Tangsang-dong No. 1, Mangyongdae District, Pyongyang, DPRK

Tel:

Fax: 850-2-381-4416

E-mail:

Export: Silkworm eggs, cocoons, perilla seeds

Import: Fertilizers, reagents, agricultural chemicals, sprayers, vinyl sheets, maize for animal feed, bean, tractors, sowing machines for barley, wheat, oat, rye, etc.

18. OCEAN SHIPPING AGENCY

Address: Kinmaul-dong No.1, Moranbong District, Pyongyang, DPRK

Tel: 850-2-18111-381-8100

Fax: 850-2-381-4531

E-mail:

Export:

Import: Separation materials, lashing materials

19. PYONGYANG GENERAL DOMESTIC FOWL CORPORATION

Address: Tongsong-dong, Central District, Pyongyang, DPRK

Tel:

Fax: 850-2-381-4410

E-mail:

Export: Duck, chicken, duck down

Import: Veterinary medicines, poultry farm equipment and accessories, duck down washing agent

20. KOREA OKRYU COMBINED CORPORATION

Address: Ansan-dong No.1, Phyongchon District, Pyongyang, DPRK

Tel: 850-2-18111-381-8092

Fax: 850-2-381-4618

E-mail:

For additional analytical, business and investment opportunities information,
please contact Global Investment & Business Center, USA
at (202) 546-2103. Fax: (202) 546-3275. E-mail: rusric@erols.com

Export: Kangso Mineral Water, marine products, Pyongyang Liquor, Ponghak Beer, cigarettes, clothes, red peppered bean paste, cold noodle, dehydrated starch noodle, cucumber, tomato, sweet pepper, nonmetallic minerals, ceramics, industrial craftworks, cement

Import: Goods for sale at shop, building materials

21. KOREA AMROKGANG TRADING CORPORATION

Address: Haebang-dong, Sinuiju City, North Phyongan Province' DPRK

    Tel: 850-2-18111-061-25-0502

    Fax: 850-2-381-2626

E-mail:

Export: Metallic silicon, pulp, processed stones, marine products, agricultural produce

Import: Fuel oil, nitrogenous fertilizer

22. ARIRANG TRADING CORPORATION

Address: Tongsong-dong, Central District, Pyongyang, DPRK

    Tel: 850-2-18111-381-8450

    Fax: 850-2-381-4789

E-mail:

Export: Vegetables, flowering plants and seeds

Import: Facilities for research into seeds of flowering plants, greenhouse building materials, agricultural chemicals

23. ASABONG TRADING COMPANY (PYONGYANG BRANCH OFFICE OF THE INTERNATIONAL ORGANIZATION OF JOURNALISTS)

Address: Othan-dong, Central District, Pyongyang, DPRK

    Tel:

    Fax: 850-2-381-4410

E-mail:

Export: Medicinal herbs

Import: Foodstuffs, photographic paper, films, cameras, cloths, electric appliances, rolling stocks

24. KOREA BUILDING MATERIALS TRADING CORPORATION

Address: Tongdaewon-dong No. 1, Tongdaewon District, Pyongyang, DPRK

Tel: 850-2-18111-381-8085

Fax: 850-2-381-4555

E-mail:

Export: Cement, asbestos, natural slate, granite, crude and processed marble stones, sponge and its goods

Import: Kraftpaper bags for packing cement, PP bags, bearings, rolling stocks, rollers for belt conveyor, electric and electronic accessories, gypsum

25. KOREA CERAMIC TRADING CORPORATION

Address: Sohung-dong, Moranbong District, Pyongyang, DPRK

Tel:

Fax: 850-2-381-4410

E-mail:

Export: Sepiolite, feldspar, ceramic craftworks

Import: Gypsum, reagents, ferromanganese, electrolytic copper, aluminium ingots, tin, paraffin, rolling stocks and parts

26. KOREA 6. 17 TRADING CORPORATION

Address: Songsin-dong No.1, Sadong District, Pyongyang, DPRK

Tel: 850-2-18111-381-8563

Fax: 850-2-381-2100

E-mail:

Export: Bottled beer, draft beer, barley tea, fermented vinegar

Import: Barley, hop, alcohol, sugar, glacial acetic acid, sodium phosphate, glycol, calcium chloride

27. KOREA CHILBOSAN TRADING CORPORATION

Address: Kansong-dong, Phyongchon District, Pyongyang, DPRK

Tel:

Fax: 850-2-381-4410

E-mail:

Export: Women's dresses (suits, skirts, vests, trousers, jumperskirts, blouses, coats, sportswear), children's clothes

Import: Cloths, cotton, sewing machines and accessories, sewing-machine oil

28. KOREA CHILMYONG TRADING CORPORATION

Address: Jungsong-dong, Central District, Pyongyang, DPRK

Tel: 850-2-18111-381-8008

Fax: 850-2-381-4593

E-mail:

Export: Cutlery, health drinks, marine products, insulating tapes

Import: Heavy-duty rolling stocks, stainless steel plates, insulating materials, packing tapes, vinyl sheets, cloths, reagents, palm oil, livestock feed

29. KOREA CHINSON PRODUCTION TRADING CORPORATION

Address: Jungsong-dong, Central District, Pyongyang, DPRK

Tel: 850-2-18111-381-8549

Fax: 850-2-381-4410

E-mail:

Export: Wheat, wheat flour, bean, vegetables

Import: Grain, fertilizers, agricultural chemicals, herbicides, vinyl sheets, fuel oil, farming machines and parts

30. KOREA CHOLBONG TRADING CORPORATION

Address: Kwangbok-dong No. 2, Mangyongdae District, Pyongyang, DPRK

Tel: 850-2-18111-381-8355

Fax: 850-2-381-2100

E-mail:

Export: Marine products

Import: Fuel oil, wire ropes, fishing tackles

31. KOREA CHOLSAN GENERAL TRADING CORPORATION

Address: Saesallim-dong, Tongdaewon District, Pyongyang, DPRK

Tel: 850-2-18111-381-8403

Fax: 850-2-381-4410

E-mail:

Export: Iron oxide, molybdenum disulphide, bentonite, metallic and nonmetallic minerals, agricultural produce, marine products, nonferrous concentrates, jade, for infrared tiles

For additional analytical, business and investment opportunities information, please contact Global Investment & Business Center, USA at (202) 546-2103. Fax: (202) 546-3275. E-mail: rusric@erols.com

Import: Vehicle parts, daily necessities, computer equipment

32. KOREA CHOLSAN TECHNICAL TRADING CORPORATION

Address: Saesallim-dong, Tongdaewon District, Pyongyang, DPRK

Tel: 850-2-18111-381-8403

Fax: 850-2-381-4410

E-mail:

Export: Kumgang yakdol (medicinal stone) tiles, leftovers of lead, aluminium and zinc

Import: Computer equipment and accessories, computer network equipment and accessories, paper

33. KOREA CHONGGIL TRADING CORPORATION

Address: Othan-dong, Central District, Pyongyang, DPRK

Tel: 850-2-18111-381-8005

Fax: 850-2-381-4452

E-mail:

Export: Potato, potato starch

Import: Rice, glutinous rice, maize, bean

34. CHONGGYECHON TECHNOLOGY TRADING CORPORATION

Address: Ryonghung-dong No. 3, Taesong District, Pyongyang, DPRK

Tel:

Fax: 850-2-381-2100

E-mail:

Export: Potato starch, nonvirus mini tuber potatoes, natural food colours, Ganoderma lucidum

Import: Vinyl sheets, kraftpaper, cloths, reagents, experimental apparatuses

35. KOREA CHONGSU TRADING CORPORATION

Address: Inhung-dong, Moranbong District, Pyongyang, DPRK

Tel: 850-2-18111-381-8263

Fax: 850-2-381-4748

E-mail:

Export: Marine products, gold concentrate, jade tiles, nonmetallic minerals

Import: Printing equipment, paper, reagents, fishing tackles

36. KOREA CIGARETTE EXPORT AND IMPORT CORPORATION

Address: Ryongsong-dong No.1, Ryongsong District, Pyongyang, DPRK

Tel: 850-2-18111-381-8199

Fax: 850-2-381-4708

E-mail:

Export: Filter cigarettes, leaf tobacco, paper

Import: Materials for cigarettes and cigarette paper, belts

37. KORYO COMMERCIAL TRUST CO. , LTD.

Address: Chongryu-dong No.1, Taedonggang District, Pyongyang, DPRK

Tel: 850-2-18111-381-8561

Fax: 850-2-381-4441

E-mail:

Export: Electrolytic lead, electrolytic zinc, molybdenum concentrate, talc

Import: Clothes, shoes, household electric and electronic goods

38. DAILY NECESSITIES INDUSTRY TRADING CORPORATION

Address: Pothongmun-dong, Central District, Pyongyang, DPRK

Tel: 850-2-18111-381-8139

Fax: 850-2-381-7807

E-mail:

Export: Cosmetics, toothbrushes, toothpaste, soap, plastic goods, toys, vinyl sheets, mini-transformers

Import: Chemical products, plastics, materials for cosmetics, industrial oil

39. KOREA DUTY-FREE CORPORATION

Address: Kansong-dong, Phyongchon District, Pyongyang, DPRK

Tel: 850-2-18111-381-8234

Fax: 850-2-381-4489

E-mail:

Export:

Import: Cigarettes, drinks, foodstuffs, raw materials for foodstuffs, cosmetics, furniture.

For additional analytical, business and investment opportunities information,
please contact Global Investment & Business Center, USA
at (202) 546-2103. Fax: (202) 546-3275. E-mail: rusric@erols.com

electronic goods

40. KOREA 813 TRADING CORPORATION

Address: Tongsong-dong, Central District, Pyongyang, DPRK

Tel: 850-2-18111-381-8251

Fax: 850-2-381-4473

E-mail:

Export: Marine products, *Kimchi* (Korean pickled vegetables), liquors, soft drinks, sponge, granite, marble, polished flagstones, agricultural produce

Import: Crude oil, agricultural chemicals, fertilizers, paints, fishing tackles

41. KOREA 8. 28 GENERAL TRADING CORPORATION

Address: Ansan-dong No.1, Phyongchon District, Pyongyang, DPRK

Tel: 850-2-18111-381-8226

Fax: 850-2-381-4410

E-mail:

Export: Rabbit furs, ragworms, marine products, agricultural produce, liquors, red peppered bean paste

Import: Paper (newspaper, vellum paper, art paper, cardboard), printing inks, paints, cloths, shoes

42. KOREA ELECTRICITY & COAL TRADING CORPORATION

Address: Tongmun-dong No.1, Taedonggang District, Pyongyang, DPRK

Tel: 850-2-18111-381-8498

Fax: 850-2-381-4541

E-mail:

Export: Amorphous graphite, ferrosilicon, serpentine, vanadium, potassium carbonate

Import: Mining facilities and materials, facilities and materials for power stations, electric wire, insulating materials

43. KOREA EQUIPMENT & PLANT CORPORATION

Address: Jungsong-dong, Central District, Pyongyang, DPRK

Tel: 850-2-18111-381-8032

Fax: 850-2-381-4498

E-mail:

Export: Complete sets of factory equipment, natural roofing-slates, ball pens, mineral waters

Import: Complete sets of factory equipment (power station, beer brewery, building materials factory, communications equipment factory, cosmetics factory, cement factory, textile mill, meat-processing factory, fertilizer factory, shoes factory, flour factory)

44. KORYO EXPORT & IMPORT CORPORATION

Address: Tonghung-dong, Central District, Pyongyang, DPRK

Tel: 850-2-18111-381-8063

Fax: 850-2-381-0441, 4416

E-mail:

Export: Songhak liquor, Insam wine

Import: Materials for hotel-keeping and service, fishing tackles, gasoline, diesel oil

45. KORYO FINANCE & TRADE COMPANY

Address: Ponghwa-dong, Pothonggang District, Pyongyang, DPRK

Tel: 850-2-18111-381-8168

Fax: 850-2-381-4033

E-mail:

Export: Electrolytic gold, marine products

Import: Electric and electronic goods

46. KOREA 56 TRADING CORPORATION

Address: Chongryu-dong No. 1, Taedonggang District, Pyongyang, DPRK

Tel: 850-2-18111-381-8076

Fax: 850-2-381-4410

E-mail:

Export: Eleutherococc extract

Import: Paper, printing inks, microphones, amplifiers

47. KOREA FOREIGN TRANSPORTATION CORPORATION

Address: Jungsong-dong, Central District, Pyongyang, DPRK

Tel: 850-2-18111-381-8053

Fax: 850-2-831-4445

E-mail:

Export:

Import:

Business line: The corporation has its branch offices at the trade ports and places adjacent to Russia and China, and arranges loading and unloading as well as transportation of cargoes.

48. PYONGYANG TRANSPORT TRADING CORPORATION

Address: Chongryu-dong No.3, Taedonggang District, Pyongyang, DPRK

Tel: 850-2-18111-381-8349

Fax: 850-2-381-4416

E-mail:

Export: Sweet potato leaf-stalks, edible herbs, embroideries

Import: Electric and electronic goods, vehicle parts, scrapped vehicles for dismantling, fibre goods, daily necessities

49. 4. 27 CORPORATION

Address: Jongphyong-dong, Phyongychon District, Pyongyang, DPRK

Tel: 850-2-18111-381-8009

Fax: 850-2-381-4767

E-mail:

Export: Designing, construction and decoration of buildings like hotels, museums and other real estates, technical service, sculptures, panoramas, semi-panoramas, mural paintings, art objects, handicrafts

Import: Equipment, materials and tools for construction of real estates, materials for heating system, sculptures, art objects

50. PYONGYANG FRIENDSHIP IMPORT CORPORATION

Address: Munsu-dong No.3, Taedonggang District, Pyongyang, DPRK

Tel: 850-2-18111-381-8998

Fax: 850-2-381-4410

E-mail:

Export:

Import: Building parts, steel, rolling stocks, diesel oil, gasoline, foodstuffs, daily necessities, electric and electronic goods, chemical materials, tropical fruits

51. KOREA GENERAL CORPORATION FOR EXTERNAL CONSTRUCTION

Address: Jungsong-dong, Central District, Pyongyang, DPRK

Tel: 850-2-18111-381-8090

Fax: 850-2-381-4611

E-mail:

Export:

Import:

Business line: The corporation takes charge of all the processes from designing to building work for different projects such as dwelling houses, public establishments, industrial buildings, structures, thermal and hydroelectric power stations, bridges, railways, roads, irrigation system, ports, airports, metros, etc., and, at the same time, conducts foreign trade for necessary equipment and materials.

52. KOREA GOLDEN TRIANGLE TRADING CORPORATION

53. GREEN (ROKSAEK) 623 PAINTS COMPANY

Address: Ryonhwa-dong No.2, Central District, Pyongyang, DPRK

Tel: 850-2-18111-381-8541

Fax: 850-2-381-4011

E-mail:

Export: Paints, reed screens

Import: Paint materials, hemp-palm thread, bamboo, PP bags, plate glass

54. KOREA HAEBANGSAN TRADING CORPORATION

Address: Oesong-dong, Central District, Pyongyang, DPRK

Tel:

Fax: 850-2-381-2100

E-mail:

Export: Software and hardware, marine products, agricultural produce, processed jewels

Import: Meteorological instruments and materials, electric and electronic equipment and accessories, fishing tackles

55. KOREA HAESONG TRADING CORPORATION

Address: Kallimgil-dong No. 2, Mangyongdae District, Pyongyang, DPRK

Tel: 850-2-18111-381-8596

Fax: 850-2-381-2100

E-mail:

Export: Marine products

Import: Wire ropes, fuel oil, ferromanganese, tin, grain

56. KOREA HAEYANG IMPORT CORPORATION

Address: Kinmaul-dong No. 1, Moranbong District, Pyongyang, DPRK

    Tel: 850-2-18111-381-8839

    Fax: 850-2-381-4528

E-mail:

Export:

Import: Equipment and building materials for vessels and docks, paints, diesel oil, heavy oil, synthetic resin, clothes

57. KOREA HAEGUMGANG COMPANY

Address: Pothonggang-dong No.1, Pothonggang District, Pyongyang, DPRK

    Tel:

    Fax: 850-2-381-2421

E-mail:

Export: Hairpins, hair bands, clips

Import: Broadcasting equipment, industrial goods, foodstuffs, vehicle parts, patent and trademark service

58. KOREA HAKBONG TRADING CORPORATION

Address: Tongan-dong, Central District, Pyongyang, DPRK

    Tel: 850-2-18111-381-8804

    Fax: 850-2-381-4410

E-mail:

Export: Marine products, Koryo (traditional Korean) medicines, contracting measurement treatment of clothes

Import: Medicines, medical facilities, electronic goods

59. KOREA HUNGSONG GROUP OF TRADING CORPORATIONS

Address: Chukjon-dong No.2, Mangyongdae District, Pyongyang, DPRK

    Tel: 850-2-18111-381-8122

    Fax: 850-2-381-4629

E-mail:

Export: Electrolytic copper, electrolytic zinc, graphite, granite, marine products, bottom paint, roof paint, distemper paints, high-pressure sodium lamps, compact lamps, gold and silver works, computer accessories

Import: Copper concentrate, waste plastics, trotyl, crude rubber, synthetic rubber, ammonium nitrate fertilizer, cotton, stainless steel plates, sodium carbonate

60. KOREA HYANGAMCHON TRADING CORPORATION

Address: Jonsung-dong, Moranbong District, Pyongyang, DPRK

Tel: 850-2-18111-381-8538

Fax: 850-2-381-4410

E-mail:

Export: Marine products (live fish, crabs, halibut, shellfishes, abalone, sea cucumber, frozen squid, seasoned sea urchin eggs, pollack), agricultural produce

Import: Electric and electronic goods and parts, glass, gasoline, diesel oil, cloths, fishing tackles

61. KOREA INDUSTRIAL TECHNOLOGY CORPORATION

Address: Sinhung-dong No. 2, Tongdaewon District, Pyongyang, DPRK

Tel: 850-2-18111-381-8025

Fax: 850-2-381-4537

E-mail:

Export: Patent programs, fingerprint verification lock

Import: Electrolytic copper, electrolytic lead, aluminium ingots, paper, galvanized iron plates, cobalt oxide, tungsten carbide, low-carbon ferrochrome, electronic elements

62. KOREA INDUSTRIAL TECHNOLOGY TRADING CORPORATION

Address: Kaeson-dong, Moranbong District, Pyongyang, DPRK

Tel: 850-2-18111-381-8181

Fax: 850-2-381-4410

E-mail:

Export: Publications on order, marine products

Import: Photographing equipment and materials, computers and accessories, printing materials

63. KOREA INHUNG TRADING CORPORATION

Address: Ansan-dong No. 1, Phyongchon District, Pyongyang, DPRK

Tel: 850-2-18111-381-8006

Fax: 850-2-381-4548

E-mail:

Export:

Import: Equipment and materials for hotels, materials for hotel-keeping and service

64. GENERAL INFORMATION TECHNOLOGY INDUSTRY CORPORATION

Address: Songyo-dong No. 2, Songyo District, Pyongyang, DPRK

Tel: 850-2-18111-381-8441

Fax: 850-2-381-4416

E-mail:

Export: Information technology goods (equipment, software), marine products, metallic and nonmetallic minerals, high-purity metals

Import: Electric and electronic goods

65. KOREA INPHUNG TRADING CORPORATION

Address: Sinmun-dong, Kanggye City, Jagang Province, DPRK

Tel: 850-2-18111-067-43-0501

Fax: 850-2-381-2524

E-mail:

Export: Concentrates of gold, silver, lead and zinc, calcium carbonate, silk thread, edible herbs, agricultural produce, essential oil

Import: Gasoline, diesel oil, lubricating oil, galvanized iron plates, sodium carbonate, steel plates, wire ropes, paints, plastic bags, cotton cloths

66. INTERNATIONAL ECONOMIC UNITED CO. , LTD.

Address: Raknang-dong No. 3, Raknang District, Pyongyang, DPRK

Tel: 850-2-18111-381-8013

Fax: 850-2-381-4032

E-mail:

Export: Marine products, agricultural produce

Import: Grain, paints, electric facilities and goods, building materials

67. KOREA INTERNATIONAL INVESTMENT DEVELOPMENT CORPORATION

Address: Chongryu-dong No. 1, Taedonggang District, Pyongyang, DPRK

Tel: 850-2-18111-381-8257

Fax: 850-2-381-4588

E-mail:

Export: Processed crude oil, marine products

Import: Batteries, crude rubber, metal goods, fittings

68. INTERNATIONAL TAEKWON-DO FEDERATION TRADING CORPORATION

Address: Chukjon-dong No. 1, Mangyongdae District, Pyongyang, DPRK

Tel: 850-2-18111-381-8721

Fax: 850-2-381-4539

E-mail:

Export: Taekwon-do uniforms, marine products

Import: Daily necessities, foodstuffs

69. KOREA JANGCHON TRADING CORPORATION

Address: Jangchon-dong, Sadong District, Pyongyang, DPRK

Tel: 850-2-18111-381-8450

Fax: 850-2-381-4789

E-mail:

Export: Vegetable seeds, vegetables, vegetable breeding and cultivating expertise

Import: Vegetable seeds, vegetables, building materials for greenhouse, fertilizers, agricultural chemicals

70. JANGCHONG TRADING CORPORATION

Address: Taedongmun-dong, Central District, Pyongyang, DPRK

Tel: 850-2-18111-381-8920

Fax: 850-2-381-4719

E-mail:

Export: Scientific books, CD-ROMs carrying scientific manuscripts

Import: Miscellaneous fibre goods, electronic goods

71. KOREA JANGHUNG TRADING CORPORATION

Address: Mansu-dong, Central District, Pyongyang, DPRK

Tel: 850-2-18111-381-8755

Fax: 850-2-381-4410

E-mail:

Export: Marine products

Import: Industrial goods, foodstuffs, fishing tackles

For additional analytical, business and investment opportunities information,
please contact Global Investment & Business Center, USA
at (202) 546-2103. Fax: (202) 546-3275. E-mail: rusric@erols.com

72. KOREA JANGSAN TRADING CORPORATION

Address: Janggyong-dong, Sosong District, Pyongyang, DPRK

Tel: 850-2-18111-381-8710

Fax: 850-2-381-2100

E-mail:

Export: Marine products, agricultural produce, minerals

Import: Fuel oil, machines, chemical products, grain, foodstuffs, electric and electronic goods, building materials, fixtures

73. KOREA JANGSU TRADING CORPORATION

Address: Kyogu-dong, Central District, Pyongyang, DPRK

Tel: 850-2-18111-381-8834

Fax: 850-2-381-2100

E-mail:

Export: Tinned red Insam, red Insam powder, Insam tonic, Insam syrup, natural red Insam, white Insam, Insam tea, vitaton, sexton, Insam wine

Import: Medicines, reagents, medical instruments, packing materials

74. KOREA JANGSUBONG TRADING CORPORATION

Address: Sochang-dong, Central District, Pyongyang, DPRK

Tel: 850-2-18111-381-8863

Fax: 850-2-381-4410

E-mail:

Export: Paper mulberry trees, spring waters

Import: Colour films and photographic paper, photographic chemicals, professional cameras, art paper, colours

75. KOREA JINHUNG COMPANY

Address: Tongmun-dong No.1, Taedonggang District, Pyongyang, DPRK

Tel: 850-2-18111-381-8675

Fax: 850-2-381-4416

E-mail:

Export: Koryo medicines, various kinds of tea, Ryongji (Ganoderma lucidum) tonic, Eleutherococc tonic, Insam Eleutherococc tonic, health drinks, liquors

For additional analytical, business and investment opportunities information,
please contact Global Investment & Business Center, USA
at (202) 546-2103. Fax: (202) 546-3275. E-mail: rusric@erols.com

Import: Reagents, equipment and materials for medical research

76. KOREA JINUNG TRADING CORPORATION

Address: Ryongnam-dong, Taesong District, Pyongyang, DPRK

Tel: 850-2-18111-381-8372

Fax: 850-2-381-4416

E-mail:

Export: Silver-water producing stone, horseradish, cultured tissue seedlings of flowering plants, software

Import: Chemical reagents, experimental apparatuses, paints, printing materials, electronic goods

77. KOREA JINMYONG TRADING CORPORATION

Address: Ansan-dong No. 1, Phyongchon District, Pyongyang, DPRK

Tel: 850-2-18111-381-8229

Fax: 850-2-381-4410

E-mail:

Export: Handicrafts, marine products, agricultural produce, rabbit furs

Import: Daily necessities, fibre goods, foodstuffs, electronic goods, glues, paper, printing and photographing materials, cloths, fruits, soft drinks

78. KOREA JONLAM TRADING CORPORATION

Address: Jungsong-dong, Central District, Pyongyang, DPRK

Tel: 850-2-18111-381-8030

Fax: 850-2-381-4410

E-mail: kiec@silibank.com

Export: Handicrafts, art works, ceramics, glassware, liquors, marine products, agricultural produce

Import: Goods for trade fair, light industrial goods, foodstuffs, publishing materials

79. KOREA JONMYONG-JOHUNG TRADING CORPORATION

Address: Chongo-dong, Taesong District, Pyongyang, DPRK

Tel: 850-2-18111-381-8606

Fax: 850-2-381-4410

E-mail:

Export: Marine products, Lentinus edodes, electrolytic zinc

Import: Goods for sale at shop

80. KOREA JONSONG TRADING CORPORATION

Address: Sangsin-dong, Sosong District, Pyongyang, DPRK

Tel: 850-2-18111-381-8662

Fax:

E-mail:

Export: Marine products, nonmetallic minerals

Import: Fishing tackles, packing materials, wire ropes, vinyl sheets, belts, paints, vehicle parts, electric and electronic goods, tropical fruits

81. PYONGYANG JONSUNG TRADING CORPORATION

Address: Jonsung-dong, Moranbong District, Pyongyang, DPRK

Tel:

Fax: 850-2-381-4416

E-mail:

Export: Photographs engraved on stones, stone products, embroideries, souvenirs

Import: Sponage leather, cloths, drinks

82. KOREA JUNMA CORPORATION

Address: Janghyon-dong, Moranbong District, Pyongyang, DPRK

Tel: 850-2-18111-381-8255

Fax: 850-2-381-4416

E-mail:

Export: AD-30 (30%-grade aluminium dross), ordered printing services

Import: Newspaper, vellum paper, art paper, printing inks, PS plates, printing equipment

83. KOREA KIYONG TRADING CORPORATION

Address: Sinri-dong, Tongdaewon District, Pyongyang, DPRK

Tel: 850-2-18111-381-8928

Fax: 850-2-381-2100

E-mail:

Export: Kumgang yakdol (medicinal stone) tiles, Kumgang yakdol powder, quartz powder, quartz works

Import: Light industrial goods

84. KOREA KORYO NAMJIN CORPORATION

Address: Jungdan-dong, Raknang District, Pyongyang, DPRK

Tel: 850-2-18111-381-8496

Fax: 850-2-381-4410

E-mail:

Export: Marine products, distilled liquors

Import: Tropical fruits, tiles, vinyl leather, cloths, electric appliances

85. KOREA KORYO-PAPER TECHNOLOGY EXCHANGING CORPORATION

Address: Jungsong-dong, Central District, Pyongyang, DPRK

Tel:

Fax: 850-2-381-4416

E-mail:

Export: Koryo paper, Korean paper made from mulberry fiber

Import: Paper manufacturing equipment, reagents, utensils and tools

86. KOREA KUMBIT TRADING CORPORATION

Address: Ryonghung-dong No.2, Taesong District, Pyongyang, DPRK

Tel: 850-2-18111-381-8335

Fax: 850-2-381-4410

E-mail:

Export: Low-grade gold concentrate, concentrates of silver, zinc, lead and molybdenum, short neck clams, base bullion, adhesives, liquors

Import: Accessories of rolling stocks, chemical products, reagents, animal feed, paper, films, photographic paper, electronic goods

87. KOREA KUMBYOL CORPORATION

Address: Mansu-dong, Central District, Pyongyang, DPRK

Tel: 850-2-18111-381-8148

Fax: 850-2-381-4624

E-mail:

Export: Commemorative coins, commemorative banknotes, circulating currency

Import:

88. KOREA KUMGANG TRADING CORPORATION

Address: Ansan-dong No.1, Phyongchon District, Pyongyang, DPRK

Tel: 850-2-18111-381-8295

Fax: 850-2-381-4668

E-mail:

Export: Gold, silver, lead, zinc and other nonferrous metals

Import: Mining equipment, chemical materials, rolling stocks

89. KOREA KUMRUNG TRADING CORPORATION

Address: Unha-dong, Pothonggang District, Pyongyang, DPRK

Tel: 850-2-18111-381-8808

Fax: 850-2-381-4410

E-mail:

Export: Concentrates of gold, lead and zinc, base bullion, pyrites, nonmetallic minerals, marine products, clothes, pure silk sashes

Import: Heavy-duty machines, rolling stocks and parts, pitch, mining equipment and materials, stone processing tools

90. KOREA KUMSOK TRADING CORPORATION

Address: Ryongbuk-dong, Taesong District, Pyongyang, DPRK

Tel: 850-2-18111-381-8703

Fax: 850-2-381-4410, 4416

E-mail:

Export: Carborundum, molybdenum disulphide, marine products, scheelite residue, concentrates of gold, lead and zinc

Import: Fuel oil, diamond powder, copper powder, electrolytic nickel, ferromanganese, wire ropes, diamond saw tooth, silicon steel sheets, bearings

91. KOREA KUNMYONG TRADING CORPORATION

Address: Kinmaul-dong No.1, Moranbong District, Pyongyang, DPRK

Tel:

Fax: 850-2-381-4416

E-mail:

Export: Marine products, publications (picture books, cartoons), art works, industrial craftworks, embroideries

Import: Printing materials, paper, electronic goods, furniture

92. KOREA KURYONGGANG TRADING CORPORATION

Address: Inhung-dong No.1, Moranbong District, Pyongyang, DPRK

Tel: 850-2-18111-381-8989

Fax: 850-2-381-4480

E-mail:

Export: Various kinds of measuring instruments and gauges

Import: Prototypes for weights and measures, measuring apparatuses, analysis reagents, electronic products and parts

93. KOREA KYONGAM TRADING CORPORATION

Address: Kuchon-dong No.4, Sariwon City, North Hwanghae Province, DPRK

Tel: 850-2-18111-041-33-0506

Fax: 850-2-381-2625

E-mail:

Export: Slates, straw carpets, agricultural produce, medicinal herbs, base bullion, Kumgang yakdol (medicinal stone)

Import: Nylon bristle, resin, chemical fibre, synthetic leather, synthetic rubber, farming materials

94. KOREA LIGHT INDUSTRY TRADING CORPORATION

Address: Pothongmun-dong, Central District, Pyongyang, DPRK

Tel: 850-2-18111-381-8139

Fax: 850-2-381-7807

E-mail:

Export: Cloths, threads, handicrafts, enamelware, raincoats, clothes, liquors, mini-transformers, art works, shoes, kaolinite

Import: Ginned cotton, tetoron cotton, cotton yarn, tetoron yarn, nylon yarn, weaving and knitting machines, rolled-metal products, rubber, paper, industrial oil, leaf tobacco

95. KOREA MANDAE TRADING CORPORATION

Address: Tongsong-dong, Central District, Pyongyang, DPRK

Tel: 850-2-18111-381-8663

Fax: 850-2-381-4410

E-mail:

Export: Marine products

Import: Building equipment and materials, electric and electronic goods, glass, fishing tackles, light industrial goods

96. KOREA MANGYONG-SOGAM TRADING CORPORATION

Address: Sonnae-dong, Mangyongdae District, Pyongyang, DPRK

Tel: 850-2-18111-381-8127

Fax: 850-2-381-4416

E-mail:

Export: Koryo (traditional Korean) medicines, medicinal drinks (rebloomon, Yanggeron, Saengmaek honey, anti-VDTS, fraktus rubi-schizandra-lycii-mel, Insam-schizandra tincture), health food (wild Insam tea, Yanggeron tea, wild Insam wine, Ganoderma lucidum wine)

Import: Raw materials for Koryo medicines, packing materials, pharmaceutical equipment

97. KOREA MARINE PRODUCTS TRADING CORPORATION

Address: Pothongmun-dong, Central District, Pyongyang, DPRK

Tel: 850-2-18111-381-8513, 8543

Fax: 850-2-381-4082, 4083

E-mail:

Export: Various kinds of fishes including pollack, flatfish and trout, and shellfishes

Import: Fishing tackles, diesel oil, lubricating oil, wire ropes

98. MANSUDAE OVERSEAS PROJECT GROUP OF COMPANIES

Address: Jongphyong-dong, Phyongchon District, Pyongyang, DPRK

Tel: 850-2-18111-381-8504

Fax: 850-2-381-4410

E-mail:

Export: Pictures (Korean paintings, oil paintings, mural paintings, publishing paintings, powdered jewel pictures), ceramic ware, embroideries, industrial art objects, sculptures, badges, bronze statues, stone sculptures, designing and manufacture of decorations of buildings

Import: Materials for art works and handicrafts

99. KOREA METAL & MACHINE EXPORT, IMPORT CORPORATION

Address: Pothonggang-dong No. 1, Pothonggang District, Pyongyang, DPRK

Tel: 850-2-18111-381-8478

Fax: 850-2-381-4410

E-mail:

Export: Tin plates and its products, rare metals, ferroalloy, nonmetallic minerals, electric wires, turbines and accessories of hydroelectric generators, tools, insulating materials, electric appliances

Import: Grain, foodstuffs

100. KOREA MORAN GENERAL CORPORATION
NO. 1 TRADING COMPANY

Address: Sonnae-dong, Mangyongdae District, Pyongyang, DPRK

Tel: 850-2-18111-381-8245

Fax: 850-2-381-4522

E-mail:

Export:

Import: Electric appliances, kitchen utensils, liquors, medicines, fibre, textiles, cosmetics, furniture, sporting goods, shoes, clocks, bags, toys

101. KOREA MORAN GENERAL CORPORATION
NO. 2 TRADING COMPANY

Address: Sonnae-dong, Mangyongdae District, Pyongyang, DPRK

Tel: 850-2-18111-381-8245

Fax: 850-2-381-4410

E-mail:

Export:

Import:

Business line: The company engages in import, transit trade and wholesale of cigarettes.

102. KOREA MORAN GENERAL CORPORATION
NO. 3 TRADING COMPANY

Address: Sonnae-dong, Mangyongdae District, Pyongyang, DPRK

Tel: 850-2-18111-381-8245

Fax: 850-2-381-4522

E-mail:

Export:

Import: Foodstuffs, household articles, electronic goods, fibre, cloths

103. KOREA MUNPHIL TRADING CORPORATION

Address: Minhung-dong, Moranbong District, Pyongyang, DPRK

Tel:

Fax: 850-2-381-4410

E-mail:

Export: Marine products

Import: Paper, electric and electronic goods

104. KOREA MUNSU TRADING CORPORATION

Address: Tongmun-dong No.1, Taedonggang District, Pyongyang, DPRK

Tel:

Fax: 850-2-381-2100

E-mail:

Export: Marine products, agricultural produce, far infrared sauna facilities, concentrates of gold, lead and zinc

Import: Industrial goods, paper, chemical goods

105. KOREA SAENAL TECHNOLOGY TRADING CORPORATION

Address: KoJungsong-dong, Central District, Pyongyang, DPRK

Tel: 850-2-18111-381-8282

Fax: 850-2-381-4410

E-mail:

Export: Dancing fountains, powdered jewel pictures, natural stones, electric motors, essential oil, programs, placer gold prospecting technique. IT service, CNC technical service

Import: Educational equipment and materials, printing materials, computers

106. KOREA MYOHYANG GENERAL TRADING CORPORATION

Address: Phalgol-dong No. 1, Mangyongdae District, Pyongyang, DPRK

Tel: 850-2-18111-381-8342

Fax: 850-2-381-4408

E-mail:
Export: Round steel, square steel, nonferrous metals, steel plates of scrapped ship
Import: Parts and materials of scrapped ship, gasoline, diesel oil

107. KOREA MYONGBONG TRADING CORPORATION

Address: Sinhung-dong No.2, Tongdaewon District, Pyongyang, DPRK
Tel: 850-2-18111-381-8333
Fax: 850-2-381-4410
E-mail:
Export: Handicrafts, grass works, marine products, liquors
Import: Industrial goods, foodstuffs, cameras and photographing materials, printing paper (art paper, vellum paper, newspaper)

108. KOREA MYONGHWA TRADING CORPORATION

Address: Okryu-dong No. 3, Taedonggang District, Pyongyang, DPRK
Tel:
Fax: 850-2-381-4410
E-mail:
Export: Cultured seedlings of **Kimjongilia**, marine products
Import: Flowering plants and their seeds, electronic goods, materials for souvenirs

109. KOREA MYONGO TRADING CORPORATION

Address: Jungsong-dong, Central District, Pyongyang, DPRK
Tel: 850-2-18111-381-8845
Fax: 850-2-381-4718
E-mail: myongo@silibank.com
Export: Electrolytic zinc, base bullion, zinc powder, amethyst, clothes
Import: Fuel oil, vehicle parts, light industrial products, machines, electric motors, marine products, steel plates

110. KOREA MYONGSIM TRADING CORPORATION

Address: Sochon-dong, Sosong District, Pyongyang, DPRK
Tel: 850-2-18111-381-8115
Fax: 850-2-381-4564

E-mail:

Export: Clothes, marine products

Import: Gold foil, gold dust, silver dust, zinc dusting powder, distemper paints, colorants, latex, fuel oil

111. KOREA NAMGANG TRADING CORPORATION

Address: Pulgungori-dong No. 2, Pothonggang District, Pyongyang, DPRK

Tel: 850-2-18111-381-8411

Fax: 850-2-381-4410

E-mail:

Export: Low-grade gold concentrate, low-grade lead concentrate, low-grade zinc concentrate, nonmetallic minerals

Import: Cloths, sugar, building materials

112. KOREA NAMSAN TRADING CORPORATION

Address: Munhwa-dong, Hanggu District, Nampho City, DPRK

Tel: 850-2-18111-039-42-0503

Fax: 850-2-381-4410

E-mail:

Export: Electronic goods, marine products, knitted goods, agricultural produce, embroideries, furs

Import: Palm oil, caustic soda, sodium carbonate, animal feed, vessel and vehicle accessories, fishing tackles, paints

113. KOREA NAMSANJAE TRADING CORPORATION

Address: Jungsong-dong, Central District, Pyongyang, DPRK

Tel:

Fax: 850-2-381-4427

E-mail: namsanjae@silibank.com

Export: Multimedia programs, programs for the retrieval of databases, programs for computer network, communication and security

Import: Computer accessories, office supplies

114. KOREA NATIONAL LAND AND ENVIRONMENT TRADING CORPORATION

Address: Pothonggang-dong No. 1, Pothonggang District, Pyongyang, DPRK

Tel: 850-2-18111-381-8340

Fax: 850-381-4434

E-mail:

Export: Marine products, pine nuts, rubble stones, sand

Import: Gasoline, diesel oil, mobile oil, cloths, wire ropes, tin plates, electrolytic copper, insecticides, herbicides

115. KOREA NATURAL GRAPHITE TRADING CORPORATION

Address: Sosan-dong, Sosong District, Pyongyang, DPRK

Tel: 850-2-18111-381-8728

Fax: 850-2-381-4055

E-mail:

Export: Natural graphite goods (graphite concentrate, graphite brushes, graphite pipes), electrolytic zinc, nonmetallic minerals, marine products

Import: Graphite production equipment, dressing reagents, gasoline, diesel oil, materials for clothes

116. KOREA 9. 26 TRADING CORPORATION

Address: Jungsin-dong, Sosong District, Pyongyang, DPRK

Tel: 850-2-18111-381-8814

Fax: 850-2-381-4410

E-mail:

Export: Commemorative coins, processed precious metals, printed matters, stamps of foreign countries

Import: Equipment for minting coins, printing equipment and parts, chemical materials, paper

117. KOREA OPHALSAN TRADING CORPORATION (1)

Address: Thongil-dong No. 2, Raknang District, Pyongyang, DPRK

Tel: 850-2-18111-381-8010

Fax: 850-2-381-4405

E-mail:

Export: Round steel, cement, plastic sashes, distemper paints, artificial marble, water-proof plates, pressurized cement roof tiles, elevators, cast iron pipes

Import: Building materials, ferrous and nonferrous metals, chemical materials, electrodes, gypsum, wire ropes

118. KOREA OPHALSAN TRADING CORPORATION (2)

Address: Sosan-dong, Mangyongdae District, Pyongyang, DPRK
   Tel: 850-2-18111-381-8576
   Fax: 850-2-381-4410
E-mail:
Export: Gold, silver, plastic sashes, sanitary ware, water-proof materials, artificial marble, distemper paints
Import: Cloths, shoes, articles for cultural use, fuel oil

119. KOREA PAEKHAK TRADING CORPORATION

Address: Janghyon-dong, Moranbong District, Pyongyang, DPRK
   Tel:
   Fax: 850-2-381-4410
E-mail:
Export: Agricultural produce
Import: Paper, industrial goods, foodstuffs, daily necessities

120. KOREA PAEKHO TRADING CORPORATION

Address: Raknang-dong No. 2, Raknang District, Pyongyang, DPRK
   Tel: 850-2-18111-381-8950
   Fax: 850-2-381-2100, 4410
E-mail:
Export: Various kinds of audio-video cassettes, silver souvenirs, pianos and fine arts
Import: Various kinds of electronic goods, equipment and materials for films, pianos, musical instruments and publications, a rich selection of nutritious foodstuffs

CULTURAL ENTERTAINMENT: JOINT AND ORDERED PRODUCTION OF CARTOON FILMS AND FEATURE FILMS, EXCHANGE OF CULTURE AND ARTS (MUSIC, DANCE AND ACROBATICS)

121. KOREA PAEKMA TRADING CORPORATION

Address: Sochon-dong, Sosong District, Pyongyang, DPRK
   Tel: 850-2-18111-381-8368
   Fax: 850-2-381-4416
E-mail:

Export: Ordered printing and sale of calendars, catalogues, trademarks, forms, books, notebooks, wallpapers, patterned papers

Import: Paper, printing materials, printing equipment and accessories, diesel oil, gasoline, mobile oil, industrial goods, foodstuffs

122. KOREA PAEKMU TRADING CORPORATION

Address: Hyesan-dong, Hyesan City, Ryanggang Province, DPRK

Tel: 850-2-18111-079-34-0502

Fax: 850-2-381-4416

E-mail:

Export: Nonmetallic minerals, edible herbs, fruits of Crataegus pinnatifida, fruits of Schizandra chinensis, blueberry jelly

Import: Fibre goods, chemical products, electric appliances, building materials, foodstuffs

123. KOREA PHYONGCHON TRADING CORPORATION

Address: Saemaul-dong No. 1, Phyongchon District, Pyongyang, DPRK

Tel: 850-2-18111-381-8568

Fax: 850-2-381-4410

E-mail:

Export:

Import: Various kinds of office supplies such as ball pens, erasers and files, steel filing cabinets, tables, laundry soaps

124. KOREA PHYONGSIN TRADING CORPORATION

Address: Kaeson-dong, Moranbong District, Pyongyang, DPRK

Tel:

Fax: 850-2-381-4410

E-mail:

Export: Marine products

Import: Papers, photographic papers and reagents

125. KOREA PHILBONG TRADING CORPORATION

Address: Munsin-dong No.1, Tongdaewon District, Pyongyang, DPRK

Tel: 850-2-18111-381-8460

Fax: 850-2-381-2100

E-mail:

Export: Sedge mats, sedge cushions, bush-clover baskets

Import: Colour photographic paper, colour films

126. PONGSU GENERAL TRADING CORPORATION

Address: Sojang-dong, Pothonggang District, Pyongyang, DPRK

Tel: 850-2-18111-381-8107

Fax: 850-2-381-4067

E-mail:

Export: Electronic goods (contracting measurement treatment), marine products

Import: Communications equipment, educational apparatuses and materials, medicines and medical instruments, fishing tackles, rolling stocks, fuel oil, articles for cultural use

127. KOREA POST & TELECOMMUNICATIONS TRADING CORPORATION

Address: Oesong-dong, Central District, Pyongyang, DPRK

Tel: 850-2-18111-381-8735

Fax: 850-2-381-4412

E-mail:

Export:

Import: Communications equipment, switching and transmission equipment, TV broadcasting and relay equipment, electronic tubes for broadcasting equipment, materials for producing optical fibre cables and copper cables

128. KOREA PUHUNG TRADING CORPORATION

Address: Jongphyong-dong, Phyongchon District, Pyongyang, DPRK

Tel: 850-2-18111-381-8175

Fax: 850-2-381-4475

E-mail:

Export: Orthoclase, molybdenum, brucite, sulfuric mud, marine products, processed stones

Import: Seamless steel pipes, welded pipes, steel plates, rolling stocks, building materials, gasoline, diesel oil, lubricating oil, mobile oil, non-freezable oil, cotton, tetoron cotton, cloths, sugar, electronic goods and parts

129. KOREA PUKSONG TRADING CORPORATION

Address: Puksong-dong No. 2, Phyongchon District, Pyongyang, DPRK

Tel: 850-2-18111-381-8683

Fax: 850-2-381-4416

E-mail:

Export: Marine products, ground fir, mica, gold concentrate

Import: Tetoron cotton, cotton, crude rubber, synthetic rubber, leather, caustic soda, sodium carbonate, fishing tackles

130. KOREA PYONGYANG TRADING CORPORATION

Address: Ryusong-dong, Central District, Pyongyang, DPRK

Tel: 850-2-18111-381-8634

Fax: 850-2-381-7805

E-mail:

Export: Clothes, knitwear, embroideries, liquors, Okryu cold noodle, red peppered bean paste

Import: Industrial products, chemical materials, raw materials for foodstuffs, essential oil, cloths

131. KOREA RAEIL TRADING CORPORATION

Address: Ryugyong-dong, Pothonggang District, Pyongyang, DPRK

Tel: 850-2-18111-381-8942

Fax: 850-2-381-4092

E-mail:

Export: Artificial bezoar, marine products, embroideries

Import: Newspaper printing facilities, paper, computers, photographing equipment and materials, reagents

132. KOREA RAKWON GENERAL TRADING CORPORATION

Address: Tongsong-dong, Central District, Pyongyang, DPRK

Tel: 850-2-18111-381-8015

Fax: 850-2-381-4474

E-mail:

Export: Cosmetics, school things, metals, concentrates of gold, molybdenum, titanium and zirconium, embroideries, marine products, agricultural produce, cement, clothes, shoes

Import: Raw materials for foodstuffs, foodstuff processing equipment, alcohol, plastics, materials for producing sponge

133. PYONGYANG RECYCLE CORPORATION

Address: Tongdaewon-dong No. 1, Tongdaewon District, Pyongyang, DPRK

Tel: 850-2-18111-381-8074

Fax: 850-2-381-4410

E-mail:

Export: Secondhand electronic amusement facilities, dry distillation of rubber

Import: Reclaimed resin

134. RIMHUNG TRADING CORPORATION

Address: Taesong-dong, Taesong District, Pyongyang, DPRK

Tel: 850-2-18111-381-8450

Fax: 850-2-381-4789

E-mail:

Export: Flower seeds, cut flowers, dried flowers, flowerpots, garden trees, cultured tissue seedlings, floricultural technology

Import: Flower seeds, building materials for greenhouse, fertilizers, agricultural chemicals, experimental equipment and apparatuses

135. KOREA ROKSAN GENERAL TRADING CORPORATION

Address: Pulgungori-dong No. 2, Pothonggang District, Pyongyang, DPRK

Tel: 850-2-18111-381-8321

Fax: 850-2-381-4695

E-mail:

Export: Marine products (octopus, hard-finned sandfish, blue crab, clam, squid, ark shell, sea weed)

Import: Sugar, universal adhesives, tiles, caustic soda, glacial acetic acid, alcohol, building parts, fishing tackles, paper

136. PYONGYANG ROKSAN CORPORATION

Address: Chungsong-dong No. 2, Raknang District, Pyongyang, DPRK

Tel: 850-2-18111-381-8033

Fax: 850-2-381-4089

E-mail:

Export: Bullets for sports rifles

Import: Cars, minibuses, heavy-duty lorries, special vehicles, heavy machines for construction, additives, paints, vehicle tools and parts

137. KOREA RUNGRA 888 TRADING CORPORATION

Address: Sinwon-dong, Pothonggang District, Pyongyang, DPRK

Tel: 850-2-18111-381-8112

Fax: 850-2-381-4608

E-mail:

Export: Medicinal herbs, agricultural produce, folkcrafts, Koryo (traditional Korean) medicines, liquors, processed Insam, canned goods, marine products, non-ferrous metals, silver-water producing stone

Import: Sodium carbonate, printing equipment and materials, crude rubber, rolling stocks and parts, electric and electronic goods

138. KOREA RYONGMA TRADING CORPORATION

Address: Yokjon-dong, Central District, Pyongyang, DPRK

Tel: 850-2-18111-381-8508

Fax: 850-2-381-4410

E-mail:

Export: Embroideries, crabs

Import: Newspaper, art paper, cloth for embroidery, thread, propylene resin

139. KOREA RYONGSAN TRADING CORPORATION

Address: Yokjon-dong, Central District, Pyongyang, DPRK

Tel: 850-2-18111-381-8908

Fax: 8f50-2-381-4410

E-mail:

Export: Embroideries, marine products, processed Kumgang yakdol (medicinal stone)

Import: Printing materials, cloths , vessel accessories, fishing tackles

140. KOREA RYONGGUNBONG TRADING CORPORATION

Address: Chilgol-dong No.1, Mangyongdae District, Pyongyang, DPRK

Tel: 850-2-18111-381-8469

Fax: 850-2-381-4416

E-mail:

Export: Processed stones, jade vessels, cinerary urns, handicrafts

Import: Latex, paper, polished glass, photographing materials, PP bags

141. KOREA RYONMOT TRADING CORPORATION

Address: Sosan-dong, Sosong District, Pyongyang, DPRK

Tel: 850-2-18111-381-8014

Fax: 850-20381-4482

E-mail:

Export: Clothes, knitwear, plant growth stimulants, leather goods, marine products

Import: Cloths, crude rubber, cotton, leather, building materials, fishing tackles

142. KOREA SAEBYOL TRADING CORPORATION

Address: Ponghak-dong, Phyongchon District, Pyongyang, DPRK

Tel: 850-2-18111-381-8072

Fax: 850-2-381-4750

E-mail:

Export: Silicate bricks, marine products, agricultural produce, grass works

Import: Factory equipment and attachments, electronic goods, industrial goods, foodstuffs, kitchen utensils, tiles, glass

143. KOREA SAESIDAE TRADING CORPORATION

Address: Sangsin-dong, Sosong District, Pyongyang, DPRK

Tel: 850-2-18111-381-8940

Fax: 850-2-381-4410

E-mail:

Export: Diatomite, processed stones, marine products

Import: Computers, electric and electronic goods, fibre goods, foodstuffs

144. KOREA SAMGAKJU TRADING CORPORATION

Address: Saemaul-dong No. 1, Phyongchon District, Pyongyang, DPRK

Tel: 850-2-18111-381-8622

Fax: 850-2-381-4410

E-mail:

Export: Marine products, agricultural produce, concentrates of gold, lead and zinc

Import: Fibre, paper, rubber, igniting materials, vehicle parts, fishing tackles, sugar, cloths

145. KOREA SAMGWANG TRADING CORPORATION

Address: Songyo-dong No. 2, Songyo District, Pyongyang, DPRK

Tel: 850-2-18111-381-8416

Fax: 850-2-381-4443

E-mail:

Export: TV sets, computers, tape recorders, video sets, electronic elements, electric fans, electric wires, distributing boards, electric and electronic goods, gauges and instruments

Import: TV sets and parts, computers and parts, printers, IC circuits and electronic elements

146. KOREA SAMHUNG CORPORATION

Address: Jungsong-dong, Central District, Pyongyang, DPRK

Tel: 850-2-18111-381-8852

Fax: 850-2-381-4496

E-mail:

Export:

Import: Motorcars, foodstuffs, vehicle parts, electronic goods, building parts

147. KOREA SANGMYONG TRADING CORPORATION

Address: Segori-dong, Pothonggang District, Pyongyang, DPRK

Tel: 850-2-18111-381-8293

Fax: 850-2-381-4752

E-mail:

Export: Paektusan Eleutherococc, marine products, red Insam powder, rough granite, medicinal herbs, medicines

Import: Vehicle parts, industrial goods, foodstuffs

148. KOREA SANGWON TRADING CORPORATION

Address: Pulgungori-dong No. 2, Pothonggang District, Pyongyang, DPRK

Tel: 850-2-18111-381-8077

Fax: 850-2-381-4521

E-mail:

Export: Cement, wood carvings, paper, furniture

Import: Cement producing equipment, mining equipment, wire ropes, power saws, belts, bearings, synthetic lath, stainless wire lath, press felt

149. KOREA SEK COMPANY

Address: Othan-dong, Central District, Pyongyang, DPRK

Tel: 850-2-18111-381-8332

Fax: 850-2-381-4757

E-mail:

Export: Cartoon films on order

Import: Movie films, fine art materials, electronic goods

150. SERICULTURE TRADING CORPORATION

Address: Mansu-dong, Kanggye City, Jagang Province, DPRK

Tel: 850-2-18111-381-2524'

Fax: 850-2-381-4410

E-mail:

Export: Processed mulberry cocoons, processed tussahs, silkworm eggs, tussahs, silkworm pupas, agricultural produce

Import: Urea fertilizer, gasoline, diesel oil, mobile oil, kraftpaper, reagents, electric appliances, cloths, sericultural facilities

151. KOREA SHOES TRADING CORPORATION

Address: Pothongmun-dong, Central District, Pyongyang, DPRK

Tel: 850-2-18111-381-8353

Fax: 850-2-381-4410

E-mail:

Export: Shoes, bags, leather goods

Import: Raw materials for shoes and tanning, materials for sponge production

152. KOREA SILK TRADING CORPORATION

Address: Pothongmun-dong, Central District, Pyongyang, DPRK

Tel: 850-2-18111-381-8350

Fax: 850-2-381-4538

E-mail:

Export: Raw silk, silk waste, silk top, spun silk, silk fabrics, silk goods

Import: Tetoron yarn, rayon yarn, dyestuffs, textile equipment, vinyl sheets

153. SINGON TRADING CORPORATION

Address: Kwangbok-dong No.2, Mangyongdae District, Pyongyang, DPRK

Tel: 850-2-18111-381-8193

Fax: 850-2-381-4053

E-mail:

Export: Marine products, molybdenum concentrate, gold concentrate, inorganic and nontoxic bottom paint, paints for building materials, clothes

Import: Heavy machines and equipment for construction, rolling stocks, fuel oil, furnishing materials, fishing tackles

154. KOREA SINHUNG TRADING CORPORATION

Address: Tongan-dong, Central District, Pyongyang, DPRK

Tel: 850-2-18111-381-8060

Fax: 850-2-381-4410

E-mail:

Export: Shellfishes, crabs, fishes

Import: Cloths, electric appliances, iron and steel materials, furniture

155. KOREA COMPUTER CENTRE SINHUNG COMPANY

Address: Sonnae-dong, Mangyongdae District, Pyongyang, DPRK

Tel: 850-2-18111-381-8825

Fax: 850-2-381-4707

E-mail:

Export: Computer software, development of software on order, bio-information programs, recognition programs, multimedia and games, massage-gel with Kwangryang mud, agar-agar

Import: Software, computers and accessories, network equipment, electronic equipment and elements

156. KOREA SINJIN TRADING CORPORATION

Address: Chilgol-dong No. 1, Mangyongdae District, Pyongyang, DPRK

Tel: 850-2-18111-381-8699

Fax: 850-2-381-4478

E-mail:

Export: Fresh and processed marine products, agricultural produce, granite, marble, processed Insam, compact lamps, medicines, single-use syringes and instillator sets, clothes

Import: Heavy machines and facilities, diesel oil, gasoline, fishing tackles, chemical goods, animal feed, electronic goods, paper producing equipment

157. SOBAEKSU UNITED COMPANY

Address: Kumsong-dong No.1, Mangyongdae District, Pyongyang, DPRK

Tel: 850-2-18111-381-8712

Fax: 850-2-381-4691

E-mail:

Export: Graphite goods, cement, coal pulverizing accelerator

Import: Coking coal, coal pitch, carborundum, paraffin, reagents

158. KOREA SOGWANG COMPANY

Address: Yokjon-dong, Central District, Pyongyang, DPRK

Tel: 850-2-18111-381-8883

Fax: 850-2-381-4410

E-mail:

Export: Kumgang yakdol (medicinal stone), Eleutherococc extract

Import: Art paper, printing inks, PS plates

159. KOREA SOGYONG TRADING CORPORATION

Address: Ryugyong-dong No.1, Pothonggang District, Pyongyang, DPRK

Tel: 850-2-18111-381-8871

Fax: 850-2-381-4724

E-mail:

Export: Marine products, base bullion, zinc, machine-woven carpets, hand-made carpets, handicrafts, furniture, agricultural produce

Import: Machines and parts, electronic goods, parts of rolling stocks, fishing tackles, chemical products, reagents, agricultural chemicals, fertilizers, fuel oil

160. KOREA SOKCHON TRADING CORPORATION

Address: Kinmaul-dong No.1, Moranbong District, Pyongyang, DPRK

Tel:

Fax: 850-2-381-2100

E-mail:

Export: Machines, building materials, minerals, agricultural produce, marine products

Import: Electric and electronic goods, machines, fertilizers, agricultural chemicals, vinyl sheets, chemical products

161. KOREA SONGCHONGANG TRADING CORPORATION

Address: Hoesang-dong No.1, Hamhung City, South Hamgyong Province, DPRK

Tel: 850-2-18111-053-22-0502

Fax: 850-2-381-2604

E-mail:

Export: Sea sand, river sand, river rubble stones, marine products, agricultural produce, handicrafts, electrolytic zinc, base bullion

Import: Pitch, fuel oil, parts of rolling stocks, reagents, electronic goods

162. SONBONG COMMERCIAL & TECHNICAL TRADING COMPANY

Address: Ryonhwa-dong No. 2, Central District, Pyongyang, DPRK

Tel:

Fax: 850-2-381-4410

E-mail:

Export: Marine products (king crabs, hairy crabs, squid, halibut, ark shell), embroideries

Import: Fibre goods, household articles, electronic goods

163. KOREA SONBONG EXPORT & IMPORT COMPANY

Address: Hasin-dong, Sosong District, Pyongyang, DPRK

Tel: 850-2-18111-381-8730

Fax: 850-2-381-4416

E-mail:

Export: Marine products

Import: Foodstuffs

For additional analytical, business and investment opportunities information,
please contact Global Investment & Business Center, USA
at (202) 546-2103. Fax: (202) 546-3275. E-mail: rusric@erols.com

164. KOREA SONGAKSAN TRADING CORPORATION

Address: Naesong-dong, Kaesong City, North Hwanghae Province, DPRK

Tel: 850-2-18111-049-35-0502

Fax: 850-2-381-2613

E-mail:

Export: Insam products (Insam extract, Insam syrup, Insam jelly, Koryo red Insam), liquors, embroideries, nonmetallic minerals, lead, zinc

Import: Iron and steel, fuel oil, fittings

165. KOREA SONGDOWON TRADING CORPORATION

Address: Wonsok-dong, Wonsan City, Kangwon Province, DPRK

Tel: 850-2-18111-057-32-0501

Fax: 850-2-381-2609

E-mail:

Export: Marine products, nonmetallic minerals, industrial art objects, embroideries

Import: Fuel oil, silicon steel sheets, wire ropes

166. KOREA SOUTH-SOUTH COOPERATION CORPORATION

Address: Jungsong-dong, Central District, Pyongyang, DPRK

Tel: 850-2-18111-381-8820

Fax: 850-2-381-4776

E-mail:

Export:

Import:

Cooperation objects: Designing, construction of and technical cooperation for ore mines, tunnels, roads, bridges, railway bridges, heavy machine factories, dwelling houses, public establishments, dams, irrigation projects, equipment assembly factories, power lines, transformer substations, power stations and cities

167. KOREA STAMP CORPORATION

Address: Yokjon-dong, Central District, Pyongyang, DPRK

Tel: 850-2-18111-381-8508

Fax: 850-2-381-4626

E-mail: admin@dprk-stamp.com

Export:

Import:

Business line: Stamps (mint and used), FDCs, postal stationeries, maxicards, stamp booklets, presentation packs, yearbooks, stamp CD-ROMs, stereophotograph cards.

168. KOREA SUNGRI TRADING CORPORATION

Address: Jangsan-dong, Sosong District, Pyongyang, DPRK

Tel: 850-2-18111-381-8018, 8310, 8633

Fax: 850-2-381-4446, 4030, 4765

E-mail:

Export: Electrolytic zinc, light-burnt magnesia, nonmetallic minerals, lubricating oil, marine products, tiles, bean-cake for animal feed

Import: Equipment and materials for mines and power stations, crude oil products, vehicles, building parts, chemical products, rubber goods, insulating materials and equipment for their production, electronic goods, paper

169. KOREA SUYANGSAN TRADING CORPORATION

Address: Sami-dong, Haeju City, South Hwanghae Province, DPRK

Tel: 850-2-18111-045-44-4060

Fax: 850-2-381-2601

E-mail:

Export: Zinc concentrate, rough serpentine, dressed olivine, titanium, sea sand, flaky graphite, marine products, agricultural produce

Import: High-pressure and low-pressure polyethelene, vinyl sheets, crude rubber, sodium carbonate, caustic soda

170. KOREA TAEDONG TRADING CORPORATION

Address: Tongan-dong, Central District, Pyongyang, DPRK

Tel:

Fax: 850-2-381-4410

E-mail:

Export: Pure silk sashes, clothes, knitwear

Import: Dyestuffs, fibre goods, daily necessities, gold threads, silver threads

171. KOREA TAEDONGGANG CORPORATION

Address: Raknang-dong No. 2, Raknang District, Pyongyang, DPRK

Tel: 850-2-18111-381-8773

Fax: 850-2-381-4097

E-mail: kdc@silibank.com

Export: Grinders, ballasts, paints, instant noodle, sanitary ware, marine products

Import: Vehicle parts, medicines, fertilizers, agricultural chemicals, machinery and parts, paper, office supplies, building materials, materials for ballasts, sanitary ware and grinders, printing materials, raw materials for vinyl production

172. KOREA TAEDONGGANG EEL CORPORATION

Address: Tangsang-dong No. 2, Mangyongdae District, Pyongyang, DPRK

Tel: 850-2-18111-381-8156

Fax: 850-2-381-2100

E-mail:

Export: Eels, marine products, agricultural produce, nonmetallic products

Import: Eel feed, equipment for eel-feed factory, fishing tackles, household articles

173. KOREA TAEDONGGANG TRADING CORPORATION

Address: Undok-dong, Phyongsong City, South Phyongan Province, DPRK

Tel: 850-2-18111-031-24-0501

Fax: 850-2-381-2603

E-mail:

Export: Amorphous graphite, ferrosilicon, silver-water producing stone, yellow lead ashes, slates, nonmetallic minerals, agricultural produce, marine products

Import: Gasoline, diesel oil, plastic goods, paper, fishing tackles

174. KOREA DAEZIN CORPORATION

Address: Ryongnam-dong, Taesong District, Pyongyang, DPRK

Tel: 850-2-18111-381-8191

Fax: 850-2-381-4470

E-mail:

Export: Processed stones

Import: Saws, drills, grinding wheels, diamonds

175. KOREA TAESONG 8 TRADING CORPORATION

Address: Janggyong-dong, Sosong District, Pyongyang, DPRK

Tel: 850-2-18111-381-8318

Fax: 850-2-381-4490

E-mail:

Export: Electrolytic gold, electrolytic silver, gold concentrate, marine products, furniture

For additional analytical, business and investment opportunities information, please contact Global Investment & Business Center, USA at (202) 546-2103. Fax: (202) 546-3275. E-mail: rusric@erols.com

Import: Palm oil, clothes, daily necessities, fibre goods, household articles, fishing tackles, medicines, gasoline, diesel oil, building materials

176. KOREA TAESONGSAN TRADING CORPORATION

Address: Taesong-dong, Taesong District, Pyongyang, DPRK

Tel: 850-2-18111-381-8338

Fax: 850-2-381-2100

E-mail:

Export: Animals, plants, seedlings, bear's gall, musk, furs, medicinal liquors, marine products, agricultural produce

Import: Animals, plants, animal feed, farming materials, veterinary medicines, building materials and equipment, recreation facilities, photographing equipment

177. KOREA TAEWON INDUSTRIES COMPANY

Address: Chukjon-dong, Mangyongdae District, Pyongyang, DPRK

Tel: 850-2-18111-381-5988

Fax: 850-2-381-5888

E-mail: dawion@silibank.com

Export: Wooden products, ferrous metals, nonferrous metals, chemical goods, refueling on the sea

Import: Crude oil products, chemical products, ferrous and nonferrous metals

178. KOREA TAEYANG TRADING CORPORATION

Address: Ryonghung-dong No. 3, Taesong District, Pyongyang, DPRK

Tel: 850-2-18111-381-8975

Fax: 850-2-381-4410

E-mail:

Export: Meat, skin and eggs of ostrich, industrial art objects, agricultural produce, marine products

Import: Farming materials, light industrial goods, animal feed

179. KOREA TEXTILE MACHINERY TRADING CORPORATION

Address: Pothongmun-dong, Central District, Pyongyang, DPRK

Tel: 850-2-18111-381-8139

Fax: 850-2-381-7807

E-mail:

Export: Sewing and knitting needles, reeds, heddles, piano frames, V-belts, iron rulers, enamel, household scissors

Import: Ferrous and nonferrous metals and their products, chemical products, paper, crude rubber, synthetic rubber, vehicle parts

180. KOREA TEXTILE TRADING CORPORATION

Address: Pothongmun-dong, Central District, Pyongyang, DPRK

Tel: 850-2-18111-381-8471

Fax: 850-2-381-4469

E-mail:

Export: Cloths, sewing threads, clothes, knitwear, shirts

Import: Loom accessories, dyestuffs, bearings

181. KOREA TONGHAE CORPORATION

Address: Tongan-dong, Central District, Pyongyang, DPRK

Tel: 850-2-18111-381-8850

Fax: 850-2-381-4620

E-mail:

Export: Marine products, grass works

Import: Diesel oil, machine parts, steel plates, rails, insulating materials, building parts, paints, light industrial goods, electronic goods

182. KOREA TONGHAENG TRADING CORPORATION

Address: Uiam-dong, Taedonggang District, Pyongyang, DPRK

Tel: 850-2-18111-381-8783

Fax: 850-2-381-7807

E-mail:

Export: Millet liquor, marine products, jade works

Import: Paper, printing inks, fishing tackles

183. KOREA UIAM TRADING CORPORATION

Address: Munsin-dong No.1, Tongdaewon District, Pyongyang, DPRK

Tel: 850-2-18111-381-8945

Fax: 850-2-381-4410

E-mail:

Export: Marine products, agricultural produce

Import: Paper, daily necessities, foodstuffs

184. KOREA ULRIM TRADING CORPORATION

Address: Sungri-dong No. 2, Raknang District, Pyongyang, DPRK

Tel: 850-2-18111-381-2210

Fax: 850-2-381-4410

E-mail:

Export: Rolling stocks and parts, processed meat nutriments, concentrates of tantalum, gold, lead and titanium, agricultural produce, marine products

Import: Caustic soda, diesel oil, lubricating oil, electric and electronic goods

185. KOREA UNBANGUL TRADING CORPORATION

Address: Pothongmun-dong, Central District, Pyongyang, DPRK

Tel: 850-2-18111-381-8914

Fax: 850-2-381-4410

E-mail:

Export:

Import: Ready-made suits, bags, household articles, cloths, fibre goods, photographic chemicals, films, photographic paper

186. KOREA UNDOK GROUP

Address: Uiam-dong, Taedonggang District, Pyongyang, DPRK

Tel: 850-2-18777-381-8965

Fax: 850-2-381-4575

E-mail:

Export: Pig iron, iron scraps and scales, low-grade gold concentrate, concentrates of molybdenum, titanium and zinc, marine products

Import: Hollow steel, silicon steel sheets, sodium carbonate, caustic soda, butanol, vehicle parts, fishing tackles, equipment and materials for oil exploration, reagents, crude rubber, computer accessories

187. KOREA UNGUM CORPORATION

Address: Jungsong-dong, Central District, Pyongyang, DPRK

Tel: 850-2-18111-381-8884

Fax: 850-2-381-4467

E-mail:

Export: Precious metal works, nonferrous concentrates
Import: Ore-dressing chemicals, soap, sugar

188. PYONGYANG VIDEO COMPANY

Address: Munhung-dong No. 2, Taedonggang District, Pyongyang, DPRK
Tel: 850-2-18111-381-8401
Fax: 850-2-381-4416
E-mail:
Export: Videorecording on order, recorded video tapes
Import: Recording heads, tapes, vehicle parts, broadcasting equipment and accessories

189. KOREA WISONG CORPORATION

Address: Phalgol-dong No. 2, Mangyongdae District, Pyongyang, DPRK
Tel:
Fax: 850-2-381-4410
E-mail:
Export: Base bullion, molybdenum concentrate, marine products, agricultural produce
Import: Electric and electronic goods

190. PYONGYANG WOMEN'S TRADING & GARMENTS CENTRE

Address: Sochon-dong, Sosong District, Pyongyang, DPRK
Tel: 850-2-18111-381-8248
Fax: 850-2-381-4410
E-mail:
Export: Clothes, cosmetics, glasses
Import: Cloths, materials for cosmetics and glasses

191. KOREA WONBONG TRADING CORPORATION

Address: Tongsin-dong No. 3, Tongdaewon District, Pyongyang, DPRK
Tel: 850-2-18111-381-8050
Fax: 850-2-381-4410
E-mail:
Export: Marine products, natural minerals, quartz, molybdenum, silver concentrate, embroideries, Koryo medicines, Armillaria edodes liquor, wooden products
Import: Gasoline, diesel oil, lubricating oil, vehicle parts, vessel parts, alcohol, cloths, engines, diving apparatuses, building parts

192. KOREA WONHWA TECHNOLOGY TRADING CORPORATION

Address: Okryu-dong No. 3, Taedonggang District, Pyongyang, DPRK

    Tel: 850-2-18111-381-8435

    Fax: 850-2-381-4783

E-mail:

Export: Cultured seedlings of Kimjongilia, liquors, pine pollen, industrial art objects, refrigerants, agricultural produce

Import: Building materials, electric appliances, reagents

193. KOREA YANGGWANG CORPORATION

Address: Sungri-dong No. 2, Raknang District, Pyongyang, DPRK

    Tel: 850-2-18111-381-8941

    Fax: 850-2-381-4410

E-mail:

Export:

Import:

Business line: Contracting measurement treatment of clothes and leather shoes, and export of calcite

194. KOREA YENUNG TRADING CORPORATION

Address: Yokjon-dong, Central District, Pyongyang, DPRK

    Tel:

    Fax: 850-2-381-4416

E-mail:

Export: Marine products, agricultural produce, books for art education, folklore articles

Import: Printing equipment and materials, daily necessities

195. KOREA YONGHUNG TRADING CORPORATION

Address: Tongan-dong, Central District, Pyongyang, DPRK

    Tel: 850-2-18111-381-8223

    Fax: 850-2-381-4527

E-mail:

Export: Freight cars, bogies, all-steel rolled wheels, rims, axles, couplers, buffers, springs, brake shoes, brake hoses, distribution valves, marine products, nonmetallic minerals, agricultural produce, electronic goods, software development and sale

Import: Rolled steel, steel plates, insulating materials, ferroalloy, bearings, chemical products, paints, fittings for passenger cars

196. KOREA YONPHUNG TRADING CORPORATION

Address: Ansan-dong No.1, Phyongchon District, Pyongyang, DPRK

Tel: 850-2-1811-381-8894

Fax: 850-2-381-4410

E-mail:

Export: Kaesong Koryo red peppered bean paste, agricultural produce, medicinal herbs, knitwear

Import: Vehicle parts, electronic goods, daily electric appliances, daily necessities, foodstuffs

197. KOREA KWANGOP TRADING CORPORATION

Address: Pothonggang-dong No. 1. Pothonggang District, Pyongyang, DPRK

Tel: 850-2-18111-381-8247

Fax: 850-2-381-4569

E-mail:

Export: Electrolytic zinc, base bullion, and concentrates of zinc, copper, lead, molybudenite, gold and scheelite, placer wolframite, talc powder, talc lumps, barite, jade, automobile batteries, sepiolite, electric motors, pumps, rock drills

Import: Coking coal, round steel, silicon steel sheets, wire ropes, seamless steel pipes, rails, tin plates, electrolytic nickel, electrolytic lead, hard alloy, copper sulfate, aluminium ingots

198. KOREA TUMANGANG TRADING CORPORATION

Address: Ingok-dong No. 2, Chongam District, Chongjin City, North Hamgyong Province, DPRK

Tel: 850-2-18111-073-23-0504

Fax: 850-2-381-4410

E-mail:

Export: River sand, embroideries, marble, talc vessels, grass works, marine products, edible herbs, rabbit furs

Import: Urea fertilizer, tetoron cotton, cloths, vinyl sheets, fittings, paints, insulating materials

199. KOREA GENERAL MAGNESIA CLINKER INDUSTRY GROUP

Address: Tongsong-dong, Central District, Pyongyang, DPRK

Tel: 850-2-018111-381-8080

Fax: 850-2-381-4634

E-mail:

Export: Magnesia clinker, slightly burnt magnesia, chlorite, firebricks, fireproof materials

Import: Equipment and accessories for mines and factories, steel, electric equipment and machines, vehicle parts, insulating materials, fibre goods, synthetic resin goods, rubber and its products, heavy oil, nonferrous metals, bean, animal feed

200. KOREA CHONGCHUN TRADING CORPORATION

Address: Tangsang-dong No. 1, Mangyongdae District, Pyongyang, DPRK

Tel: 850-2-18111-381-8345

Fax: 850-2-381-4410

E-mail:

Export:

Import: Foodstuffs, industrial goods, electric appliances, metal goods, vehicle parts

201. KOREA FORESTRY TRADING CORPORATION

Address: Taedongmun-dong, Central District, Pyongyang, DPRK

Tel: 850-2-18111-381-8618

Fax: 850-2-381-4410

E-mail:

Export: Sawn timber, wooden products, wooden chips, charcoal, Abies nephrolepis oil, pine-leaf oil

Import: Wire ropes, formalin, vinyl sheets, power saws and accessories, rolling stocks and parts, cloths, bearings

202. KOREA SAENAL TRADING CORPORATION

Address: Ryugyong-dong No. 1, Pothonggang District, Pyongyang, DPRK

Tel: 850-2-18111-381-8345

Fax: 850-2-381-4410

E-mail:

Export: Art objects (oil paintings, colour-fast pictures, embroideries), souvenirs, health foods, cement hardener

Import: Non-ferrous metals and their products, household articles, paper, printing equipment

LARGEST PRODUCERS AND EXPORTERS

1. WONSAN LEATHER SHOES FACTORY

Maebongsan-brand products produced by the Wonsan Leather Shoes Factory that has existed for over 60 years are drawing public interest at home.

The factory consists of designing section, injection-moulding workteam, uppers and shoemaking workshops and other production processes.

So far it has taken a large share in improving the living standards of Wonsan citizens. Recently, it made good progress in enhancing the quality of its products by upgrading injection-mould machine and other equipment and applying uppers paster, a program-aid device for measuring different shapes of feet and other technical findings. Especially, the laser cutter made it possible to save labour and materials and raise the efficiency in cutting process.

With due attention to designing, a primary process in shoemaking, the factory organized prize contests on a regular basis and introduced worthwhile designs into production. As a result, it has made remarkable achievements in the effort to diversify the products in terms of kind, shape and colour and make them lighter.

In addition, it strives to make shoes that satisfy the tastes and physical constitution of clients and meet the mental features according to their age as well as seasonal conditions with vinyl chloride and synthetic leather from the February 8 Vinalon Complex and the Phyongsong Synthetic Leather Factory.

In this way the officials and other employees are working hard to raise the quality of their products to the maximum.

2. KOREA PAEKYON TRADING COMPANY

The Korea Paekyon Trading Company, established in March Juche 98 (2009), has developed in a short period as a comprehensive base for production, scientific research, sale and service to order.

The company has the Rangnang Finishing Material Factory that produces wallboards and other materials for decoration, as well as production bases for truss, plastic window frames, concrete blocks, switchboards, water sterilizers and air conditioners including those that ensure sanitary safety of buildings. It is striving to corner domestic and international markets.

By introducing cutting-edge technology, the production bases have set up a well-regulated production management system and conduct production according to the rigid regulations and standards for quality control, thus making ordered goods of high quality that require high technology.

The company has also established Paekyon Shop that sells many kinds of fittings, fixtures and other building materials.

According to its enterprising business strategy, it is making sustained efforts to introduce cutting-edge technology, develop new products, step up modernization, increase the variety of products and improve their quality. It is also promoting cooperation and exchanges with foreign countries while strengthening its material and technical foundations.

3. TANCHON PORT IN THE EAST SEA OF KOREA

Tanchon Port, which adjoins the Tanchon Refinery, a giant nonferrous metal producer, and Tanchon Magnesia Factory, a large refractory producer, is a trade port with a great cargo traffic capacity.

Inaugurated in May 2012, it has a wide open-air storage ground with a loading capacity of hundreds of thousands of tons, a depot of thousands of square metres, a clinker storehouse of hundreds of thousands of square metres, and wharfs Nos. 1, 2, 3 and 4, where even ships of hundreds of thousands of tons can be tied up.

The port had large cranes, truck cranes, hydraulic shoves, forklifts and an exclusive railroad.

It is a fully-equipped trade port with a control centre which is perfect in formative art to meet the requirements of the new century and a lighthouse which can guide ships safely from afar.

The main cargos of the port include lead and zinc products, light burned magnesia, high-grade magnesia clinker, cereals and fertilizer.

It has organs for customs control, sanitary inspection and transport of cargoes to ensure promptness in cargo procedures and entry into and departure from the port.

Today it is playing with credit its role as an international trade port.

4. STONES TURN INTO WORKS OF ART

These days, the Pyongyang Stonework Exhibition Hall is drawing public interest as it develops processed articles with locally available stone resources.

On display at a newly furnished room in the exhibition hall are samples of various natural stones, building materials, craftwork and stone-processing facilities.

The country abounds in deposits of high-quality stones valuable as building materials, and demand for them is on the rise.

The hall has a base for producing different sizes of slabs and handrails made of granite, marble and serpentine.

It also makes architectural decorations of various patterns and colours to order, which are durable, attractive and hygienic.

They have been applied to the construction of hotels, department stores and many other service facilities, winning public favour.

Stone craftwork is also well received by customers.

It has natural colours, patterns and lustre.

The hall attracts more people day by day as there are exhibits developed with latest science and technology including art works and photos on stones and Kumgang medicinal stone.

5. NEW GOAL, NEW START

The modernization project of the Pyongyang Children's Foodstuff Factory has been completed in a little over ten months.

The project consisted of the upgrading of buildings and equipment and the construction, extension and rebuilding of dozens of facilities. Among them are a bean silo with a capacity of thousands of tons and a Tetra Pak packaging building.

All the processes ranging from feeding of raw materials to production, packaging, storage and transport are equipped with latest facilities and fully automated, and all the elements of the production sites are germ- and dust-free, ensuring hygienic safety of products.

The production line of soya yogurt that is supplied to children at nurseries and kindergartens is equipped with the CIP system, making it possible to increase production 1.5 times more than before.

The integrated production system established in the factory is a multidimensional one capable of optimizing all matters related to production and business activities. The factory has also a general analysis room for accurate quality inspection.

It developed a variety of new products that suit the physical constitutions of Korean children in the last one year. Among them are the powdered milk for babies who develop allergy to cow's milk, powdered rice, thin gruel, powdered vegetable and rice, nutritive candy and powdered soya milk.

The powdered milk for babies is made of soya bean and is virtually breast milk. It is highly digestive and used for babies who have allergic reaction to powdered milk made of cow's milk. The powdered rice is soluble even in cold water and the soft and highly nutritious thin gruel is for children above four months old. There are different kinds of powdered vegetable and rice that preserve the flavour and colour peculiar to vegetables and the nutritive candy made with bean and sea tangle is delicious and fragrant. The powdered soya milk is harmoniously composed of calcium and vitamin D, so it is helpful for the growth of school-age children.

The factory that fully guarantees scientific accuracy and promptness in quality control produces 13 kinds of 32 items of children's foods.

6. KOREA POSOK TRADING COMPANY

The Korea Posok Trading Company turns out as its major products jewellery and other gem ornaments.

Covering a wide area, it is equipped with jewel-processing machines like diamond working machine, angle-forming machine and cutter and also with facilities for producing precious metals like medium-frequency induction furnace, precision casting machine and rolling mill. It ensures high precision and quality of the products.

The main products of the company are jewellery made of natural gems like olivine, garnet, crystal and agate, and it also conducts bonded processing of imported gems.

The processed goods including necklaces, earrings and rings made of gold and silver and medals made of precious metals are the main export index of the company and it has a decades-long tradition in thisfield.

It also mass-produces bronze products with good mechanical properties, peculiar colour and resonance to order.

It concentrates on developing the goods in great demand and modernizing the bases for producing export goods, while promoting exchanges and cooperation with many countries.

7. PYONGYANG CATFISH FARM RENOVATED

The Pyongyang Catfish Farm has been renovated into a model fish farm.

More than 50 buildings have been reconstructed or newly constructed in an area of over 100 000 square metres, including the general control room, cold storage and workshops for feed, fodder additives, protein, fermentation and general feed processing and smoking.

It has been furnished with an intelligent, informatized and digitized integrated production system with the installation of underwater cameras at the hatching, young catfish raising and fattening grounds and gauges at over 100 outdoor ponds, making it possible to measure and control in real time the water temperature, pH and the amount of oxygen in the indoor and outdoor ponds and regulate the water supply and amount of feed in accordance with the growth of catfish.

A labour- and water-saving fish farming has come true as it has made the water recycling system science-based while establishing a triple hot water supply system in the hatching ground and an automatic control system for hot water supply to all ponds and making the most of the waste water from the East Pyongyang Thermal Power Station.

It has introduced solar water heater and covered vinyl sheets over some 40 outdoor ponds, providing a guarantee for raising catfish all the year round.

Storage of raw materials and fodder processing have been updated, the production process of microbial additives automatically controlled, fixed and mobile automatic feed sprinklers installed in all ponds and catfish hauling machine and other modern equipment introduced.

The farm's catfish production process is scientific and intensive, with its production capacity 2.5 million fry a year and a grown catfish weighing over 1.2 to 2 kg, and 3 kg at maximum, within six months after hatching.

This year the farm has produced over 1 800 tons of catfish, which is more than double the amount of catfish production in the past.

It is now working to produce 1.4 times more catfish in 2016 than this year and cut the feed consumption and production cost of fish.

And it also works as a flagship provider of scientific and technological information on catfish farming.

For additional analytical, business and investment opportunities information,
please contact Global Investment & Business Center, USA
at (202) 546-2103. Fax: (202) 546-3275. E-mail: rusric@erols.com

8. BY WORKING STRENUOUSLY

At the 30th national sci-tech festival held in April last one particular exhibit was wood-plastic composite planks. One of the visitors said, "These look smart and strong. That light brown plank seems to be suitable for the living room." Another one said, "Look at the yellow plank for the wall of the dining room. It feels cosy and is water resistant. It'll be a favourite with housewives." Hearing them many other people turned their eyes to the goods presented by the Korea Sangwon Trading Company.

The company has always maintained an important principle in developing and producing new things. It is to pay primary attention to the country's actual condition and people's needs in all consideration.

Two years ago the company decided to lay a new process for production of wood-plastic composite planks. At the time Kwon Thae Song who was in charge of the task said, "We must make goods quite different from the existing kind. This is not simply for our company's popularity. Our company exists to produce the people's favourite goods and render a help to the country's economic development." He asked the workers to put out new ideas for the project.

All of them rose as one to develop high-quality goods. In this course, they all agreed that the primary problem was to improve the goods' water-resistant capacity.

Kim Yong Bok, an officer for technical affairs, knew by studying latest data and making repeated experiments that a clue of water resistance might be to denature the surface of the filler (sawdust). He verified the possibility in several research institutes and buckled down to the making together with technicians and workers.

On the other hand, Kwon produced an idea that would help further decrease the production cost. It was to increase the ratio of the cheap filler while maintaining the quality index. Though some opinions were raised about the fear that a higher ratio of the filler might weaken water resistance, most of the workers wanted the two ideas to be pushed ahead with simultaneously. They believed there is nothing impossible to a willing heart.

After months of painstaking researches and repeated experiments and analyses, the sci-tech problems were solved to prevent humidity by denaturing the filler's surface. In addition, a reasonable ratio of combination of the filler, PVC and auxiliary additives was found out. At last the new kind of plank was developed, which is resistant to water, heat and decay. A gravitational water supply system was introduced in the moulding process after the workers' ingenious idea, and a new sub-process was added in which the goods are cut as required by users. A year later the company cut the production cost of the planks by 20 per cent, while improving the impact stress and pressure intensities 1.5 times.

As the users' demand for planks is steadily growing and becoming varied, the workers are making strenuous efforts to produce cheaper and better goods in greater quantity.

9. POPULAR FOODSTUFFS

Taeha-brand foods of the Unha Taesong Foodstuff Factory are now popular with customers at the shops and stalls of the air terminal of Pyongyang International Airport, and Pyongyang Department Store No. 1, Kwangbok Area Supermarket and other commercial networks in Pyongyang.

The factory produces over 250 kinds of foodstuffs.

Confectionary, processed meats and soft drinks are coming out of the germ-and dust-free production processes.

Particularly, processed meats are favoured by customers as they use natural additives.

Unique are the flavour and fragrance of sausages smoked with pine needles and oak leaves, hams made of the finest and freshest meats, salamis tasting like dried meat and pork sausages.

Milk biscuits added with functional ingredients like laver, barley, sesame and pumpkin seed, calcium cakes and chocolate-coated peanut flavour cake strips are mouth-watering.

Other popular products include lollipops and other sweets and various kinds of breads with a variety of shapes, patterns, colours, tastes and fragrance, and juices and beers made from fruits of Rosa davurica that are rich in vitamins.

10. THE SANGWON CEMENT COMPLEX

The Sangwon Cement Complex situated in Sangwon County, North Hwanghae Province, went into operation in April 1989. Consisting of a cement factory which is the core of the complex, a limestone mine and a refractory factory, the complex has a general control room which automatically operates all the production processes, a maintenance shop, a repairs shop, a kiln shop, a steel foundry and a transport shop. Its workers live in a modern residential district on the scenic shore of the Sangwon River, which is provided with public service facilities, a worker's culture hall, a hospital, schools, a kindergarten, a day nursery and trade networks which cater for the convenience of the residents in their everyday life. Since it started operation, the complex has produced tremendous quantities of cement for the economic construction of the country. By conducting the technical control of the processes scrupulously and carrying out various forms of technical reconstruction, it has produced a large amount of cement, and is now vigorously conducting many scientific research works including new technical researches on the production of fire bricks in keeping with the requirements of the developing times and the work of further modernizing the production processes.

In addition, it is developing joint venture with foreign enterprises for increasing production. For its concentration of the production processes and its clean environment, the complex is known as a model of factory building.

For additional analytical, business and investment opportunities information, please contact Global Investment & Business Center, USA at (202) 546-2103. Fax: (202) 546-3275. E-mail: rusric@erols.com

11. CVD CEMENTED CARBIDE TOOLS

The Pyongyang CVD Tool Development Corporation is boosting production and export of various CVD cemented carbide tools.

Its factory, which is equipped with high-pressure press, vacuum-type sintering furnace, chemical evaporator and washing machine, is turning out various types of indexable inserts with cemented carbide powder. It is also furnished with modern machines like NC milling machine and electric discharge machine for processing toolholders for inserts. The characteristics of the tools are that the indexable inserts can be inserted into the toolholders.

Inserts for external and internal machining, external thread milling, slotting and face milling are in wide use in CNC machining centres, universal centre lathes and other up-to-date machines.

Round and hexagonal drawn dices are diverse in size and ensure high efficiency and long service life.

The various CVD cemented carbide tools exported by the corporation have won worldwide recognition as they have been highly appreciated at tool exhibitions held in many countries of the world.

In the future, the corporation plans to be proactive in accessing to global tool markets, while putting efforts into developing new types of CVD cemented carbide tools.

12. KOREA KYONGHUNG TRADING CORPORATION

Inaugurated in Juche 76 (1987) the Korea Kyonghung Trading Corporation engages in exporting and importing goods. The main categories of its business are commercial and public catering, foodstuff and clothes processing, shipbuilding, wholesale trade, IT development and equity and contractual joint ventures.

It has scores of enterprises and branches at home and abroad, and conducts trade transactions with several corporations in Southeast Asia and Europe.

As a state-run corporation its business categories are diverse and it is fully equipped with facilities and staffed with powerful technical forces, thus gaining its strength every year.

Regarding introduction of CNC technology and automation in production, creating bases of high profitability, keeping credible dealings with its partners, and ensuring service and convenience on a high level as its management strategy, it has achieved rapid progress in recent years.

With a great concern on commercial circulation, it has set up service outlets in Pyongyang and other major cities.

Foodstuffs, electronic appliances, household articles, furniture, textile goods and building materials are sold in its several outlets including the Taesong Department Store, Kyonghung Shop, Chukjon Shop and Hyangmanru Shop. These shops offer delivery service to order for clients.

The large-scale Hyangmanru Restaurant as well as Kyonghung, Chukjon and Unhasu restaurants serve various Korean dishes including Pyongyang cold noodle, specialty of Korea, as well as Western dishes.

It has entered into contracts with foreign companies in order to produce various kinds of textiles, garments and toys.

The Kyonghung Information Technology Company develops and sells various programs and other electronic goods.

It is making positive efforts to expand the scope of cooperation and exchanges with its foreign partners in exchanging commodities, technology and materials needed in foodstuff processing and conducting equity and contractual joint ventures.

13. KUMGANGSAN INTERNATIONAL TOURISM DEVELOPMENT CORPORATION

Located in 128° 11' longitude and 38° 44' latitude, Mt. Kumgang covers an area of 530 sq km in Kosong and Kumgang counties, Kangwon Province. Midway down the east coast of Korea, it extends 60km from north to south and 40km from east to west. It is renowned for its splendid landscape, an ensemble of mysterious ridges, clean sea and lakes, and biodiversity.

The Kumgangsan International Tourism Development Corporation directs primary attention to turning the mountain into a world-famous tourist resort.

The corporation has invested in building infrastructure and welfare service facilities for the convenience of tourists: Kosong port, Kumgangsan railway station, railways and roads; Kumgangsan, Oegumgang, Mokran, Onjong and other hotels that can accommodate more than 4 000 guests on a daily basis; hall of culture, spa, golf course, sledge course and bathing resort.

It also pays due concern to developing the tourist area into a multi-purpose and multi-functional resort that is friendly to environment protection and introducing modern and high-speed means of traffic and communications to ensure their promptness and safety.

It plans to develop the mountain into a base for eco-tourism, history tourism and international winter sports, and the Lagoon Samil-Sea Kumgang area into a large-scale resort by taking advantage of its natural beauty and flat land. Also on the drawing board is construction of various recreational facilities, folklore and other parks, venues for international conferences and expositions, and other comprehensive tourist establishments and lodgings.

It focuses its attention on developing the Mt. Kumgang International Tourism Special Zone into a hub of commerce, culture, banking and green industry.

To speak nothing of corporate bodies, natural persons and other economic organizations of foreign countries, overseas Korean compatriots and relevant organs and units in the DPRK are allowed to invest in this special zone.

Currently in operation there are a wide variety of businesses run by over 10 foreign-invested enterprises and scores of domestic companies–hotel, restaurant, shop, duty-free business and recreations.

The corporation encourages investment in the special zone, affords investors preferential treatment in their economic activities, and provides a legal guarantee for their capital, legitimate income and rights. For this purpose, it will promote exchanges and cooperation with international tourism organizations and tourism agencies of other countries.

14. PYONGYANG CORN PROCESSING FACTORY

Situated in Rangnang District, Pyongyang, the factory consists of a basement and a two-storey building.

Covering an area of over 12 800 square metres and a total floor space of 8 600 square metres, it has an annual capacity of producing 10 000 tons of corn products.

The factory turns out over ten kinds of corn products, including noodles, biscuits, steamed breads, oil, riced corn, corn grits, sweet jelly and popcorn.

Provided with various production processes, it has a sample display room, general control room, sci-tech dissemination room, experiment and analysis room and gym.

In the milling process, corn flour and grits are produced through such stages as peeling off the corn, separating the embryo and degeneration. Their yield and the rate of fine grinding are very high.

All the production processes ranging from material input to packaging have been put on the unmanned, dust-free and germ-free basis. An integrated production system has been established in order to carry on the control of all the production lines and the management of the factory in a comprehensive way.

The factory has introduced a bio-microscope combined with CCD camera and other sophisticated analyzing instruments to thoroughly ensure the hygienic safety of corn products and guarantee the quality control on a scientific basis.

In the sci-tech dissemination room the workers have access to various information on different sectors including corn processing technology and food-safety management, and to tele-education.

They play volleyball, basketball, tennis and other sports games in the gym. The factory is also provided with a mess hall and other cultural and welfare facilities for the sake of its workers.

The delicious corn products of high nutritive value are supplied to the restaurants specializing in corn foods, making substantial contributions to improving the Pyongyang citizens' diet. They are coming into great favour among buyers.

15. KOREA ILLUMINATION CENTRE

The centre is located in Songyo District, Pyongyang. The main categories of its business are research, production and sale of illumination-related apparatuses.

It has integrated all business activities ranging from design, scientific research, development of technology, production, technical service and after-sale service.

The assembly bases of LED lights and electronic elements of lamps, covering a total area of nearly 3 000 sq m, and other production bases mass-produce various kinds of illuminators including LED floodlight, LED rod, LED focus and illuminated signboard.

Electronic elements are processed to order and accessories for solar panels and other electric apparatuses are assembled by means of modern equipment like CNC cutter and moulding press.

Competent designers and other technical personnel have developed different kinds of illuminators and other solar power units, both smart and suited to national sentiments, in order to make effective use of green energy.

The structures decorated by the centre include Chollima Statue, Victorious Fatherland Liberation War Museum, Grand People's Study House, Okryu, Taedong and other bridges, May Day Stadium, Munsu Water Park and Rungna People's Pleasure Ground. They add beauty to the night view of Pyongyang.

The products of the centre render a significant contribution to splendidly decorating buildings, big and small, in Wonsan, Hamhung and other cities of the country.

It concentrates efforts on developing hi-tech equipment.

For additional analytical, business and investment opportunities information, please contact Global Investment & Business Center, USA at (202) 546-2103. Fax: (202) 546-3275. E-mail: rusric@erols.com

Better quality and low cost constitute part of its business strategy and, to satisfy the ever-growing demands, it strives to increase the proportion of locally-available raw and other materials.

Having made its business activities multifarious, it satisfies orders for production of illuminators and their installation. It also maintains close ties with foreign partners on the principles of mutual benefit, profitability and credit-first.

16. JONGHUNG J.V. COMPANY

Inaugurated in 2013, the Jonghung J.V. Company specializes in producing goods from wood fibre pulp including writing paper, newsprint and disposable tampon.

The company is furnished with a flow line with a capacity of producing more than 1 000 tons of paper and intellectualized equipment of producing disposable hygienic goods so as to mass-produce wood fibre pulp goods demanded by customers.

The company produces different kinds and various sizes of paper according to the technical agreement with the clients, and ensures the quality of its products, thus enjoying great popularity among clients.

Nano-high polymer absorbents, and indigenous essential oil and medical agents are used in the production of disposable tampon that is hygienic and convenient to use, so the number of clients is increasing day by day and the amount of annual production has reached millions of pieces.

While focusing its concern on producing cheap and quality fibre processed goods, the company is promoting exchanges and cooperation with other companies across the world with a view to strengthening its production foundations, introducing the latest achievements of advanced technology and increasing the variety of its products.

17. KOREA JOYANG TEXTILE JOINT VENTURE COMPANY

Situated in Songyo District, Pyongyang, the Korea Joyang Textile Joint Venture Company was established in May Juche 99 (2010).

The company specializes in producing and exporting various towels with high-grade cotton yarn.

Furnished with state-of-the-art CAD weaving machines, it specializes in production and sales of towels and processed goods.

The company actively introduces achievements of the advanced textile technology and sensitively reflects clients' demand to develop various kinds of Joyang-brand products, with the result that its products are enjoying popularity at home and abroad.

The company's products including towels for washing and bathing, bedspread, baby covers, pillow towels, napkins and bathing robes of diverse types and patterns have won quality certification diplomas from several countries including Russia and Mongolia.

The company exports millions of products annually to many countries in Asia and Europe.

Demand for its products is increasing with each passing day for their excellent absorbability, soft sensibility, refined pattern and convenience in use.

As the dying materials that are used for the production of goods are activated ones which have won international patent, they give no harmful effect to human beings. They are popular among women, in particular mothers with babies.

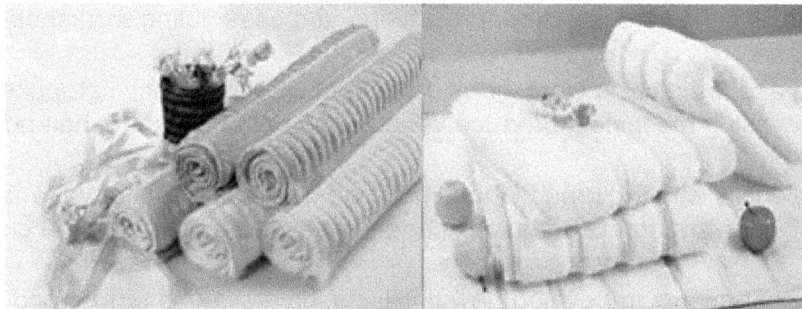

The company is making tangible efforts to further strengthen its material and technical foundations and turn out products that are contributable to making people's life more bountiful.

18. KOREA HAEBARAGI TRADING CORPORATION

The Korea Haebaragi Trading Corporation is affiliated to the Pyongyang Plastic Pencil Factory.

The major exports of the corporation are plastic pencils and ball-point pens of various sizes and the major imports are raw materials and equipment needed for operating the factory.

The factory has all the workshops for producing plastic pencils and ball-point pens in large amounts, like the lead, ejection, processing and assembling workshops.

The ejection and processing workshops, furnished with automatic catapults and precision-processing machines, produce various parts of pencils and ball-point pens.

The plastic pencils with the brand Chotuijong and ball-point pens of various brands are of a variety of kinds and forms and user-friendly. They are enjoyed by the customers.

The factory endeavours to develop new products, diversified in form, good to the eye and comfortable to the hand.

While concentrating investment on long-term and sustainable modernization of equipment, the corporation is making efforts to improve the quality of its products.

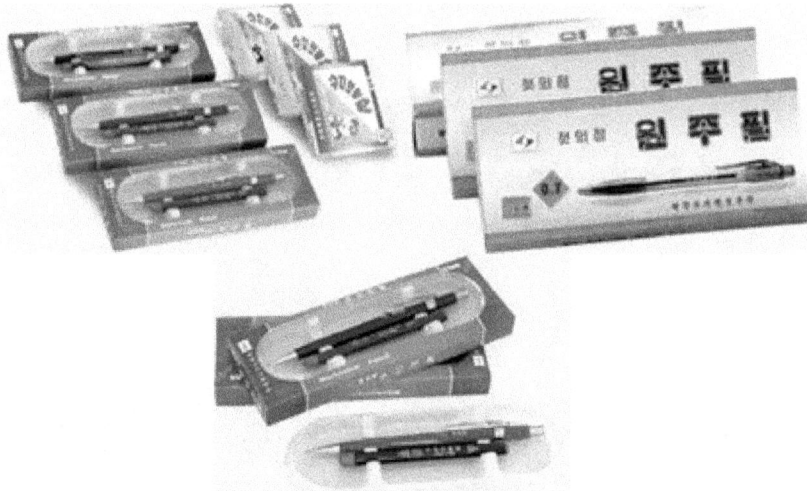

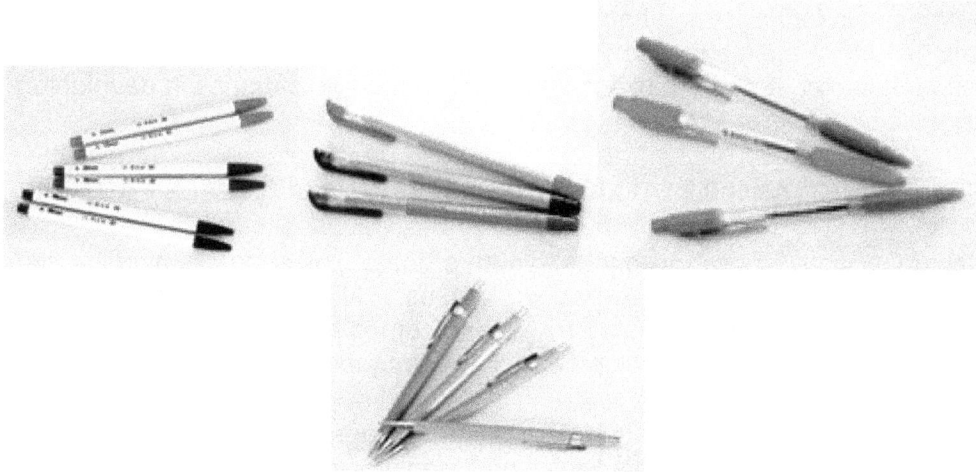

19. TOKJUNG TRUCK JOINT VENTURE COMPANY

Tokjung Truck J.V. Company, set up in June 2013, is a producer of different types of truck.The company has set up a highly-effective assembly workshop of truck whose total floor space is over 3 000 sq m at the Sungni Motor Complex.

Work for every process of the assembly line including the assembly of different kinds of wiring, pipe, spring and axle and engine and gearbox is conducted delicately by the highly skilled workers and the assembled trucks go through a thoroughgoing test.

As the trucks' output of power is relatively higher than their rated capacity and their whole bodies are two-folded, they are well resistant to dynamic strength and their electronic devices are high in performance and individualized.The kinds of Sungni-branded trucks are more than ten, including 2.5-ton semi-freight car, 5-, 8-, 10- and 25-ton platform trucks and container cars and its annual output is thousands of units.

The company channels its great efforts into fully supplying the domestic demand for trucks and increasing the proportion of home-made major parts by making effective use of the technical force and production capacity that have already been established at the Sungni Motor Complex.

Better quality, increase of variety and credit-first principle—these are the company's management strategy.

For additional analytical, business and investment opportunities information, please contact Global Investment & Business Center, USA at (202) 546-2103. Fax: (202) 546-3275. E-mail: rusric@erols.com

The company is further strengthening its own technical force and production foundations to take the lead in the domestic truck market and gain access to the international market. It also maintains close ties with other countries in developing exchanges and cooperation.

20. PYONGYANG METALLIC CONSTRUCTION MATERIALS FACTORY

The factory with its 60-year history has youth process workshop, illumination fittings workshop, mirror workshop and several workteams. A kitchen unit workshop was added to the factory in 1982. It was donated by Korean compatriots in Japan out of patriotic desire for the prosperity and development of their motherland.

Now the factory produces various kinds of metallic construction materials needed for major projects like Mirae Scientists Street and Mangyongdae Schoolchildren's Palace.

The kitchen unit workshop equipped with a 500-ton hydraulic press, a 110-ton press, a 35-ton bender, a hydraulic cutter, a grinder and other facilities produces kitchen utensils, foodstuff production facilities and their parts.

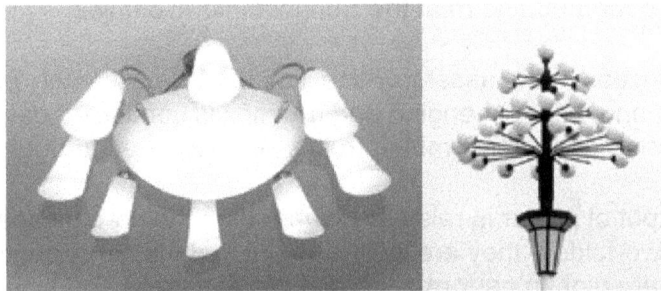

The glass plates from the Taean Friendship Glass Factory are completed as mirrors of various sizes and forms through cleaning, high-vacuum evaporation, plating and processing procedures at the mirror workshop.

Besides, the factory produces lamp ornaments, hinges, shelf-style three-row towel hangers and sink covers.

The products are well accepted by consumers for their high quality.

TRADE AND EXPORT CONTACTS

Research on North Korean Economy
¤· Offer economic information collected through about 100 Overseas Korea Trade Centers
¤· Analyze contemporary economic issues and present the result
¤· Issues books focusing on economic data
¤· Establish electronic database on economic data
¤· Research areas

- *Basic information on politics, economy, society and culture*
- *Products and industries*
- *International economic policies*

- Systems and regulations on investment and trade
- International trade status
- Foreign investment into North Korea
- Development on the Intra-Korean trade
Support for the Inter-Korean Trade
¤· Assist South Korean firms in trading with North Korea, outsourcing through process- on-commission and investing in partnership.
¤·Offer consulting service in relation to doing business in North Korea.
Support for a joint investment into North Korea between a South Korean concern and a foreign counterpart.
¤· Play a match-making role to connect partners
¤· Supply English-version data on North Korea¡¯s investment environment
¤·Offer assistance in negotiating with North Korean counterpart
Operation of North Korea Economic Information Center
¤· Being furnished with a combination of 3,000 kinds of books, periodicals and research thesis with regard to North Korea.
¤·Open all materials to visitors along with consultation services.

Team/Division	Name	Consulting Areas	Contact
North Korea Department	Dong-Chul Lee (Director General)		
	Ho-Sang Yoo (Director)	¤·Economic institutions and corporations ¤·Joint investment	hosang@kotra.or.kr
	Sam-Sik Kim	¤·Trade between Europe and North Korea ¤·Economic Trend	sk7192@kotra.or.kr
	Chang-Hak Lee	¤·Economy and Trade ¤·North Korea-Japan relation ¤·Analysis of trade trend ¤·Statistics of trade	chlee@kotra.or.kr
	Kwang-IL Kim	¤·Support for the Inter-Korean trade ¤·Offer consulting service ¤·North Korea-China relation	guangri@kotra.or.kr
	Kyung-Hee Koo	¤·Inquiry on homepage ¤·KOTRA NK Club ¤·North Korea-Russia, Asia relation	judykoo@kotra.or.kr
	Hyun-Jung Lee	¤·Sales of KOTRA-published data	northjung@hanmail.net
	Min-A Cho	¤·Introduction on utilization of the economic center and information furnished in it	keaima@hanmail.net

TRADING CORPORATIONS

Name of company	Chosun Kwangmyong General Trading Co.		
Address	Central District, Pyongyang	**TLX**	36022 KW KP
Telegraph code	KWANGMYONG Pyongyang		
Tel	850-2-381-4111	**FAX**	850-2-381-4410, 4494, 4416
Details of business	Established in 1976 • The trading company is a central trading organization administering regional trading in North Korea, and has 10 regional trading companies and 2 directly managed trading companies. • The Business range of the General company covers agency work for exporting of products from various places in North Korea and importing of goods necessary for regional and private needs. • It¡¯s connected to about 400 trading companies in around 90 nations. ++ Items dealt with: (Export) nonferrous metals and processed products (lead, zinc, cadmium of which export volume amounts to thousands of tons and the qualities of lead, electrolytic lead, electrolytic zinc have good reputation in the international market.). Non-metallic minerals (granite, slate, talc, calcite, barite and black lead), agricultural and marine products (wild ginseng, ginseng, a kind of milk vetch, maximowiczia chinensis, Chinese matrimony vine, parsley, fern brake, various seeds including pumpkin seed, ginseng seed, mushroom, peppermint oil, cocoon, kidney bean, etc) * Shrimp, octopus, squid, maximowiczia chinensis, ginseng, Chinese matrimony vine, shiitake mushroom, various health food among agriculture and marine products are sold actively. (Import) Raw materials for light industry, pesticide, fertilizer, feed, vegetable oil, sugar, soap and tire, etc		

NATIONAL ECONOMIC COOPERATION FEDERATION

Past subsidiary Organization of Foreign Economic Committee, Council of State Affairs of North Korea, which is in charge of the issue of economic cooperation with South Korea. Changed its name to ¡®National Economic Cooperative Federation¡¯ at the end of May, 1998

The federation is composed of Kwangmyongsung General Corp., Samcholli General

Corp., Gaesun Trading Corp., Mt. Kumgang International General Tourism Corp., and Koryo Commercial Bank.

The headquarters in Pyongyang is composed of chairman-Jung Woon-up, vice chairman-Lee Chang-ho, Chief Secretary-Lee Ei-duk

Currently Yun Won-chol (head), Shim Gi-sup and Kim Jin-su are in charge of the business of Peking Representative Office.

Address: No.601, 66ho-dong, New Central Street, Dongsung-gu, Peking, China

Tel: (8610) 6592-0268

Jeon Sung-gun (head) and Kim Jong-sung are in charge of Dandong Representative Office.

Address: Rm No.201, Jangsung Hotel, 5ho, 11 Gyung-ro, Jinhung-gu, Dandong, Yoryong Province, China

Tel: (86-415) 212-4027

ASIA-PACIFIC PEACE COMMITTEE

The affiliated people with Asia-Pacific Peace Committee, a distant organization of the Party, are promoting mainly social, cultural and sport fields in Peking, however they also undertake economy related major businesses

Without permanent staff or office in Peking, a unit composed of 2 people performs business by commuting between Pyongyang and Peking when there happens some business to deal with.

The heads of units are Lee Sung-duk, Hwang Chul and k-sun and Cho Gwang-ju, Kim Tae-ee and Kim Gwang-il participate in the actual work.

THE COMMITTE FOR THE PROMOTION OF INTERNATIONAL TRADE OF THE DPR KOREA

Location	Central District, Pyongyang		
Tel	850-2-18111(8054)	Fax	850-2-381-4440
Main Business	The Committe for the Promotion of International Trade of the DPR Korea , established in 1952, is a comprehensive organization for promoting foreign trade and economic relations between the DPRK and foreign countries. Recently, the CPIT's activities have been focused on the introduction of transactions and of investment from western countries.		
Noteworthy	The head of the Committee is Kim Yong Mun.		

details	

THE COMMITTEE FOR THE PROMOTION OF EXTERNAL ECONOMIC COOPERATION

Location	Central District, Pyongyang		
Tel	850-2-381-6163	Fax	850-2-381-4498, 850-2-381-4630
Main Business	Past subsidiary organization of Committee for External Economy. Especially Peking Representative Office is mainly in charge of investment consultation business of Rajin-Sunbong Region in the field of South and North Korea Economic Cooperation.		
< details Nteworthy>	Kim Jong-woon (head), Won Chang-jung and Mun Song-won are permanently stationed in Peking Representative Office The place for the chairman of Pyongyang headquarters is vacant, and currently Kim Yong-sul is the acting chairman. Jang Kwang-ho is in charge of main business		

KOREA FOREIGN COMMODITY INSPECTION COMMITTEE

Location	Central District, Pyongyang		
Telegraph code	KFCIC PYONGYANG	TLX	5972 TECH KP
Tel	3816252	Fax	ii
Details of business	This committee inspects and appraises exporting and importing cargos as an official inspection institution for those.		
Noteworthy details	The committee belongs to Foreign Economic Committee of the Cabinet. The committee operates branch committees in major ports such as Nampo, Haeju, Hungnam, Wonsan, Chongjin, Rajin and Songlim.		

KOREA INTERNATIONAL EXHIBITION CORPORATION

Location	Jungsong-dong, Central District, Pyongyang		
Telegraph code	ZENRAM PYONGYANG	TLX	5952 ZR KP
Tel	850-2-381-6054	FAX	850-2-381-4440
Main Business	Business related to hosting of North Korean Exhibition and exhibiting in a foreign country		

For additional analytical, business and investment opportunities information,
please contact Global Investment & Business Center, USA
at (202) 546-2103. Fax: (202) 546-3275. E-mail: rusric@erols.com

	Business related to participating in international sample exhibition hosted in a foreign country and exhibiting
	Receiving and accepting of the hosting of a foreign exhibition in North Korea and its related business
	Overseas PR and advertisement

ECONOMIC AND BUSINESS CONTACTS

ORGANIZATIONS RELATED TO ECONOMY AND TRADE

National Economic Cooperation Federation

Past subsidiary Organization of Foreign Economic Committee, Council of State Affairs of North Korea, which is in charge of the issue of economic cooperation with South Korea. Changed its name to 'National Economic Cooperative Federation' at the end of May, 1998

The federation is composed of Kwangmyongsung General Corp., Samcholli General Corp., Gaesun Trading Corp., Mt. Kumgang International General Tourism Corp., and Koryo Commercial Bank.

The headquarters in Pyongyang is composed of chairman-Jung Woon-up, vice chairman-Lee Chang-ho, Chief Secretary-Lee Ei-duk

Beijing Representative office

Address: No.601, 66ho-dong, New Central Street, Dongsung-gu, Beijing, China Tel: (8610) 6592-0268

Dandong Representative Office. Address: Rm No.201, Jangsung Hotel, 5ho, 11 Gyung-ro, Jinhung-gu, Dandong, Yoryong Province, China Tel: (86-415) 212-4027

Asia-Pacific Peace Committee

The affiliated people with Asia-Pacific Peace Committee, a distant organization of the Party, are promoting mainly social, cultural and sport fields in Peking, however they also undertake economy related major businesses

Without permanent staff or office in Beijing, a unit composed of 2 people performs business by commuting between Pyongyang and Beijing when there happens some business to deal with.

The Committe for the Promotion of International Trade of the DPR Korea

Location	Central District, Pyongyang		
Tel	850-2-18111(8054)	Fax	850-2-381-4440
Main Business	The Committe for the Promotion of International Trade of the DPR Korea , established in 1952, is a comprehensive organization for promoting		

	foreign trade and economic relations between the DPRK and foreign countries. Recently, the CPIT's activities have been focused on the introduction of transactions and of investment from western countries.
Noteworthy details	The head of the Committee is Kim Yong Mun.

The Committee for the Promotion of External Economic Cooperation of DPRK

Location	Central District, Pyongyang		
Tel	850-2-381-6163	Fax	850-2-381-4498, 850-2-381-4630
Main Business	Past subsidiary organization of Committee for External Economy. Especially Beijing Representative Office is mainly in charge of investment consultation business of Rajin-Sunbong Region in the field of South and North Korea Economic Cooperation.		
	Kim Yong-sul is the acting chairman.		

Korea Foreign Commodity Inspection Committee

Location	Central District, Pyongyang		
Telegraph code	KFCIC PYONGYANG	TLX	5972 TECH KP
Tel	3816252	Fax	
Details of business	This committee inspects and appraises exporting and importing cargos as an official inspection institution for those.		
Noteworthy details	The committee belongs to Foreign Economic Committee of the Cabinet. The committee operates branch committees in major ports such as Nampo, Haeju, Hungnam, Wonsan, Chongjin, Rajin and Songlim.		

Korea International Exhibition Corporation

Location	Jungsong-dong, Central District, Pyongyang		
Telegraph code	ZENRAM PYONGYANG	TLX	5952 ZR KP
Tel	850-2-381-6054	FAX	850-2-381-4440
Main Business	Business related to hosting of North Korean Exhibition and exhibiting in a foreign country Business related to participating in international sample exhibition hosted in a foreign country and exhibiting Receiving and accepting of the hosting of a foreign exhibition in North Korea and its related business Overseas PR and advertisement		

JOINT OPERATION AND JOINT VENTURE COMPANIES

Chosun Yukyung Joint Operation Company

Address	Moranbong-gu, Pyongyang City		
Tel	850-2-3814252	FAX	850-2-3814497
Details of business	The company was established in 1988 as a jointly invested and operated company between the unit related to the Sport Ministry of North Korea and Japanese company. The company operates a restaurant, shop and company in Dandong, China.		

Chosun Jonjin Joint Operation Company

Address	Pyongchon-gu, Pyongyang City	TLX	5344 PC KP
Tel	Jonjin Pyongyang	FAX	850-2-3814410
Details of business	The company owns a clothing processing factory. The factory holds high class designers and fashion designers. The company mainly exports to Japan, and also China and the Middle East. The company produces and processes clothing such as wool mixed spinning, silk fabric, cotton, cotton mixed spinning and other chemical textile. ++ Items dealt with: Clothing (Shirt, jacket, winter clothes, suit, vest, half-coat and mountain climbing clothes)		

Chosun Kumgang Motor Joint Operation Company

Address	Dongdaewon-gu, Pyongyang City	TLX	5975 MT KP, 36041 KG KP
Tel	850-2-3814102	FAX	850-2-3814495
Details of business	The company was established in Oct. 1993 A subsidiary company related to Machinery Ministry of North Korea and East-West General Fuel-Oil Corporation jointly invested and operate the company. The company produces thousands of gasoline engines every year and sells		

them to many nations in the world.

The Kumgang branded 5.3 horsepower, 6hp and 7hp gasoline engines are mainly used for a rice transplanter, pesticide sprayer, rice collector, weeder and small transporting vehicle.

In addition, the company produces a gasoline pump used for drinking water supply and small gasoline motor used for light bulb and heating.

++ Items dealt with: Gasoline engine

Chosun Pyongyang Piano Joint Operation Company

Address	Mangyungdae-gu, Pyongyang City		
Tel	850-2-3814393	FAX	
Details of business	The company produces high quality PACO pianos ++ Items dealt with: Piano		

Chosun Rainbow Joint Operation Company

Address	Jung-gu, Pyongyang	TLX	5340 MJVC KP
Tel	850-2-3184358	FAX	850-2-3814410
Details of business	The company is jointly operated with Hohwa Co.,Ltd of Japan. The company established branches in major regions such as Yongjung and Yanji, China. Clothing processing trade, light industry products and food consigned processing and relaying trade The company holds a food factory, clothing factory and research institute. ++ Items dealt with: Clothing and food		

Chosun Daedong River Electronic calculator Joint Operation Company

Address	Daedong River-gu, Pyongyang City	TLX	
Tel		FAX	850-2-3814416/1210
Details of business	The company is jointly operated between Chosun Computer Center and JIAGE Limited Corporation of Taiwan		

	The company's land area is 17,000 sqm, and building area is 14,600 sqm. The company produces 1,200 units of 386 and 486 class computers (CPU, monitor and keyboard) annually, and 300,000 printing circuit board annually. ++ Items dealt with: Computer

Chosun International Chemicals Joint Operation Company

Address	Mangyungdae-gu, Pyongyang City	TLX	36007 KUKXEI KP
Telegraph code	850-2-3814256	FAX	850-2-3816124
Details of business	The company is jointly invested and operated between Chosun Yunbong General Company and International Trading Co., Ltd (Jochongryun vice chairman of Commerce and Industry Federated Association, Yeo Sung-geun operates). The company treats abundant monajite and produces and exports about 20 kinds of rare earth element products. The company's major export regions are China, Japan, Spain and Hong Kong, etc. ++ Items dealt with: Rare earth element		

Chosun Rungra Joint Operation Company

Address	Jung-gu, Pyongyang City		
Telegraph code	RUNGRA Pyongyang		
Tel	850-2-3816065	FAX	850-2-3814495
Details of business	The company produces 12,000 various burlap bags every year. The company produces nylon water-resistant sacks and shoulder bags, women's handbags and sport bags made of artificial leather. The company undertakes clothing consigned processing and deals with food. The company is consolidating relaying trade through its Shimyang branch in China and is scheduled to set up a Joint Operation Company in Dandong, China. ++ Items dealt with: Sacks, burlap bags and bags		

Chosun Yunha Machinery Joint Operation Company

Address	Mangungdae-gu, Pyongyang City		TLX	37019 MC KP
Tel	850-2-3814215	FAX	850-2-3814215	
Details of business	The company holds a specialized research institute and factory The research institute is developing the processing technology using mainly electric sparks and the factory produces machinery products based on this sort of research. (The company exports 500B type and 260A type Yunha branded lathes.) ++ Items dealt with: (Electric spark) Cutting lathe			

Chosun Nakwon Garment Co.

Address	Sosung-gu, Pyongyang City		TLX	
Tel	850-2-18111, 0333186711	FAX	850-2-3814416/4410, 0333140690	
Details of business	The company was established in Nov, 1985. The company is jointly invested and operated by Nakwon Co. and Sunghwa Co., Ltd. The company holds a clothing factory and research institute, and produces 200,000 units of garments annually. The company participates in various garment exhibitions in Japan and Southeast Asia. The company developed newly designed 20 types of garments in 1995. The company also produces garments following the design made by a customer. ++ Items dealt with: Half-coat, long-coat, jacket, women's blouse, T-shirt, one piece, two pieces and skirt, etc			

Chosun Hoisung Co.

Address	Nakrang-gu, Pyongyang City		
Tel	850-2-3818980	FAX	850-2-3814595
Details of business	The company was jointly ventured with Mazda Co., Ltd, Japan in July 1991. The company produces ECM-319 series microphones, portable microphones, 6 channel 100W amplifiers, 50W speakers, cassette tape		

	recorders and records.
	The company exports to Japan and Southeast Asia.
	The company developed a 400W amplifier and 480W speaker.
	The company is related to Saga Co., Ltd., Japan in business.

Chosun Mt. Gold. New Future Joint Venture Company

Address	Jung-gu, Pyongyang City		TLX	850-2-3812100
Tel	850-2-318111 (Representative No.): 346590	FAX		
Details of business	The company is a joint venture between Chosun Mt. Gold Trading Company and Japanese New Future Limited Responsibility Corporation. The company mainly manages jewelry processing and the processed products, and owns a mine and a jewelry processing factory. It has some high quality jewelry processing staff. The jewels dealt with by the company are cone type (diameter: 2-10mm) and oval type (4*3-12*16mm). Every year it exports 50,000ct. The company carries out consignment processing according to the sample of an orderer and hire processing Cotton crafted pieces, embroidery products and colored stone animal shaped crafted pieces and paintings, etc ++ Items dealt with: Ornaments of gold and silver and other jewels (ring, broach, ear ring, necklace and necktie pin, etc)			

Chosun 12.29 Fertilizer Joint Venture Company

Address	Jung-gu, Pyongyang City		TLX	5972 TECH
Tel	850-2-3816025	FAX	850-2-3814537	
Details of business	The company is a joint venture between Chosun Industrial Technology Company, a subsidiary of Chosun Science & Technology Committee and China Green Technology Development Center. The company produces and exports composite fertilizer. The company owns a composite fertilizer factory and it produces 20,000 tons of the fertilizer annually. All the processes ranging from fertilizer mix			

For additional analytical, business and investment opportunities information,
please contact Global Investment & Business Center, USA
at (202) 546-2103. Fax: (202) 546-3275. E-mail: rusric@erols.com

and packaging to product forwarding are mechanized.

The company has produced and exported hundreds of composite fertilizer since it started to produce in Feb. 2002. (If 750-1,000kg of composite fertilizer per 1ha is used, the food production can increase 20-30%.)

The composite fertilizer contains nitrogen, phosphoric acid, 25% of kali, 5% of humic acid, over 100 million of germs, below 12% of water, 80% of granularity 1-8mm and its hardness is 2N.

++ Items dealt with: Composite fertilizer

Chosun Kwangyoung Furniture Joint Operation Company

Address	Hyungjesan-gu, Pyongyang City		
Tel		FAX	850-2-81455
Details of business	The company was established in June 1993. This company is a Joint Operation Company between a furniture factory, a subsidiary of the Ministry of Building Material Industry and China Shimyang National Machinery Facility Sales Agency Corporation The company produces about 18,000 pieces of furniture annually The company produces a chest, table, bed, sofa, tea table and round table by using a thorny ash tree, fir, spruce and short aromatic tree. ++ Items dealt with: Furniture		

Chosun Koryo Mt. Shinduk Mineral Water Joint Venture Factory

Address	Daedong River-gu, Pyongyang City	TLX	5967 KLGJVC KP
Tel	850-2-3816040	FAX	850-2-3814578
Details of business	The company was established in 1995. The company is a joint venture between Chosun International Joint Operation General Corporation and a Jochongryun related company. The company is located about 30km away from Pyongyang. Building area is 10,000sqm. Three lines of 0.5-0.9 liter, 1.8 liter and 18.9 liter are operated. Daily production amount is about 300 tons. Mineral water components: Ph7.2, SO4 17.82mg/1, Cl 12.4mg/1, F 0.41mg/1 and CaCo330.16mg/1		

| | ++ Items dealt with: Spring water |

SPECIALIZED BUSINESS COMPANIES

Chosun Foreign Construction General Corporation

Address	Jung-gu, Pyongyang City		
Tel		FAX	850-2-3814416/1210
Details of business	The company, established in 1961, is the only national construction company getting contracts of various constructions.> The company's headquarters is in Pyongyang and construction agencies are in Libya, Yemen, Arab Emirate and a liaison office is in Bladivostok. The company mainly designs, constructs a kitchen, public construction, road, bridge, water supply and drainage, thermoelectric power plant, hydroelectric power plant, irrigation, railroad and port, carries out agency work for facilities and materials introduction and also undertakes loan of finance and joint venture related to labor. The company owns a design research institute, design office, training center for high quality technicians, construction company, modernization construction facility and construction material production base, and about 30,000 employees are working for the company. (Among them, about 1000 employees are professional engineers.) The company has constructed about 250 cases of construction in 60 countries worldwide.		

Chosun Mansudae Foreign Development Company Group

Address	Pyongchon-gu, Pyongyang City	TLX	37073 KORYO KP
Telegraph code	KORYOMUYOK Pyongyang		
Tel	850-2-3816104	FAX	850-2-3814646
Details of business	Various monuments, sculptures and crafted pieces managed by the group were all created by Mansudae Creative Company belonging to this Group. The group owns an art creative base and made monuments, commemorating towers and large sculptures. Mansudae Creative Company produced the 50th anniversary commemorating tower for the establishment of the Workers' Party of North Korea on Oct. 10 1995. The group produces monuments, commemorating towers and sculptures		

	upon the orders from its clients.

Chosun Technology Company

Address	Jung-gu, Pyongyang City		TLX	5972 TECH KP
Telegraph code	KONGOBKISUL Pyongyang			
Tel	850-2-3816025	FAX	850-2-3814537	
Details of business	The company is an agent in dealing with invention, patented technology data and related products, transfer of the technology knowledge and exchange business. The company participated in the 24th Geneva international invention, new technology and new product exhibition. ++ "Technology connecting opening of the wrinkled pipe of Aluminum", "Natural mushroom", "Medium electric wave emitting heat treating instrument for cancer" received the Gold Prize, "Diagnosing device for distinguishing one's physical constitution by finger print", "Plant growth promotive" and "Robot with stone carving" were awarded the Silver Prizes.			

Chosun Pyongyang Natural Spices and Aromatic Essence Research Center.

Address	Jung-gu, Pyongyang City		TLX	37025 SN KP
Tel	850-2-381-3214249	FAX	850-2-3812100/4410	
Details of business	The center was established in Apr. 1984. The center researches various spices and aromatic essence. The center is composed of research room for spices for daily use, research room for edible spices, analysis room, chemical facilities and apparatus research room, assortment of spices and application research room, data research room, and it owns a spices factory. About 50 PhD and master degrees' holders who are spices and aromatic essence experts are working in the center. In the subsidiary factory, natural aromatic essences such as a wild rose, clove bud, thymus quinqecos, snake radish, pine needle, tangerine, apple, strawberry and banana and edible spices have been produced and exported. ++ Items dealt with: Spice and aromatic essence			

EXPORTS GOODS PRODUCING COMPANIES

For additional analytical, business and investment opportunities information, please contact Global Investment & Business Center, USA at (202) 546-2103. Fax: (202) 546-3275. E-mail: rusric@erols.com

Chosun Mangyungdae Garment Corporation

Address	Pyongyang		TLX	36024 KNY KP
Telegraph code	PONGHWA Pyongyang			
Tel	850-2-3816023	FAX	850-2-3814444	
Details of business	Factory land area is 12,900 sqm The corporation produces 120,000 men's suits and 60,000 coats annually. The corporation's producing room for men's suit is equipped with automatic sewing machines and various steam irons, and the whole process is controlled by computers. The corporation produces pure wool, wool mixed spinning (wool: 50%, polyester: 50%), pure cotton, cotton mixed spinning. Hire processing according to the design by a client and raw material providing The produced products are sold by the agent, "Chosun Bonghwa General Corporation". ++ The contact numbers mentioned above are those of "Chosun Bonghwa General Corporation".			

Chosun 43 Comprehensive Factory

Address	Dongdaewon-gu, Pyongyang City		TLX	36041 KG KP
Tel	850-2-18555-381-8102	FAX	850-2-3814495	
Details of business	The factory is a machine tool production and exporting base of North Korea The factory is equipped with international class lathes such as figure control lathes and super large lathes. It sells No. 3,6 and 10 multi purpose lathes, multi purpose praise lathes and drilling machines in many places. The No.104 figure control lathe can store about 100 complex product processing procedures, and its capacity is 32 KB. It can be equipped with 12 processing blades and blade exchanging time does not exceed 0.8 seconds. The factory undertakes customized production. "Chosun Lathe Trading Co." is selling the products of the factory under the agency contract. ++ The Contact Numbers are those of "Chosun Lathe Trading Co."			

Chosun 918 Factory

Address	Dongdaewon-gu, Pyongyang City	TLX	5957 MT KP 36041 KG KP
Telegraph code	KIGYE Pyongyang		
Tel	850-2-3814102	FAX	850-2-3814495
Details of business	The factory was established and started to produce in Apr. 1986. The factor is one of the major bearing factories in North Korea. 918 Factory produces mainly locomotives and various bearings with inner diameter from 4mm and outer diameter up to 1m such as cargo vehicles' bearings and general bearings. The factory is equipped with automated assembly lines, computerized production technology and automated measurement facilities measuring angles of bearings and inner & outer diameters. "Chosun Machinery General Trading Corporation" is selling the products of 918 Factory under the agency contract. ++ The contact numbers mentioned above are those of "Chosun Machinery General Trading Corporation."		

Chosun Moranbong Garment Factory

Address	Moranbong-gu, Pyongyang City		
Tel	850-2-3814156	FAX	850-2-3814410, 3814416
Details of business	The factory is equipped with mobile and fixed cutters and automatic embroidery machine. The factory has an assembly line controlled by computers. The factory produces about 200,000 men's clothes mainly including pure wool, pure cotton, mixed spinning (cotton-polyester, cotton-linsey. It undertakes customized production according to a client's design. "Chosun Hyangsan General Corporation" is selling the products of the factory under the agency contract. ++ The contact numbers mentioned above are those of "Chosun Hyangsan General Corporation".		

Chosun 65 Electrical Integrated Factory

Address	Dongdaewon-gu, Pyongyang City		TLX	5975 MT KP, 36041 KG KP
Telegraph code	KIGYE Pyongyang			
Tel	850-2-3814102	FAX	850-2-3814495	
Details of business	The factory is an old porcelain production base located in Gyongsung Region, North Hamgyung Province, North Korea. The Gyongsung Region has over 100 million tons of clay reserve such as kaolin, which is a major raw material base for the porcelain industry and construction material industry of North Korea. 65 Factory produces hundred thousands of various porcelain electrical devices every year by using this regional advantage. Major products are high pressure power transmission line insulation stuff, insulation stuff for a power plant and transformer substation electrical facilities and various porcelain parts for low and high pressure electrical devices (facilities). The factory is equipped with an assembly production line and various equipments such as a grinder, drying facility, vacuum clay blender, porcelain coating sprayer, 1800KV voltage impact experiment generator, 1000KV low frequency experiment transformer. "Chosun Machinery General Trading Corporation" exports the products of the factory. ++ The contact Numbers mentioned above are those of "Chosun Machinery General Trading Corporation".			

FINANCIAL INSTITUTIONS

Chosun Joint Operation Bank

Address	Jung-gu, Pyongyang City		TLX	36001 KJB KP
Tel	850-2-3814151	FAX	850-2-3814497	
Details of business	The bank is jointly operated by Chosun International Joint Operation General Corporation and Jochongryun Joint Operation Business Promotion Committee. The bank has business cooperation agreements with around 40 banks in such nations as Japan, Britain, Belgium, Hong Kong, Austria, China, Russia, Germany, Malaysia, Canada and Australia. The bank's major clients are joint operation companies and individuals The bank carries out deposit, remittance settlement, foreign exchange			

For additional analytical, business and investment opportunities information, please contact Global Investment & Business Center, USA at (202) 546-2103. Fax: (202) 546-3275. E-mail: rusric@erols.com

	settlement, L/C settlement and loan business. General depositing and Time depositing account for large share of the whole business. In addition, the bank researches the international financial market situation and provides services such as interest rate and foreign exchange rate information.

SELECTED TRADING COMPANIES

KOREA FERROUS METALS EXPORT & IMPORT CORP.

Address	Pothonggang-dong No. 2, Pothong-gang District, Pyongyang, DPRK		
Cable address	"KUMSOK" Pyongyang		
TEL	850-2-18111 (EXT) 381-8078	FAX	850-2-381-4569, 850-2-381-4633
Information	The Korea Ferrous Metals Export & Import Corporation is an authoritative trading corporation specializing in the export of ferrous metal products. With 45 years of export history, the corporation conducts business transactions with more than 120 firms and companies in over 60 countries and regions the world over. It has under its control the iron ore and steel production centres including the Musan Mining Complex and the Kim Chaek Iron and Steel Complex with an annual production capacity of several million tons of steel. It has representative and branch offices in many countries and regions throughout the world.		
Exports	Structural alloy steel and other steels, cold-rolled, galvanized and other steel sheets and plates, square steel and other rolled steel, ferrosilicon, oxidizing roasting pellets, magnetite concentrates, etc.		
Imports	Cokes, steel materials including high-, medium- and low carbon ferromanganese; seamless steel pipes for boilers, oxygen blow-in pipes, artificial graphite electrodes, coal tar pitch, sisal, ore-dressing reagents, crude rubber, tyres, bearings, steel cord conveyor belts, nylon belts and wire ropes.		

KOREA NONFERROUS METALS EXPORT & IMPORT CORP.

Address	Pothonggang-dong No. 2, Pothonggang District, Pyongyang, DPRK		
Cable address	"YUSAEK" Pyongyang		
TEL	850-2-18111 (EXT) 381-8247	FAX	850-2-381-4569, 850-2-381-4633
Information	The Korea Nonferrous Metals Export & Import Corporation is an authoritative trading corporation which engages in the export of non-ferrous metals and non-metallic minerals. The corporation conducts trading business in reliance upon scores of large-sized smelteries and mines including the Komdok Mining Complex with an annual production capacity of millions of tons of minerals. It has long years of experience in manufacturing "KM" brand electrolytic zinc, one of its main export items, which has been registered in London Metal Exchange 35 years ago. It also undertakes the processing work of lead and zinc concentrates, according to buyers' request.		
Exports	Non-ferrous metals including electrolytic zinc and cadmium; non-metallic minerals such as barytes, talc and granite; and various non-ferrous metal ore concentrates including zinc and lead concentrates.		
Imports	A wide range of chemical products, reagents, oils, machinery, equipment and		

	their accessories for mines and smelteries.

KOREA MAGNESIA CLINKER EXPORT & IMPORT CORP.

Address	Oesong-dong, Central District, Pyongyang, DPRK		
Cable address			
TEL	850-2-18111 (EXT) 381-8080	FAX	850-2-381-4634
Information	The Korea Magnesia Clinker Export & Import Corporation is an authoritative trading corporation marketing magnesia clinker and its products. The corporation has a powerful magnesite production base, the world's leading magnesite producer. On this basis, it exclusively handles trading business in magnesia clinker. Thanks to a huge investment, the magnesia clinker producing centre has been further expanded in recent years. Accordingly, the corporation is now in a position to meet the overseas demand for magnesia clinker.		
Exports	Magnesia clinker, magnesite, light magnesia, magnesia bricks, chamotte bricks, cyanite, bentonite, diatomite, talc, etc.		
Imports	Cokes, various kinds of industrial oils, chromite, wire ropes, conveyor belts, bearings, insulators, hard alloys, mining machinery and edible oils.		

KOREA BUILDING MATERIALS TRADING CORP.

Address	Tongdaewon District, Pyongyang, DPRK		
Cable address			
TEL	850-2-18111 (EXT) 381-8085	FAX	850-2-381-45555
Information	The Korea Building Materials Trading Corporation is an authoritative trading corporation which carries on the export of a wide variety of building materials including "KIMGANG" Port-land cement. The corporation undertakes trading business with more than 160 firms and companies in over 40 countries and regions of the world. It has up-to-date cement and building materials producing centres including the Sunchon Cement Complex with an annual production capacity of millions of tons. "KUMGANG" Portland cement, a gold medal winner in international commodity exhibition, has been exported to many countries of the world. It fully accords with BSS-12/1978 standard.		
Exports	Various kinds of cement; non-metallic minerals; water taps, valves and other metal fittings; glassware, tiles in diverse colours, designs and sizes; and washbasins, toilet stools and other sanitary ware.		
Imports	Gypsum, PP bags, complete sets of equipment for cement factory and their accessories; tyres, caustic soda, asbestos, and raw materials and fuels for the production of building materials.		

KOREA GENERAL MACHINERY TRADING CORP.

For additional analytical, business and investment opportunities information, please contact Global Investment & Business Center, USA at (202) 546-2103. Fax: (202) 546-3275. E-mail: rusric@erols.com

Address	Tongsin-dong No. 3, Tongdaewon District, Pyongyang, DPRK		
Cable address	"KIGYE" Pyongyang		
TEL	850-2-18555 (EXT) 381-8102	FAX	850-2-381-4495
Information	The Korea General Machinery Trading Corporation is an authoritative trading corporation which engages in the export and import business of all sorts of machinery, equipment and their accessories. The general corporation has several affiliated enterprises such as the Ryongsong Associated Machinery Bureau, Taean Heavy Machine Complex and Rakwon Machine Complex. It has become widely known as an influential corporation throughout the world. Upon buyer's request, it is ready to supply promptly modern machinery and equipment including 125,000 kVA hydraulic generators, 50,000 kVA steam turbines, 10,000 kW motors, large-size excavators, 10,000-ton presses, 7,000 hp 8-axle electric locomotives and extra-large oxygen plants. In addition, it conducts joint ventures in the production of machinery and equipment, as well as processing trade of tyres.		
Exports	Hydraulic turbines, generators, transformers, motors, insulator, electric wires and other electric machinery and related products, accessories for ships and vehicles such as trucks and tractors, farming machines, general machinery including reduction gears, compressors, superhigh-pressure presses, various gears, bolts and nuts, bearings, valves, motor-driven generators, hutches, coal waggons, etc.		
Imports	Ferromanganese, silicon steel sheets, tin, antimony, aluminium, industrial oils, chemical products including lacquer and thinners, rubber, tyres, insulating papers, diamond pencils and cotton threads.		

KOREA MACHINE TOOLS TRADING COPR.

Address	Tongdaewon District, Pyongyang, DPRK		
Cable address			
TEL	850-2-18555 (EXT) 381-810	FAX	850-2-4495
Information	The Korea Machine Tools Trading Corporation handles the export business of machine tools.		
Exports	Various kinds of machine tools		
Imports	Materials and accessories for machine tools		

KOREA UNHA GENERAL TRADING CORP.

Address	Rungra-dong No. 1, Taedonggang District, Pyongyang, DPRK		
Cable address			
TEL	850-2-18111 (EXT) 381-8236	FAX	850-2-381-4506

Information	The Korea Unha General Trading Corporation is an authoritative trading corporation which conducts the export business of clothes. The general corporation has several subsidiary trading corporations and branch offices, and runs clothing and embroidery institutes and clothing factories at home and abroad. It handles garment processing trade, as well as the arrangement of transportation of trade cargoes on shipowners' or shippers' consignment.
Exports	A rich selection of clothes, towels, embroideries, shoes and natural mineral waters (Koryo Phalbong and Koryo Changphyong).
Imports	Equipment and accessories for the manufacture of various fibres, cloths, dyestuffs and garments; shoe materials, packing materials and zinc concentrates.

KOREA KWANGMYONG TRADING GROUP.

Address	Jungsong-dong, Central District, Pyongyang, DPRK		
Cable address			
TEL	850-2-18111 (EXT) 381-8111	FAX	850-2-381-4410, 850-2-381-4416
Information	The Korea Kwangmyong Trading Group is an authoritative trading corporation specializing in the export of agricultural produce, marine products and non-metallic minerals. The group has several subsidiary trading corporations and garments joint venture companies. It set up branch offices abroad. It also undertakes different trade arrangements such as processing trade, re-export trade and border trade, as well as joint ventures.		
Exports	Agricultural produce including edible herbs and seeds; marine products, non-metallic minerals, chemical products, liquors and wines, hops, furs, essential oils, plaited articles, hardware and handicrafts.		
Imports	Chemical products, edible oils, powdered sugar, laundry soaps, tyres, clothes, machines and tools, and crimped nylon yarn.		

KOREA NAMHUNG GENERAL TRADING CORP.

Address	Sinri-dong, Tongadewon District, Pyongyang, DPRK		
Cable address			
TEL	850-2-18111(EXT) 381-8974	FAX	850-2-4623, 850-2-381-4416
Information	The Korea Namhung General Trading Corporation is an authoritative trading corporation which deals in the export and import business of chemical products and their raw materials. The corporation is taking active measures to promote trading business, relying on scores of chemical enterprises including the Hungnam Fertilizer Complex, Namhung Youth Chemical Complex and February 8 Vinalon Complex, the country's leading manufacturers of chemical materials and products. In addition, the corporation undertakes different trade arrangements such as		

	joint ventures, processing trade and re-export trade. Chemical materials and products exported by the corporation enjoy a good reputation among its business partners for their excellent quality.
Exports	Chemical fertilizers, carbide, polyvinyl alcohol, acetic acid, liquefied gas, waste pulp fluids, high-tenacity vinalon fibre, vinyl chloride compounds, high-pressure polyethylene, chemical products and their raw materials, and various medicines including diosgenine.
Imports	Raw materials for chemicals and reagents, and complete sets of equipment for chemical plants and their accessories.

KOREA COALS TRADING CORP.

Address	Pothonggang-dong No. 2, Pothonggang District, Pyongyang, DPRK		
Cable address			
TEL	850-2-18111(EXT)381-8205	FAX	850-2-381-4503
Information	The Korea Coals Trading Corporation is an authoritative trading corporation which mainly exports coals.		
Exports	Non-metallic minerals including soft and hard coals, amorphous graphite and perlite; welded pipes, spiral pipes, charcoal and pots.		
Imports	Mining equipment and their accessories, tyres, crude rubber, industrial oils and various insulators.		

KOREA SAMGWANG TRADING CORP.

Address	Songyo-dong No. 2, Songyo District, Pyongyang, DPRK		
Cable address			
TEL	850-2-18111 (EXT) 381-8987	FAX	850-2-381-4416, 850-2-381-2100
Information	The Korea Samgwang Trading Corporation is a trading corporation dealing in the export and import business of electronic and automation products. Its business scope also includes joint ventures and processing work for electric appliances and their accessories. It also conducts the export and import business of ultra-modern technology in the fields of electronics and automation industry, as well as lighting fixtures and medical appliances.		
Business Lines	Electronic products including TVs and their parts; refrigerators, electric irons, voltage stabilizers, distributing boards, special and ordinary bulbs, medical appliances such as various kinds of prosthetic and surgical appliances, semiconductors, measuring instruments, electronic valves, ordinary valves, integrated circuits, etc.		

KOREA LIGHT INDUSTRY PRODUCTS EXPORT & IMPORT CORP.

Address	Sinri-dong, Tongdaewon District, Pyongyang, DPRK		
TEL	850-2-18111 (EXT) 381-8963	FAX	850-2-381-4538
Cable address			

Information	The Korea Light Industry Products Export & Import Corporation specializes in the export of light industrial products. The corporation also conducts processing trade in the fields of production of electronic products, clothings and enamelware.
Exports	Ceramics, hardware, embroideries, wood carvings, plaited articles, cosmetics, essential oils, liquors and wines, canned goods and non-metallic minerals.
Imports	Chemical products including plastics and sodium carbonate; edible and industrial oils and other raw materials needed in light industry.

KOREA JONGIL TRADING CORP.

Address	Tongmun-dong No. 1, Taedonggang District, Pyongyang, DPRK		
TEL	850-2-18111(EXT) 381-8972	FAX	850-2-4518
Cable address			
Information	The Korea Fishery Trading Corporation is an authoritative trading corporation specializing in the export of marine products. The corporation is provided with modern fishing boats, 14,000-ton factory ships and refrigerating transport ships. It has branch offices in many countries all over the world. It also conducts joint ventures in the field of fishing industry.		
Exports	Lead powder, zinc dust, ferrosilicon, plankingsteel, etc.		
Imports	Chrome ore, ferro-alloys including ferromanganese; equipment and raw materials for power stations and power distribution stations including electric power measuring instruments and meters: aluminium foils. PP resin and fuels.		

KOREA FISHERY TRADING CORP.

Address	Pothongmun-dong, Central District, Pyongyang, DPRK		
TEL	850-2-18111 (EXT) 381-8513	FAX	850-2-381-4416
Cable address			
Information	The Korea Fishery Trading Corporation is an authoritative trading corporation specializing in the export of marine products. The corporation is provided with modern fishing boats, 14,000-ton factory ships and refrigerating transport ships. It has branch offices in many countries all over the world. It also conducts joint ventures in the field of fishing industry.		
Exports	Live fish, shellfish and crab-halibut, flatfish, pollack, short-necked clam, hairy crab and King crab. Frozen fish and shellfish-flatfish, lockington, squid, herring and oyster. Dried fish-pollack, squid, sea-cucumber and abalone. Salted fish-jellyfish and pollack roe. Seaweeds-fresh and dried sea tangle and dried laver.		
Imports	Oils and accessories for vessels, fishing gears and packing materials.		

KOREA PHYONGCHON TRADING CORP.

Address	Tongan-dong, Central District, Pyongyang, DPRK		
TEL	850-2-18111 (EXT) 381-8224	FAX	850-2-381-4527
Cable address			
Information	The Korea Phyongchon Trading Corporation is a trading corporation which mainly exports rolling stocks for railways.		
Exports	Waggons, passenger cars, rolled wheel tyres, shafts and driving wheels, hardware, clothings and knitted goods.		
Imports	Insulators, waggons, fittings for passenger cars, painting materials, and accessories and materials for rolling stocks.		

KOREA UNDOK GROUP

Address	Uiam-dong, Taedonggang District, Pyongyang, DPRK		
TEL	850-2-18111 (EXT) 381-8965	FAX	850-2-381-4575
Cable address			
Information	The Korea Undok Group specializes in the export and import of ferrous and non-ferrous metals, and non-metallic minerals. The group opens an individual bank and has several large-size cargo ships. It has branch offices in many countries and regions all over the world. It engages in different trade arrangements such as re-export trade, processing work, chartering and joint ventures for repairing of construction machinery. It also undertakes the import business of petroleum prospecting and mining equipment and materials, as well as the development of ultra-modern technology.		
Exports	Ferrous and non-ferrous metals, rare earth metals and their oxide, and knitwear.		
Imports	Machines and equipment needed for the modernization of factories, petroleum prospecting and mining equipment and their accessories.		

KOREA HYOPDONG TRADING CORP.

Address	Othan-dong, Kangan Street, Central District, Pyongyang, DPRK		
TEL	850-2-18111(EXT) 381-8011	FAX	850-2-381-4454
Cable address			
Information	The Korea Hyopdong Trading Corporation is a trading corporation which engages in the export of mineral ores and a great variety of ordinary products, as well as in the processing of garments.		
Exports	Chitin, lead powder, soft lead iron concentrates, iron oxide, calcium carbonate, garments, knitted goods, towels, plaited articles, essential oils, chicken feather and down, and stone carvings.		
Imports	Clothings, spinning yarn, and public service facilities and their accessories.		

KOREA MANNYON HEALTH CORP.

Address	Othan-dong, Central District, Pyongyang, DPRK		
TEL	850-2-18111 (EXT) 381-8905	FAX	850-2-381-4546
Cable address			
Information	The Korea Mannyon Health Corporation is an influential trading corporation specializing in the export of health foods and various Koryo medicines. The corporation has established joint venture companies in many countries and regions throughout the world.		
Exports	Health foods, Koryo medicines, medicinal herbs and their processed items.		
Imports	Medicines and their raw materials, packing materials, medicinal herbs, and medical appliances and equipment.		

KOREA UNBYOL GENERAL TRADING CORP.

Address	Ansan-dong, Phyongchon District, Pyongyang, DPRK		
TEL	850-2-18111(EXT) 381-8226	FAX	850-2-381-4499
Cable address			
Information	The Korea Unbyol General Trading Corporation has under its control a large number of export bases including the computer technical trading centre and the export clothing factories.		
Exports	Clothings, marine products, electrolytic zinc, some of ferrous and non-ferrous metals.		
Imports	Computers, sound facilities, electronic musical instrument, sporting goods and refrigerators.		

KOREA DAESONG GENERAL TRADING CORP.

Address	Pulgungori-dong No. 1, Pothonggang District, Pyongyang, DPRK		
TEL	850-2-18111 (EXT)381-8208	FAX	
Cable address	"DAESONG DA" Pyongyang		
Information	The Korea Daesong General Trading Corporation is an authoritative trading corporation with engages in the export and import of various commodities including heavy and light industrial products, jewellery and agricultural produce. It has under its control over ten subsidiary export and import corporations, and conducts transit trade and shipping trade. There are over ten light industrial factories for the production of jewellery and embroideries, and scientific research institutes affiliated to the general corporation. The general corporation is in an advantageous position to cooperate in the form of joint ventures with foreign firms and companies, as well as with individuals.		
Exports			
Imports			

KOREA DAESONG SEIL TRADING CORP.

Address	Pulgungori-dong No. 1, Pothonggang District, Pyongyang DPRK		
TEL	850-2-18111 (EXT) 381-8188	FAX	850-2-381-4431, 850-2-381-4432
Cable address	"DAESONG A" Pyongyang		
Information			
Exports	Non-metallic minerals including anthracite and serpentine; machinery, cutting tools, gold and silver jewellery including rings, earring and necklaces: glassware, ceramics, handicraft, wood carvings, feather works, plaited articles, etc.		
Imports	Machinery and equipment needed for the modernization of factories and enterprises, and various kinds of raw materials. The corporation conducts joint ventures in the processing of diamond and other gems with many countries of the world.		

KOREA DAESONG JEI TRADING CORP.

Address	Pulgungori-dong No. 1, Pothonggang District, Pyongyang, DPRK		
TEL	850-2-18111 (EXT) 381-8213	FAX	850-2-381-4431, 850-2-381-4432
Cable address	"DAESONG B" Pyongyang		
Information			
Exports	Knitted goods such as sweaters and sportswear; down products, children's clothes, one-piece dresses, blouses, pajamas, leather quilts, towels and embroideries.		
Imports	Acrylic and nylon cotton, and nylon threads.		

KOREA DAESONG JESAM TRADING CORP.

Address	Pulgungori-dong No. 1, Pothonggang District, Pyongyang, DPRK		
TEL	850-2-18111 (EXT)381-8562	FAX	850-2-381-4431
Cable address	"DAESONG R" Pyongyang		
Information	The corporation engages in the commercial services at foreign crew's clubs. It sells at wholesale light industrial products, marine products, agricultural produce, natural mineral waters, embroideries, handicrafts, etc. The corporation carries on barter trade and transit trade, as well as the import business of a variety of commodities.		

KOREA DAESONG JEO TRADING CORP.

Address	Pulgungori-dong No. 1, Pothonggang District, Pyongyang, DPRK		
TEL	850-2-18111 (EXT) 381-8132	FAX	850-2-381-4431, 850-2-

			381-4432
Cable address	"DAESONG H" Pyongyang		
Information	The corporation undertakes both barter trade and transit trade in all items of general commodities with neighbouring countries through its branch offices set up in port and frontier cities. Main export products handled by the corporation include trepang, sea urchine egg paste, abalone, pollack roe and shellfishes, and a rich variety of agricultural produce.		
Exports			
Imports			

KOREA DAESONG JERYUK TRADING CORP.

Address	Pulgungori-dong No. 1, Pothonggang District, Pyongyang, DPRK		
TEL	850-2-18111 (EXT) 381-8143	FAX	850-2-381-4431, 850-2-381-4432
Cable address	"DAESONG K" Pyongyang		
Information	The corporation specializes in the import of complete sets of equipment for factories, vehicles, electronic products, materials for publication and sundry goods.		

KOREA NONFERROUS METALS EXPORT & IMPORT CORP.

Address	Pothonggang-dong No. 2, Pothonggang District, Pyongyang, DPRK		
Cable address	"YUSAEK" Pyongyang		
TEL	850-2-18111 (EXT) 381-8247	FAX	850-2-381-4569, 850-2-381-4633
Information	The Korea Nonferrous Metals Export & Import Corporation is an authoritative trading corporation which engages in the export of non-ferrous metals and non-metallic minerals. The corporation conducts trading business in reliance upon scores of large-sized smelteries and mines including the Komdok Mining Complex with an annual production capacity of millions of tons of minerals. It has long years of experience in manufacturing "KM" brand electrolytic zinc, one of its main export items, which has been registered in London Metal Exchange 35 years ago. It also undertakes the processing work of lead and zinc concentrates, according to buyers' request.		
Exports	Non-ferrous metals including electrolytic zinc and cadmium; non-metallic minerals such as barytes, talc and granite; and various non-ferrous metal ore concentrates including zinc and lead concentrates.		
Imports	A wide range of chemical products, reagents, oils, machinery, equipment and their accessories for mines and smelteries.		

KOREA MAGNESIA CLINKER EXPORT & IMPORT CORP.

For additional analytical, business and investment opportunities information,
please contact Global Investment & Business Center, USA
at (202) 546-2103. Fax: (202) 546-3275. E-mail: rusric@erols.com

Address	Oesong-dong, Central District, Pyongyang, DPRK		
Cable address			
TEL	850-2-18111 (EXT) 381-8080	FAX	850-2-381-4634
Information	The Korea Magnesia Clinker Export & Import Corporation is an authoritative trading corporation marketing magnesia clinker and its products. The corporation has a powerful magnesite production base, the world's leading magnesite producer. On this basis, it exclusively handles trading business in magnesia clinker. Thanks to a huge investment, the magnesia clinker producing centre has been further expanded in recent years. Accordingly, the corporation is now in a position to meet the overseas demand for magnesia clinker.		
Exports	Magnesia clinker, magnesite, light magnesia, magnesia bricks, chamotte bricks, cyanite, bentonite, diatomite, talc, etc.		
Imports	Cokes, various kinds of industrial oils, chromite, wire ropes, conveyor belts, bearings, insulators, hard alloys, mining machinery and edible oils.		

KOREA BUILDING MATERIALS TRADING CORP.

Address	Tongdaewon District, Pyongyang, DPRK		
Cable address			
TEL	850-2-18111 (EXT) 381-8085	FAX	850-2-381-45555
Information	The Korea Building Materials Trading Corporation is an authoritative trading corporation which carries on the export of a wide variety of building materials including "KIMGANG" Port-land cement. The corporation undertakes trading business with more than 160 firms and companies in over 40 countries and regions of the world. It has up-to-date cement and building materials producing centres including the Sunchon Cement Complex with an annual production capacity of millions of tons. "KUMGANG" Portland cement, a gold medal winner in international commodity exhibition, has been exported to many countries of the world. It fully accords with BSS-12/1978 standard.		
Exports	Various kinds of cement; non-metallic minerals; water taps, valves and other metal fittings; glassware, tiles in diverse colours, designs and sizes; and washbasins, toilet stools and other sanitary ware.		
Imports	Gypsum, PP bags, complete sets of equipment for cement factory and their accessories; tyres, caustic soda, asbestos, and raw materials and fuels for the production of building materials.		

KOREA GENERAL MACHINERY TRADING CORP.

Address	Tongsin-dong No. 3, Tongdaewon District, Pyongyang,DPRK		
Cable address	"KIGYE" Pyongyang		
TEL	850-2-18555	FAX	850-2-381-4495

	(EXT) 381-8102		
Information	The Korea General Machinery Trading Corporation is an authoritative trading corporation which engages in the export and import business of all sorts of machinery, equipment and their accessories. The general corporation has several affiliated enterprises such as the Ryongsong Associated Machinery Bureau, Taean Heavy Machine Complex and Rakwon Machine Complex. It has become widely known as an influential corporation throughout the world. Upon buyer's request, it is ready to supply promptly modern machinery and equipment including 125,000 kVA hydraulic generators, 50,000 kVA steam turbines, 10,000 kW motors, large-size excavators, 10,000-ton presses, 7,000 hp 8-axle electric locomotives and extra-large oxygen plants. In addition, it conducts joint ventures in the production of machinery and equipment, as well as processing trade of tyres.		
Exports	Hydraulic turbines, generators, transformers, motors, insulator, electric wires and other electric machinery and related products, accessories for ships and vehicles such as trucks and tractors, farming machines, general machinery including reduction gears, compressors, superhigh-pressure presses, various gears, bolts and nuts, bearings, valves, motor-driven generators, hutches, coal waggons, etc.		
Imports	Ferromanganese, silicon steel sheets, tin, antimony, aluminium, industrial oils, chemical products including lacquer and thinners, rubber, tyres, insulating papers, diamond pencils and cotton threads.		

KOREA MACHINE TOOLS TRADING COPR.

Address	Tongdaewon District, Pyongyang, DPRK		
Cable address			
TEL	850-2-18555 (EXT) 381-810	FAX	850-2-4495
Information	The Korea Machine Tools Trading Corporation handles the export business of machine tools.		
Exports	Various kinds of machine tools		
Imports	Materials and accessories for machine tools		

KOREA UNHA GENERAL TRADING CORP.

Address	Rungra-dong No. 1, Taedonggang District, Pyongyang, DPRK		
Cable address			
TEL	850-2-18111 (EXT) 381-8236	FAX	850-2-381-4506
Information	The Korea Unha General Trading Corporation is an authoritative trading corporation which conducts the export business of clothes. The general corporation has several subsidiary trading corporations and branch offices, and runs clothing and embroidery institutes and clothing factories at home and abroad. It handles garment processing trade, as well as		

	the arrangement of transportation of trade cargoes on shipowners' or shippers' consignment.
Exports	A rich selection of clothes, towels, embroideries, shoes and natural mineral waters (Koryo Phalbong and Koryo Changphyong).
Imports	Equipment and accessories for the manufacture of various fibres, cloths, dyestuffs and garments; shoe materials, packing materials and zinc concentrates.

KOREA KWANGMYONG TRADING GROUP.

Address	Jungsong-dong, Central District, Pyongyang, DPRK		
Cable address			
TEL	850-2-18111 (EXT) 381-8111	FAX	850-2-381-4410, 850-2-381-4416
Information	The Korea Kwangmyong Trading Group is an authoritative trading corporation specializing in the export of agricultural produce, marine products and non-metallic minerals. The group has several subsidiary trading corporations and garments joint venture companies. It set up branch offices abroad. It also undertakes different trade arrangements such as processing trade, re-export trade and border trade, as well as joint ventures.		
Exports	Agricultural produce including edible herbs and seeds; marine products, non-metallic minerals, chemical products, liquors and wines, hops, furs, essential oils, plaited articles, hardware and handicrafts.		
Imports	Chemical products, edible oils, powdered sugar, laundry soaps, tyres, clothes, machines and tools, and crimped nylon yarn.		

KOREA NAMHUNG GENERAL TRADING CORP.

Address	Sinri-dong, Tongadewon District, Pyongyang, DPRK		
Cable address			
TEL	850-2-18111(EXT) 381-8974	FAX	850-2-4623, 850-2-381-4416
Information	The Korea Namhung General Trading Corporation is an authoritative trading corporation which deals in the export and import business of chemical products and their raw materials. The corporation is taking active measures to promote trading business, relying on scores of chemical enterprises including the Hungnam Fertilizer Complex, Namhung Youth Chemical Complex and February 8 Vinalon Complex, the country's leading manufacturers of chemical materials and products. In addition, the corporation undertakes different trade arrangements such as joint ventures, processing trade and re-export trade. Chemical materials and products exported by the corporation enjoy a good reputation among its business partners for their excellent quality.		

Exports	Chemical fertilizers, carbide, polyvinyl alcohol, acetic acid, liquefied gas, waste pulp fluids, high-tenacity vinalon fibre, vinyl chloride compounds, high-pressure polyethylene, chemical products and their raw materials, and various medicines including diosgenine.
Imports	Raw materials for chemicals and reagents, and complete sets of equipment for chemical plants and their accessories.

KOREA COALS TRADING CORP.

Address	Pothonggang-dong No. 2, Pothonggang District, Pyongyang, DPRK		
Cable address			
TEL	850-2-18111(EXT)381-8205	FAX	850-2-381-4503
Information	The Korea Coals Trading Corporation is an authoritative trading corporation which mainly exports coals.		
Exports	Non-metallic minerals including soft and hard coals, amorphous graphite and perlite; welded pipes, spiral pipes, charcoal and pots.		
Imports	Mining equipment and their accessories, tyres, crude rubber, industrial oils and various insulators.		

KOREA SAMGWANG TRADING CORP.

Address	Songyo-dong No. 2, Songyo District, Pyongyang, DPRK		
Cable address			
TEL	850-2-18111 (EXT) 381-8987	FAX	850-2-381-4416, 850-2-381-2100
Information	The Korea Samgwang Trading Corporation is a trading corporation dealing in the export and import business of electronic and automation products. Its business scope also includes joint ventures and processing work for electric appliances and their accessories. It also conducts the export and import business of ultra-modern technology in the fields of electronics and automation industry, as well as lighting fixtures and medical appliances.		
Business Lines	Electronic products including TVs and their parts; refrigerators, electric irons, voltage stabilizers, distributing boards, special and ordinary bulbs, medical appliances such as various kinds of prosthetic and surgical appliances, semiconductors, measuring instruments, electronic valves, ordinary valves, integrated circuits, etc.		

KOREA LIGHT INDUSTRY PRODUCTS EXPORT & IMPORT CORP.

Address	Sinri-dong, Tongdaewon District, Pyongyang, DPRK		
TEL	850-2-18111 (EXT) 381-8963	FAX	850-2-381-4538
Cable address			
Information	The Korea Light Industry Products Export & Import Corporation specializes in the export of light industrial products. The corporation also conducts processing trade in the fields of production of		

	electronic products, clothings and enamelware.
Exports	Ceramics, hardware, embroideries, wood carvings, plaited articles, cosmetics, essential oils, liquors and wines, canned goods and non-metallic minerals.
Imports	Chemical products including plastics and sodium carbonate; edible and industrial oils and other raw materials needed in light industry.

KOREA JONGIl TRADING CORP.

Address	Tongmun-dong No. 1, Taedonggang District, Pyongyang, DPRK		
TEL	850-2-18111(EXT) 381-8972	FAX	850-2-4518
Cable address			
Information	The Korea Fishery Trading Corporation is an authoritative trading corporation specializing in the export of marine products. The corporation is provided with modern fishing boats, 14,000-ton factory ships and refrigerating transport ships. It has branch offices in many countries all over the world. It also conducts joint ventures in the field of fishing industry.		
Exports	Lead powder, zinc dust, ferrosilicon, plankingsteel, etc.		
Imports	Chrome ore, ferro-alloys including ferromanganese; equipment and raw materials for power stations and power distribution stations including electric power measuring instruments and meters: aluminium foils. PP resin and fuels.		

US NON-GOVERNMENTAL ORGANIZATIONS (NGOS) IN NORTH KOREA

US NGO ACTIVE IN NORTHE KOREA

Adventist Development and Relief Agency
American Friends Service Committee
American Red Cross
Catholic Relief Services
Christian Reformed World Relief Committee
Church World Service
Direct Relief International
Food for the Hungry
Heifer Project International
Interchurch Medical Assistance
Latter-day Saint Charities
Lutheran World Relief
Mercy Corps International
Refugees International
United Methodist Committee on Relief
World Vision US

FOR MORE INFORMATION:
InterAction: 1717 Massachusetts Avenue NW, Suite 801, Washington DC 20036   Tel: 202/667-8227; Fax: 202/667-8236; E-mail: ia@interaction.org
NGOs: Mary Hope Schwoebel at (202) 667-8227 x106 or mhschwoebel@interaction.org   Media: Mike Kiernan at (202) 667-8227 x116 or mkiernan@interaction.org

ADVENTIST DEVELOPMENT RELIEF AGENCY

12501 Old Columbia Pike
Silver Spring, MD 20904

Media Contacts:	
Richard Kajiura	Beth Shaefer
Tel: (301) 680-6340	Tel: (301)680-6355
Fax: (301) 680-6370	Fax: (301) 680-6370
E-mail: 74617.1365@compuserve.com	

The Adventist Development and Relief Agency (ADRA) began working with the Democratic People's Republic of Korea (DPRK) after its government's initial appeal for emergency food aid in September 1995. To date, ADRA has provided more than $2 million in medicines and supplies, 150 tons of rice, 30 tons of milk powder, 12 tons of baby food and 14,300 cartons of instant noodles (not including recent shipments).

For additional analytical, business and investment opportunities information,
please contact Global Investment & Business Center, USA
at (202) 546-2103. Fax: (202) 546-3275. E-mail: rusric@erols.com

In November 1996, under the auspices of ADRA, a 17-member heart surgery team from Loma Linda University Medical Center in Loma Linda, California, visited the DPRK. The team worked at the Kim Man You Hospital, performing open-heart surgery on 12 patients and vascular surgery on four patients. Twenty diagnostic cardiac procedures were also done, including two coronary stent interventions, the first such procedure in the country. A heart/lung machine and other supplies and equipment worth more than $250,000 were left with the Korean Cardiac Society.

AMERICAN FRIENDS SERVICE COMMITTEE
1501 Cherry Street
Philadelphia, PA 19102

Media Contact:
Mustafa Malik
Tel: (215) 241-7149
Fax: (215) 241-7026
E-mail: MMalik@afsc.org

Since the fall of 1995 the American Friends Service Committee (AFSC) Korea Relief Fund has raised over $200,000 for food relief. These funds have been used to purchase rice through Caritas Hong Kong for shipment to the DPRK. Contributions from the Mennonite Central Committee (MCC) and fundraising by Korean American groups have been a significant part of this effort.

Following a visit by AFSC to the Sambong Cooperative Farm in Pyongan Province, AFSC purchased 480 tons ($102,000) of urea fertilizer in China and delivered it to the farm in early July 2002. Further assistance to support agricultural production is planned, including a fall shipment of barley seed and relief supplies.

An AFSC delegation first visited North Korea in 1980. AFSC sponsored a visit to the United States by representatives of the Korean Committee for Solidarity with World People (KCSWP) in November 1995 and a delegation of Quaker educators visited the DPRK in July 1996. A return delegation from the KCSWP is scheduled to visit the AFSC in the fall of 2002. A delegation from the DPRK Women's Union is expected in 1998.

AFSC's Northeast Asia International Affairs representatives are based in Japan and provide the primary program contact with DPRK.

AMERICAN RED CROSS
2025 E Street, NW
Washington, DC 20006

Program Contact:	Media Contact:
Mark Preslan	Ann Stingle
Tel: (202) 728-6633	Tel: (703) 206-7803
Fax: (202) 728-6404	Fax: (703) 206-7741
E-mail: preslanm@usa.redcross.org	E-mail: stingle@usa.redcross.org

Since September 1995, the International Federation of Red Cross and Red Crescent Societies (Federation) and the Democratic People's Republic of Korea Red Cross (DPRK Red Cross) have been assisting more than 130,000 beneficiaries (26,000 families) with regular food distributions representing a daily ration of 450 grams per person. The American Red Cross has supported these efforts through the facilitation of contributions totaling nearly $275,000 in cash; and in-kind donations of 350 MT of wheat flour; 18,000 liters of vegetable oil; and a shipping container full of first aid supplies.

In operations supported by three Federation appeals, the DPRK Red Cross/Federation have been assisting beneficiaries in 15 counties in five affected provinces (North Pyongan, Jagang, North Hwanghae, South Hwanghae and Kangwon). The DPRK Red Cross/Federations selects the following beneficiaries: families who lost everything in the floods; and vulnerable groups, such as single mothers, elderly, widows, disabled, families with many children, and pregnant and lactating mothers. Beneficiaries of the Red Cross program are not served by the Public Distribution System (PDS).

The first appeal, for $4,151,000, was 84% covered; and the second appeal, for $6,390,000, 77% covered. This response ensured that the 130,000 Red Cross beneficiaries regularly received their full daily 450g rice/wheat ration. The shortfall in the appeal coverage was reflected in a reduced distribution of supplementary food (soy beans and vegetable oil).

Following a Federation assessment mission carried out in May 2002, the third appeal, which runs through November 2002, was expanded to include the provision of emergency food rations to 740,000 beneficiaries in 19 counties. In addition, the Red Cross operation now includes a health component which will provide essential medicines and medical supplies to 106 Ri-Hospitals and 343 Ri-Polyclinics, which are first level health centers, in the same 19 counties where food distributions are being carried out. (One Ri-Hospital covers a population of 20,000-22,000. One Ri-Polyclinic covers a population of 1,000/1,500 - 3,000/4,000.) Medical supplies in these hospitals and clinics have been at critically low levels.

The following items have been distributed to the target beneficiaries as of June 2002. Figures in brackets show quantities provided in the first two appeals:

Food: 31,830 Metric Tons (MT) of rice/wheat flour/corn [16,723 MT], 817 MT of soy beans [697 MT], 100,000 packs of instant noodles, 171 MT of vegetable oil (130 MT in pipeline), 120 MT of milk powder.

Clothing: 24,900 pieces jackets (9,200), 2,708 meters of cloth

Quilts/blankets: 124,005 pieces (23,980)

Medical: 1,512 medical/first aid kits (457 kits in pipeline)

Building materials (locally purchased - for reconstruction of 1,900 houses destroyed by floods): 5,415 MT of cement; 3,420 cubic meters of timber; 22.99 MT of steel.

For additional analytical, business and investment opportunities information,
please contact Global Investment & Business Center, USA
at (202) 546-2103. Fax: (202) 546-3275. E-mail: rusric@erols.com

The DPRK Red Cross has carried out the distributions, and the Federation has maintained a representative in the country since 1995 to ensure continued assistance to the DPRK Red Cross in planning, purchasing, monitoring and reporting. In summer 2002, the Federation staff in Pyongyang will be increased to four: a Head of Delegation, two logistics/monitoring delegates, and a Health Delegate to administer the health component. In addition, liaison delegates will be posted in Beijing and in Seoul to help coordinate the purchase and transport arrangements for food.

The Federation office in Pyongyang reports excellent support and cooperation from both the government and the Red Cross Society of the DPRK.

An American Red Cross representative visited the DPRK in June, 2002 to observe the food distribution operation. The American Red Cross continues to facilitate donations for the appeal.

CATHOLIC RELIEF SERVICES

209 West Fayette Street
Baltimore, MD 21201

Program Contact:	Media Contact:
Lisa Kuennen-Asfaw	Tom Price
Tel: (410) 625-2220 x3515	Tel: (410) 625-2220 x3246
Fax: (410) 234-3121	Fax: (410) 234-2992
E-mail: lkuennen@catholicrelief.org	E-mail: tprice@catholicrelief.org

Since the fall of 1995, Catholic Relief Services (CRS), a member organization of Caritas Internationalis (CI), has provided assistance to the DPRK via CI member agencies located in Asia.

In 1995 and 1996, CRS supported the food assistance programs of Caritas Hong Kong, providing $86,195 for the purchase of corn/soya blend and rice. In 2002, CRS contributed $60,000 to the relief efforts of Caritas Japan, also for the purchase of rice. Caritas Hong Kong and Caritas Japan receive additional sponsorship from other CI member agencies. Both agencies work in conjunction with the DPRK's Flood Damage Rehabilitation Program, and Caritas Hong Kong's large assistance program coordinates with the World Food Programme for the purposes of monitoring and accountability.

CHRISTIAN REFORMED WORLD RELIEF COMMITTEE
2850 Kalamazoo Ave. SE
Grand Rapids, MI 49560

Media & Program Contact:
Madeline Robins
Tel: (905) 336-2920
Fax: (905) 336-2920
E-mail: robinsm@crcna.org

Christian Reformed World Relief Committee has participated in the Canadian Foodgrains Bank response to North Korea since the Bank first learned about the emerging food deficit in that country back in the fall of 1995. Together with several other Foodgrains Bank partners, three local purchases of Thai rice and a shipment of Canadian wheat have been provided to date. In late July, Canadian Foodgrains Bank partners -- including CRWRC -- made further commitments totaling $1million that would be used to arrange either a local purchase of rice or a shipment of wheat from Canada. It is our plan to have this additional food provided prior to the North Korean harvest in September/October.

CWRC contributed $20,000 to the 1996 shipment of 1,800 mt of Thai rice and $90,000 towards our 13,500 mt shipment of Canadian wheat on early 2002. An additional shipment is planned in 2002 with CWRC contributing $30,000.

CHURCH WORLD SERVICE
475 Riverside Drive, Room 616
New York, NY 10115-0050

Media Contact:
Victor W.C. Hsu
Tel: (212) 870-2371
Fax: (212) 870-2225
E-mail: victor@ncccusa.org

CWS serves as the lead agency, on behalf of Action by Churches Together, Canadian Foodgrains Bank, Caritas International, Food for the Hungry International, Mercy Corps International and World Vision International in staffing the Food Aid Liaison Unit of the World Food Program.

Church World Service (CWS) provides food and grains including rice, corn and barley to the hungry in the DPRK. Barley seed was distributed in Byoksong, Kangnam, Jinghwa and Sinchon counties, and Sungbo and Samsok Districts. Corn seed was planted mainly in Daechong Cooperative Farm, and food and rice distribution was nationwide.

CWS also provides anti-cholera medication and other medicines in Hwanghae province and blankets and clothing throughout the country. CWS participates in a consortium for cooperative farming and integrated development program in Unpa County of North Hwanghae Province.

Medication, food, blankets and rice benefited Korean Christians Federation with a membership of about 50,000 people. About 3,500 tons of barley was harvested in June in four cooperative farms.

CWS receives funding from a combination of private donors and USAID. Among the top concerns for CWS is the lifting of economic and trade sanctions against North Korea to enable free flow of aid and long-term development assistance.

DIRECT RELIEF INTERNATIONAL
27 South La Patera Lane
Santa Barbara, CA 93117

Media & Program Contact:
Mike Hayes
Tel: (805) 964-4767
Fax: (805) 681-4838
E-mail: dri@rain.org

In response to the situation in the DPR Korea, Direct Relief has worked in partnership with the National Committee for Rehabilitation of Flood Disaster to distribute medical commodities to health facilities. Since January 1996 more than 18,000 pounds of specifically requested pharmaceuticals and medical supplies have been dispatched, valued at over $255,000.

FOOD FOR THE HUNGRY
7729 East Greenway Road
Scottsdale, AZ 85260
Program Contact:
Dwight Vogt
Tel: (800) 248-6437
Fax: (602) 951-9035
E-mail: dwightv@fh.org

Media Contact:
Sally Digges or Dwight Vogt
Tel: (800) 2HUNGER
Fax: (602) 951-9035
E-mail: sallyd@fh.org

Food for the Hungry International (FHI) began shipping requested supplies to North Korea immediately after the July-August 1995 floods. During the past two years, FHI has sent 29 containers food, seeds, and medical supplies valued at $4.54 million. The agency expects to deliver another 760 tons of wheat flour in the coming months.

Ted Yamamori, President of Food for the Hungry International (FHI), is personally directing the organization's assistance effort to North Korea. He visited famine areas of North Korea twice in 1996 and again in July 2002 to verify FHI shipments and to learn firsthand the condition of the people and their needs.

Food for the Hungry is actively encouraging the public, governments, and other humanitarian agencies to get involved in advocacy. FHI is part of the "Committee to Stop Famine in North Korea," a coalition of relief and development organizations that is urging the U.S. government to mount a swift response to the crisis in North Korea.

FHI shipments to date include:

17 containers of food (rice, corn, dehydrated fruit, wheat flour)
10 containers of medical supplies
2 containers of vegetable seeds

Shipments planned:
760 MT wheat flour (from Dandong China by rail)

All aid is channeled through the government's Flood Damage Rehabilitation Committee (FDRC). Food is designated for Kwangwan Province, Sinuiju, and other areas where most needed. The medical supply consignee is Kim Man Yu hospital which has a network of 4,000 hospitals and clinics in all of North Korea. To assist with monitoring, FHI is one of five agencies that provided funding for the posting of an NGO representative (approved by the DPRK) in Pyongyang to monitor the shipment of goods coming from the NGOs.

HEIFER PROJECT INTERNATIONAL
1015 Louisiana Street
Little Rock, AR 72202

Field Contact:
Dr. Pu Jiabi
Heifer Project China Country Director
Hong Kong Garden (Xiang Gang Huayuan)
International Metropolitan (Buo Ji Da Du Hi)
Pixian hengdu
Sichuan 611731, CHINA

US Program and Media Contact:
Mr. Tom Peterson
Tel: (800) 422-1311
Fax: (501) 376-8906
E-mail: tom@heifer.org

Heifer Project China has been engaged in a Small Animals for Food Security and Peace Program at a cooperative farm. The overall aim of the project is to increase food security of participating families, and to develop a model of food production/animal agriculture useful for other parts of the country.

HPI/China team will distribute dairy goats, rabbits, and poultry. Agroforestry practices will be implemented to ensure soil quality. Trees and shrubs that are appropriate to the region will be planted in selected areas within the cooperative. Dairy goats will be selected from regional Asian stock that have at least half European blood, and can produce at least 300 kg of milk per lactation. Selected families will receive 10. Rabbits will be Californian or New Zealand breed from Asian stock and already adapted to the region. Poultry will be one of several local multipurpose types, and distributed in groups of ten per family. The 100 dairy goats will be managed by larger units within the cooperative with full-time care. A local facilitator will be used part-time to represent HPI's objectives for the duration of the project.

Training for the project will be provided before the animals are delivered and ongoing training will be available for families in the cooperative. Nutritionists will educate both husbands and wives on gaining the best nutritional value from animal products.

This program is funded in full by private donors.

INTERCHURCH MEDICAL ASSISTANCE
Box 429, Blue Ridge Building
New Windsor, MD 21776

Program & Media Contact:
Paul Derstine
Tel: (410) 635-8720
Fax: (410) 635-8726
E-mail: I_M_A@ecunet.org

Interchurch Medical Assistance (IMA) made three shipments of donated and purchased pharmaceuticals, medical supplies, and IMA medicine boxes to the DPRK during the last fiscal year. These shipments, which were made to three hospitals and several clinics in Pyongyang, had a product value of $523,000.

Two of IMA's affiliated organizations, ADRA and Church of the Brethren, were the agency's main facilitating partners and funding sources. Thirteen mostly Protestant denominations are full affiliates of IMA. Future shipments will be made at the request of these affiliates.

LATTER-DAY SAINT CHARITIES
50 East North Temple
Salt Lake City, UT 84150

Media Contact:
Isaac C. Ferguson
Tel: (801) 240-3026
Fax: (801) 240-1964
E-mail: fergusonic@chq.byu.edu

Program Contact:
Garry R. Flake
Tel: (801) 240-5627
Fax: (212) 240-1964
E-mail: flakegr@chq.byu.edu

Latter-day Saint Charities provides the following types of relief:
Food relief, i.e. basic staple foods to support the Public Distribution System and Red Cross programs.
Medical relief through basic first aid materials and blankets for public clinic and hospital use. Latter-day Saint Charities responds to requests for medical assessment, with potential training program follow-up.

For additional analytical, business and investment opportunities information,
please contact Global Investment & Business Center, USA
at (202) 546-2103. Fax: (202) 546-3275. E-mail: rusric@erols.com

Cold weather clothing is provided to the most vulnerable.
Latter-day Saint Charities provides seed, fertilizer, insecticides for immediate cropping.
Latter-day Saint Charities is developing a longer term agricultural development program to enhance production capacity.

Food relief has been delivered to World Food Program, DPRK Red Cross (with IFRC Coordination and monitoring), and most recently the DPRK Flood Rehabilitation Committee. Medical materials have been consigned to DPRK Red Cross. Agricultural inputs have been consigned to the Agriculture Commission and the Daechong and other communal farms.

Latter-day Saints have shipped or planned shipments totaling 2,500 tons of food, 40 tons of first aid materials and blankets, 20 tons of cold weather clothing, 400 tons of fertilizer, 2.5 tons of insecticide, cabbage and radish seeds.

Latter-day Saint Charities is funded in full by the Church of Jesus Christ of Latter-day Saints.

LUTHERAN WORLD RELIEF
390 Park Avenue South
New York, NY 10016

Program and Media Contact:
Kenlynn K. Schroeder
Tel: (212) 532-6350
Fax: (212) 213-6081
E-mail: kschroeder@lwr.org

Lutheran World Relief's activities in North Korea are designed to support the Action By Churches Together (ACT) network project which aims to alleviate famine in North Korea by providing the following:

1. Emergency food shipments of rice, maize, wheat, blended food, spring barley seed, and plastic sheeting (to protect seedlings during the winter).

2. Relief supplies including cholera antibiotics, rehydration tablets, blankets, hospital supplies, beef and rice.

3. Assist a double-cropping experiment in which barley seeds were planted in March and harvested in June, after which rice was planted.

This assistance is distributed throughout North Korea in the areas of greatest need and is coordinated by an International Officer of the Non-Government Organization Food Liaison Unit of the WFP Pyongyang office. He serves as liaison officer with the North Korean Government on behalf of international relief agencies. This post is supported in part by ACT.

Shipments in 2002 include 500 tons of barley seeds, 200 tons of plastic sheeting, 10 tons of spinach seeds, and 2,000 tons of rice. For example, the 200 tons of rice was distributed in South and North Pyongyang Provinces to seven counties and an estimated 444,444 beneficiaries each received 450 grams over a ten day period. Another 360 tons of emergency biscuits and corn soya blend were due to arrive in late August.

Local and international implementing/facilitating partners include Action by Churches Together (ACT), which is a Geneva-based worldwide network of churches and their related agencies meeting human need through coordinated emergency response and common identity. The ACT network consists of many donor and implementing organizations in developing countries. ACT is based in the Lutheran World Federation (LWF) and the World Council of Churches (WCC) and is a coordinating rather than operational office. North American Members include LWR, CWS, and UMCOR among others.

MERCY CORPS INTERNATIONAL
2852 Ontario Road, NW
Washington, DC 20006

Program Contact:
Shannon Horvath
Tel: (503) 796-6800 x224
Fax: (503) 241-2850
E-mail: shorvath@mercycorps.org

Media Contact:
Nancy Lindborg
Tel: (202) 518-9466
Fax: (202) 518-9465
E-mail: MercyCorps@aol.com

Mercy Corps has played a lead role in providing humanitarian aid to North Korea since March 1996. Mercy Corps' goal is to avert wide-spread famine and starvation in North Korea as it faces a second year of severe food shortages, while laying the foundation for prevention of future food emergencies in the DPRK. Our humanitarian efforts include food and medical aid, agricultural rehabilitation, education/advocacy efforts, and increasing the exchange of visitors between North Korea and the United States. To date, Mercy Corps has:

Food and Medical Aid
Shipped medical supplies and medicines (valued at over $1 million) and 120 MT of rice. Participated in establishment and funding of a Food Aid Liaison Unit within the World Food Programme in Pyongyang to coordinate NGO relief efforts and monitor food shipments.
Arranged to send a series of shipments of medicines, medical supplies, and medical equipment valued at approximately $7 million from August through November 2002, along with future food shipments.

Agricultural Rehabilitation/Food Security
Developed a comprehensive proposal for barley seeds to introduce double cropping for summer harvest.
Shipped 100 MT of barley seed, 35 MT of high-yielding corn seed, and 3 MT of soybean seed, which are expected to yield enough grain to feed approximately 700,000 people during the critical months before the next harvest.
Shipped 24,000 lbs. of green bean seeds valued at $30,000.
Launched a 3-year model integrated farm project on the Daechong Farm in the flood-damaged county of Unpa to demonstrate methods to increase food production and promote food security.

Advocacy
Convened Musgrove I conference for key U.S. NGO players that led to increased humanitarian aid to the DPRK.
Co-convened Musgrove II conference in Seoul to open dialogue among South Korean NGOs, international NGOs and UN groups to catalyze collaborative efforts for immediate food aid to North Korea.
Founding member of Committee to Stop Famine in North Korea.
Ellsworth Culver, Senior Vice President, is chairman of the executive committee of an NGO coalition which negotiated with US and DPRK officials to allow NGO monitoring of 55,000 MT of US food aid.

Delegations to DPRK
Ells Culver has led six fact-finding delegations since July 1996 to visit flood damaged farms, hospitals, and clinics; monitor seed projects; discuss longer-term agricultural projects; and negotiate increased monitoring of food shipments as well as an increase in delegations to and from the DPRK.

Mercy Corps is working with cooperative farms in the counties of Hwangju, Kangdong, Onchon, Pyongwon, Sukchon, Unpa and the districts of Mankyondae, Ryongsong and Samsuk. In country, Mercy Corps works with the World Food Programme, the Flood Damage Rehabilitation Committee, the Agricultural Commission, and the Academy of Agricultural Science.

To date, Mercy Corps has raised over $350,000 through private contributions and 14 partner organizations (ADRA, CARE, Church of the Brethren, Church World Service, Cornerstone Ministries, MAP International, Maryknoll Missioners, Newman's Own, Northwest Medical Teams, S.G. Foundation, Stewardship Foundation, World Concern, World Touch, and World Vision) to support direct famine relief and ongoing agricultural rehabilitation and development activities.

OPERATION USA

8320 Melrose Ave. #200
Los Angeles, CA 90069

Program Contact:
Richard Walden and Neil Frame
Tel: (213) 678-7255
Fax: (213) 653-7846
E-mail: opusa@opusa.org

Operation USA was contacted two years ago by the DPRK UN Mission for assistance. Since then our project had focused on health needs at the clinic & hospital level.

Operation USA has at least two 40-foot sea containers of medical supplies and equipment ready for shipment to the Relief Committee. They total approximately a half ton at an estimated value of $250,000++.

REFUGEES INTERNATIONAL

2639 Connecticut Ave., NW Ste 202
Washington, DC 20008

Program Contact:
David Shore
Tel: (202) 828-0110
Fax: (202) 828-0819
E-mail: don@refintl.org

Refugees International has worked to mobilize public opinion and to induce governments to act in response to the food crisis in North Korea.

On June 2nd, Refugees International (RI) President Lionel Rosenblatt and Board member Shep Lowman of the U.S. Catholic Conference published an opinion piece in the Washington Times calling for increased international food assistance to North Korea, especially from Japan.

On June 10th, Rosenblatt gave a speech at the residence of the British Ambassador in Tokyo in which he again called for increased international aid for North Korea. The Japan Times subsequently interviewed him and published an article titled "A Hungry Child Knows No Politics." RI distributed the text of the press article to Japanese diplomats and press representatives in Washington.

UNITED METHODIST COMMITTEE ON RELIEF

1601 North Kent Street, Suite 1010
Arlington, VA 22209

Program Contact:
Maggie Partilla
Tel: (703) 276-1010
Fax: (703) 276-0509
E-mail: akeys@clark.net

Media Contact:
Wendy Whiteside
Tel: (212) 870-3814
Fax: (212) 870-3624
E-mail: wendyw@gbgm-umc.org

In September 1996 UMCOR received approval from the Department of Commerce to ship $6,650,000 worth of humanitarian relief. The shipment will consist of 100,000 "family boxes" and 3,000 tons of rice. Each "family box" contains rice, powdered milk, canned meat, shortening, chocolate, a comb & brush set, and two garden hand tools. A "family box" will feed a family of five for one week. An additional 3,000 tons of rice will be distributed as a supplement to the "family boxes", sustaining the same 100,000 families for an entire month. To utilize its church network in the U.S. and elsewhere, UMCOR is mobilizing member churches to assemble these boxes. On July 22, 1,362 "family boxes" were shipped, and additional boxes are expected to be shipped in September.

In April 2002, UMCOR contributed $100,000 to Action by Churches Together (ACT) who shipped 2,000 metric tons of rice to North Korea. This shipment is estimated to provide 444,444 beneficiaries with 450 grams of rice over a 10 day period. ACT representative Erich Weingartner is now in North Korea working with the World Food Program to monitor the donation.

UMCOR has also been a member of the Committee to Stop Famine in North Korea since May, 2002.

WORLD VISION US
34834 Weyerhaeuser Way South
Federal Way, WA 98001

Media Contacts:
Kathleen Brown
Tel: (202) 547-3743
Fax: (202) 547-4834
E-mail: Kathleen_Brown@wvi.org

World Vision has sent four relief assessment and response teams into the DPRK at the invitation of the North Korean government since the autumn of 1996.

Since 1995, World Vision has provided to North Korea with nearly $5 million worth of assistance including 1,500 tons of rice and shipments of medicines and medical supplies, clothing and seeds. The supplies are being distributed through World Food Program, a United Nations agency, which works through 193 government distribution centers.

In June 2002, World Vision announced its plan to provide assistance to children in 12 provincial children's centers which house more than 2,400 children younger than five years, many of them orphans. An assessment team has just returned from visiting five such centers and conducting the first systematic measurement of children from July 15 to 22, 2002. It reporting that 85% of the children are suffering from malnutrition, and of those, 60% are suffering moderate to severe forms.

In addition to children's centers, World Vision hopes to expand other aid to North Korea, including food and agricultural support and the development of noodle factories.

Along with 18 other non-governmental organizations, World Vision has formed the Committee to Stop Famine in North Korea to advocate that the US government provide leadership in feeding the starving people of North Korea and to educate the American public about the famine.

NORTH KOREA INDUSTRY: STRATEGIC EXPORT OPPORTUNITIES AND CONTACTS

NORTH KOREAN MACHINE TOOL INDUSTRY

Seung-bum Ha, KOTRA-North Korea Dept.

Recently, North Korea announced that it is manufacturing high-tech machine tools via domestic and foreign media. Machine tools are used to make other machines, so they are called the Mother of All Industries and considered an important source of national competitiveness. The great attention North Korea is giving to enhance its machine tools represents its special effort at enforcing its industrial competitiveness.

Since North Korea did not have the basis of nurturing machine engineering at the time of its independence, it needed help from Eastern European countries such as Czechoslovakia, Hungary and East Germany, which had relatively developed technologies.

This report summarizes the status of machine tool industry there to help domestic companies that are interested in North Korean competitiveness in the field and its development potential or that want to import machinery, especially machine tools from North Korea

DEVELOPMENT OF NORTH KOREAN MACHINE TOOL INDUSTRY

In 1953-1956, the North Korean machine tool industry reached full-scale development. In that period, the nation established machine tool factories with aid from Eastern European countries such as Czechoslovakia and Hungary. In 1954, Huicheon Machine Tool Factory was founded with Czech help, and in 1955 Guseong Machine Tool Factory was started with aid from Hungary.

Thanks to these efforts, they were able to manufacture pilot processing machines such as belt-type lathes, drills, forgers and presses. In March 1955, they succeeded in manufacturing low-level machine tools at Huicheon Machine Tool Factory.

During 1957-1960, they started to manufacture general machine tools that do not need precision, such as lathes and boring machines with support from Czechoslovakia and Hungary. At the end of 1959, the machine tool industry foundation was in place with the completion of Guseong Machine Tool Factory, which had an annual 1,000 unit capacity.

Between 1961-1970, they focused on quality diversification and high-quality machine development, as well as making larger products, and on localization. So they could manufacture medium-to-large machines such as a 6,000 ton press. They began producing general machine tools at Huicheon and Guseong, the largest machine tool factories in North Korea. Thus far, the machine tool industry development had occurred

For additional analytical, business and investment opportunities information, please contact Global Investment & Business Center, USA at (202) 546-2103. Fax: (202) 546-3275. E-mail: rusric@erols.com

without much difficulty, even though it still depended on machines imported from the Soviet Union and Eastern Europe.

In the early 1970s, the focus was on mass production and quality enhancement. In the late 1970s and early 80s, machine tool production goals were raised to 50,000 units (1984), and production of automatic and semi-automatic machines such as large machine tools, special machine tools and hydraulic lathes increased as the localization of machinery were accelerated. However, the production goal, which was '50,000 units per year' was not reached due to poor facilities and depressed production.

From the late 1980s to early 1990s, North Korea could annually manufacture 20 6,000-ton presses and large lathes and began to diversify. They even exported machine tools, not just satisfy domestic demand.

In 1991, they completed "Guseong Factory No. 104" in Guseong Machine Tool Factory. It enhanced the precision of machine tools and stimulated automation of all processes, thus expediting automation of the whole machinery sector.

LEVEL OF MACHINE TOOL INDUSTRY

In the 1980s North Korea tried to produce NC machine tools with aid from a Japanese company, without fruit. The failure to manufacture NC machine tools had a negative influence on North Korean machine tool development. Although exporting machine tools to Pakistan and India in the 1970s, they were no longer able to export machines in general in the 1980s, since they did not meet international NC trends.

The machine tool industry, which was depressed for a while, showed progress in 1995 when NC (Numerical Control) machine tools were developed at Huicheon Comprehensive Machine Tool Factory. These were able to process complicated products, since a program could control it automatically.

Thanks to that success, it is known that they had exported hundreds of NC machine tools were shipped to 10 Southeast Asian countries between 1998 and 2000.

In early 2001, North Korea announced it had developed CNC-attached machine tools by itself, which cut machine parts by entering numeric values into a computer. Representative products are machine tools such as CNC Guseong-No. 10, Guseong 125- 160 and Guseong 125-160-3.

Especially, Guseong 125-160-3 can cut complicated parts that need multiple processing by several machine tools such as lathes and NC milling machines. North Korea claimed that these machine tools were made 100 % thorough its own efforts, from design to part processing and assembly. At the 5th Pyongyang International Product Exhibition in 2001, North Korea exhibited these products to explore their export possibilities.

[Guseong 125-160-3 Machine Tool]

Today, the judgment that North Korea can manufacture large machine tools and has good level of technology in the machine tool industry, but still lacks of general heat treatment technology in the material production sector. From the perspective of design and technology, it is assumed that technology is fair to good, but there is still a lack of design capability for high-precision and NC machine tools.

MACHINE TOOL MANUFACTURING CAPACITY

It is estimated that North Korea can produce 35,000 units (2003). However because of the shortages of energy and raw material, the operation rate is at most 30%, so actual production is probably 10,000 to 15,000 units.

North Korea's economy has a characteristic of self-containment. It has sought to localize over 90% of machine tool production, excluding NC lathes. In the lathe sector, the nation imports some bearings like main axial ones and switches and in the milling sector; it imports main axial bearings, switches and hydraulic parts. In the boring segment, it imports some electric parts, ball laces and some precision parts.

MAJOR FACTORIES

<Huicheon Comprehensive Machine Tool Factory >

This is a special-level company in Hwacheon, Jagangdo. It is called the "Mother Factory of Machine Engineering" in North Korea. It is on 1,070,000§³land, with 200,000§³ of building space and 8,000 employees. It produces 500 copying lathes, 1,500 milling machines, 1,500 radial drilling machines, 500 grinding machines, 500 gear cutting machines and 500 shapers per year.

¤· History
- 1951. 12 Factory started with technical support from Czechoslovakia
- 1954. 5.   First lathe production in North Korea.
- 1954. 12. Operation of the first completed part began
- 1975. 7.   Supplemented approximately 50 kinds (177 units) of machines
- 1979. 10. Automation completed
- 1989. 10. First-phase operation of Huicheon-Soviet Union Gorky Joint Company

[Company View]

<Guseong Machine Tool Factory (April 3 Factory)>

This is the second biggest machine tool factory. It is famous for the Guseong series machine tools and is located in Namsan, Guseong, Pyungbuk. It is on 495,900§³ land and has an 81,100§³ building space and 5,800 employees.

It produces lathes, drills, hobbing machines, shapers, presses, program lathes, hydraulic copying lathes, watering machines, tractor parts, agricultural equipment, compression facilities, presses and robots for welding material supply.

For additional analytical, business and investment opportunities information, please contact Global Investment & Business Center, USA at (202) 546-2103. Fax: (202) 546-3275. E-mail: rusric@erols.com

¤· History

- 1955 Factory started with technological support from Hungary
- 1965 ~ 69 Facilities Expanded
- 1979. 12. Expansion of cast-iron division completed
- 1991. 2.   No. 10 branch factory completed

<Mangyeongdae Machine Tool Factory>

This is one of the main machine tool factories in North Korea, composed of Cutting, Processing, Assembly, Comprehensive Assembly and Everyday Goods Divisions, a Cast-iron Branch Factory and an attached design lab. It is located in Palgol-dong, in the Mangyeogdae area of Pyongyang. It is on 57,600§³ land and has 3,000 employees, who produce machine tools (shapers, lathes, plane grinding machines, air compressors, etc.) and general machines. It can produce 3,000 units per year.

¤· History

- 1959. 2. Construction initiated
- 1964.   Operations started
- 1982. 6. Expansion completed
- 1990.   Electronic calculator introduced

EVALUATION

The North Korean machine tool industry has insufficient performance because most production facilities are old (supported from Eastern Europe and the Soviet Union in the late 1950s and early 1960's) and have not received part support. Parts were replaced by North Korea's own technology and equipment, leading to degraded performance.

Additionally, there is an imbalance between each procedure because of the mixed use of new and old equipment, and reduced productivity because of the shortage in skilled workers. Manufacturing remains at 10,000-15,000 unit level per year.

(Sept. 19, 2004 KOTRA-North Korea Dept., Seung-bum Ha, Tel: 82 -2-3460-7415)

SOFTWARE TECHNOLOGY AND DEVELOPMENT INSTITUTES OF NORTH KOREA[1]

Editor's Note: This is an edited summary of reports presented by North Korean participants at the technology presentation session of the nation's 1st Exhibition of Software Products held in Beijing from Apr. 20 to 22, 2004.

Prospects for the Development of North Korea Software Technology by Kim Ho (Mathematics Research Center, North Korean Academy of Science)

---

[1] By Woo-suk Nam, North Korea Dept., KOTRA

1. DEVELOPMENT OF SOFTWARE TECHNOLOGY

☐ 1st Phase: Computing Software (1960's - early 1980's)

▯ Software was developed during this period mainly for scientific and technological computation by universities and research institutes.

▯ Major equipment was large computers such as ODRA, Iris, EC1043 and MITRA, processing system was the RS series including RS 760 and major languages were Cobol, Fortran and system Assembler.

▯ Software was mainly developed by scientists at Kim Ilsung University, Mathematic Research Center of the Academy of Science, Kim Chaek Institute of Technology, College of Science, College of Construction and Mathematic Engineering Research Center of Academy of Science.

▯ Major achievements during this period were the manufacture of large vacuum tube computers, development of basic design computation methods, differential methods, and development of dynamic computation algorithms using the finite element method.
▯ The development was equal to that of any advanced country.

☐ 2nd Phase: Microcomputer Software (mid-1980's - mid-1990's)

▯ With the arrival of IBM PCs and micro computers, software development was concentrated on desktop PC's, and S/W application scope was expanded for diverse purposes, not just computation.

▯ Major equipment used was IBM PCs mounted with 80 series CPUs including 80286s or Machintosh, OS was DOS, Windows 3.0 or below, or Mac, and major languages were Basic, C, Turbo C, C++, Pascal, Fortran, Fox or System Assembler.

▯ Development expanded to software for 3D computing, business administration, language information processing, games and manufacturing control systems.

▯ Development was led for the most part by the research centers under the Academy of Science, Kim Ilsung University, Kim Chaek Institute of Technology, College of Science, Chosun Computer Center and Pyongyang Information Center.

▯ Contests and exhibitions for improved document preparation technology and computer program development have been held every year since 1990 and can be considered the major achievement of the period.

☐ 3rd Phase: Golden Age of Software Development (mid-1990's -2000)

▯ Software development changed to use for Pentium computers, and the system software development improves speed and quality. Network system also established.

▯ Pentium computers were chiefly used. The principal OS was Windows 95 or higher and Mac OS. MFC, C++, MATLAB, JAVA, ASP and Assembler were the main languages.

▯ Applications for domestic network construction, databases, artificial intelligence S/W including language information processing, multimedia games, manufacturing control, 3D graphics for movie production and medical support were comprehensively developed.

▯ The foundations for internet service were prepared by constructed networks at many places such as the Academy of Science, Kim Ilsung University and People's Grand Study Hall. Joint development of software with institutes abroad, as the result of enhanced foreign interest in North Korea's software technology.

☐ 4th Period: Renaissance of Software Development (since 2000)

▯ The overall computerization currently in progress in North Korea gives software developers many technical problems to be solved, and demands for expanded applications scope for S/W has increased.

▯ As the interest in computer networks and demand for the Korean OS increases, North Korea is enjoying its heydays for software development.

2. Results of Software Development

▯ North Korea develops thousands of S/W items every year, and hundreds of them are registered with the state agency after due consideration.

▯ Developed software includes: a Korean OS, Korean character input systems, Korean document editors, Korean character input support systems, Korean character recognition systems, voice recognition systems, translation applications, musical note recognition systems, fingerprint authenticators, personal image authenticators, physical constitution diagnostic systems, a seven-language dictionary, the Samheung dictionary, educational multimedia, Eun Baduk (Korean chess), collections of Korean folk plays, intelligent wrestling, football and basketball strategy support S/W, banking and business management support systems, manufacturing supervision and control systems, mold CAD/CAM and medical diagnostic systems.

3. Specialized Software Development Institutes

▯ Korea Computer Center, Pyoungyang Information Center, Programming Research Center, Mathematics Research Institute of the Academy of Science (AOS) and Research Center of Kim Ilsusng University (KIU), Information Center of Kim Chaek College of Technology (KCCT) take the lead in developing software technology in North Korea.

4. Improvement of Software Development Environment

◊ North Korea owes its development of software technology to an improved development environment.

◊ Investment in the relevant institutes has increased, and the developers (who record remarkable achievements) are more highly esteemed.

◊ Classes on IT have increased, and numerous superior graduates are choosing IT as a career. As a result, degree-earners in the IT field increase every year.

◊ National objectives and guidelines for overall software technology development including development, quality inspection, management, service and applications have been established.

5. Prospects

☐ Main Target of Software Development

◊ The number of IT users in North Korea is increasing rapidly in accordance with the country's growing computerization.

◊ To meet user needs, a Korean OS for general use will be developed as soon as possible, along with software for artificial intelligence fields such as voice recognition, character recognition, language processing and machine translation mounted with the Korean OS system.

◊ The construction of a computer network system, including a portal server for network searching, will be finished soon. Much effort is being exerted to introduce the latest technology to network services, including network and communication systems security, multimedia communications, and B 2 B and e-commerce service.

◊ North Korea will develop software to support science and technology, including energy engineering, bioengineering and material engineering to promote the computerization of technical development as well as the development of industrial software technology for cyber design, manufacturing control and the like.

◊ Development of general-purpose software with commercial value will be encouraged.

◊ To achieve these objectives, practical problems must overcome first, such as raising of the necessary funds, preparing the basics for development and lack of time. Our firm determination and positive assistance to partners will help us to attain the targets.

☐ Prospects for Environment and Human Resources for Software Development

◊ The environment for software development should be further improved to achieve the set target of IT development. For this purpose, the equipment and network systems will be upgraded quickly for increased developmental speed.

Ꭰ Efforts on a national scope are currently being exerted to foster human resources in the IT field. Cooperation with foreign IT development businesses and institutes are being strengthened to secure the necessary human resources through diverse means such as practice, visits and training, in all respects including development, management and service.

☐ Software Development Method and Quality Improvement

Ꭰ Active effort to establish an advanced development process organization to improve the quality and speed of software development.

Ꭰ Each development unit accepts the UML design method for software design, and that method, along with a protocol for joint development using local or wide networks, will be in operation in the near future.

Ꭰ Useful tools for software development are being encouraged to develop, to improve development speed.

Ꭰ The inspection system will be improved to assure software quality, and standards as well as the naming system of various versions will be improved and unified, according to relevant international standards.

☐ Protection of Software Copyrights

Ꭰ All necessary measures will be taken to protect intellectual proprietorship for all software, with copyrights developed in North Korea and abroad, to promote the zeal of developers and to secure the safe and steady development of the IT industry.

☐ Joint Development of Software

Ꭰ Positive efforts are being made to develop software and enter the market in tandem with foreign institutes, businesses and friendly countries. The principles of respect for mutual rights and interests in conducting cooperative projects such as software development, investment, technology management, technology transfer, management, human resource training, sales, financial management and protection of rights are strongly held.

Ꭰ The exhibition is an important occasion for solving problems. It will contribute to enlarging mutual understanding among developers, develop businesses and users, and establish a foothold to the market and for developing new products in partnership that will contribute to IT development.

PYONGYANG INFORMATION CENTER (PIC)

by Yu Jong-cheol

Ꭰ Established on July 15, 1986 to develop programs in demand at home and abroad in many fields, as well as research and manufacture of computer hardware, Pyoungyang Information Center has been widely known as North Korea's computer program development base.

☐ Hundreds of specialists educated at famous colleges including Kim Ilsung University, Kim Chaek Institute of Technology, College of Science and Computer Technological College are engaged in developing programs and computer-related devices at PIC. Dozens of them are professors or holders of doctorates.

☐ PIC is roughly divided into two divisions. Division No. 1 undertakes projects concerned with ☐ Korean character processing in every OS, and research on the construction and use of the most efficient network, ☐ development of design programs for architecture, apparel and shoes, and business administration programs for factories and businesses, ☐ establishment of a program development process unique to North Korea, integrated storing, use and arrangement of program resources developed at PIC and research planning.

☐ Division No. 2 undertakes projects concerned with ☐ the development of the Korean word processor Changdeok, ☐ development of a Korean-language publishing program for all publications and the establishment of an electronic publishing system, ☐ development of voice recognition, voice composition, character recognition and machine translation programs to complete the integrated Korean language processing system focusing on Changdeok, ☐ the development of the computer character type most appealing to the taste and sentiment of the people, ☐ general research into multimedia technology and the production of multimedia
publications of the result.

☐ In addition, PIC undertakes the commercialization and advertising of programs, overseas marketing, development and introduction of hardware and fostering of computer specialists.

☐ For the past 16 years, PIC has developed and introduced more than a thousand programs needed by domestic units, and contributed to the computerization of the country. PIC has many users at home and abroad for its many developed and commercialized programs.

☐ PIC meets the requirements of China, Singapore and Japan by executing development projects requested by them, based on its accumulated technology.

☐ PIC established a Korean-language electronic publishing system composed of character recognition, voice recognition, voice composition and machine translation programs centering around Korean-word processor and publishing programs, to retain the national identity in the field of information industry.

☐ PIC surpasses its competitors in the development of programs such as design support programs including 3D architecture, diverse multimedia products and musical accompaniment on screen, especially the construction of a screen accompaniment

For additional analytical, business and investment opportunities information,
please contact Global Investment & Business Center, USA
at (202) 546-2103. Fax: (202) 546-3275. E-mail: rusric@erols.com

music system for portable electronic terminals using the internet and business administration programs.

◻ PIC achieved remarkable results its research on 3D modeling and rendering, CAD engines and virtual reality, and is currently manufacturing multimedia based on these results.

◻ PIC conducts science and technology exchanges and cooperation with many countries and promotes joint research and development.

KIM ILSUNG UNIVERSITY INFORMATION CENTER (KIUIC)[2]

◻ Established on May 5, 2002

◻ KIUIC was established as a research-centered institute with the purpose of reinforcing science education using the latest computer network technology, and to develop research software.

◻ KIUIC has about ten rooms doing research on computer networks, OSs, data security, multimedia contents and software engineering.
◻ What makes KIUIC distinct from other institutes is that it applies the latest achievements of basic science to its program development projects. Dozens of the best students of natural science at Kim Ilsung University are sent every year to apply their knowledge to developing new computer programs. (The realistic seawater processing scene in the movie "The Living Souls" is a 3D image processed by combined physical and mathematical knowledge.

◻ Many social science departments such as history, language and literature, along with the departments of natural science such as biology, mathematics, geography and geology conduct joint R&D at KIUIC. Software such as Search System for Juche Idea Study Material, Korean Language Study Program, English-Korean Dictionary, Electronic Handbook of Korean Fauna and Flora all owe their existence to these joint development projects.

◻ KIUIC develops software conveying an extensive area of technology, such as Business Support System of 3-tiered Server-Client Method, Information Service System of Wide Band Network Method, Korean Character Input Program, AI Game Program, and 3D Computer Image Processing Tool.

◻ KIUIC rapidly applies new trends of the computer industry to its research. It has already developed foreign language conversation and game programs that can be played on palm computers in anticipation of the great popularity of mobile computers.

◻ KIUIC will exert its efforts in the future to develop internet animation contents, multimedia contents, game software, applications for mobile computers, applications for

---

[2] by Park Du-ho

For additional analytical, business and investment opportunities information, please contact Global Investment & Business Center, USA at (202) 546-2103. Fax: (202) 546-3275. E-mail: rusric@erols.com

mobile telephones based on IMT2000, natural language processing programs and Linux distribution programs for multilingual processing.

KIM CHAEK INSTITUTE OF TECHNOLOGY (KCIT)[3]

▯ KCCT has the College of Information Science and Information Center under its jurisdiction.

▯ The college research group is composed of young scientists (in their 20's) including many professors and PhDs.

▯ The college research group has achieved notable results in various fields of information technology such as pattern recognition, voice and image processing, natural language processing, computer graphics and specialist systems.

▯ Such programs as Shindong 2004, a multilingual document recognition program for Korean, Chinese, Russian, Japanese and English; fax communication; picture processing; and data concealment are widely sold abroad as well as at home.

▯ Shindong 2004 recognizes documents printed in five languages (Korean, Chinese, Japanese, Russian and English) and directly transmits the results via Word, Excel, Internet Explorer and Acrobat Reader, while supporting various specialized functions such as correspondence to an ADF scanner and the multiplex processing of files. It works under all OS's including Windows 95 and Windows XP as well as various language versions of English, Chinese and Japanese.

▯ Fax communication programs support communication between a fax machine and a computer, and it works just like a facsimile machine.

▯ A picture processing program lets the users restore, compose and edit image data uploaded from a digital camera or scanner, with ease.

▯ KCTC also showed at the exhibition a virtual-reality driving education program that enables the user to learn how to drive a car with the sense of real driving.

KOREA APROKGANG TECHNICAL DEVELOPMENT COMPANY (KATDC)[4]

▯ KATDC has led the IT industry in North Korea since the 1990's with research on security using authentication technology of living matter and web service technology.

▯ KATDC has over 400 specialists in the fields of IT and organism information technology.
▯ KATDC consists of an organism system development team, a safety device

---

[3] by Ju Mun-young

[4] by Kang Young-il

For additional analytical, business and investment opportunities information, please contact Global Investment & Business Center, USA at (202) 546-2103. Fax: (202) 546-3275. E-mail: rusric@erols.com

development team and an IT development team. The IT development team possesses web service, database and internet/intranet and multimedia technology.

I For the past ten years KATDC has shipped security products based on its fingerprint authentication technology and personal authentication system to China, Thailand, Japan and Nigeria.

I The fingerprint authentication system and fingerprint key won first prize at Geneva Technology Fairs, Switzerland, in 1990 and 1994 and enjoys a good reputation among users.

I KATDC has developed the latest in organism authentication products based on intensive research on the human body. Organism-related products developed and distributed by the company are roughly divided into those for public security and those for civil security.

I Fingerprint authentication systems for investigation and identification systems are for public security, while fingerprint keys as well as personal authentication systems and fingerprint attendance checking systems are for civil security. All KATDC products use the newest organism processing technology developed by the company itself, and its own unique electronic technology.

I Demand for security technology, particularly if based on organism authentication and network technology, is rapidly increasing in keeping with the world-wide development of the IT industry. KATDC will meet the demand from its customers by developing excellent organism technology and electronic products.

I KATDC satisfactorily supports the development of XML-based solution S/W products and outsourcing. It also strives to develop diverse solutions such as ERP, CRM and SCM products based on network connection, DB construction and multimedia technology, to meet the overseas demands.
I KATDC will grow to an IT business with over 600 specialists, and will continue to exert itself in research, development and technical collaboration, in partnership with competent IT businesses in many countries.

BREEDING INDUSTRY OF NORTH KOREA[5]

Reports on breeding in North Korea have increased recently, indicating that the country is strengthening its efforts to foster the industry.

North Korea's emphasis on the breeding industry seems to be part of its attempt to make up for deficiencies in subsidiary foodstuff and protein, caused by smaller catches of fish due to outworn equipment and aggravated economic circumstances.

---

[5] by Seung-bum Ha North Korea Dept., KOTRA

For additional analytical, business and investment opportunities information,
please contact Global Investment & Business Center, USA
at (202) 546-2103. Fax: (202) 546-3275. E-mail: rusric@erols.com

The assessment is that North Korea's breeding industry has not expanded from early-stage, simple production, centering on a few items such as tropical catfish and seaweed.

This report is based on articles from domestic and foreign press materials, including those from North Korea over the past ten years.

I. North Korea's Fish Breeding Industry

[Freshwater Fish]

General Conditions

North Korea has set detailed guidelines for the development of the fish breeding industry, including ▲ research and development of breeding species, ▲ supplying superior breeds to fish farms and ▲ introduction of advanced culturing methods to purpose to promote the industry as part of the Movement by All People to solve the subsidiary food problem and improve nourishment.

Since the late 1990s, when the country's breeding sector entered the take-off stage, relevant North Korean agencies have been concentrating on expanding the industry. As part of these efforts, the agencies ordered each province at least 100ha and each district to construct fish farms of at least 20 to 30ha, to culture fish including tropical catfish.

As a result, over 200 fish farms or tropical catfish factories had been constructed, repaired or expanded by November 2000, with a total area of thousands of hectares, according to North Korea.

Many tropical catfish farms, the most successful of the freshwater fish projects, are throughout the country. Considering a report that as much as 1 ton a day of cultured tropical catfish are consumed in Pyongyang, the success of this enterprise seems to be well underway.

Attempts to culture other fish, such as eunjeongeo (carp) and dandubang (carp), however, have seemingly not succeeded yet. Fish that feed on soybean dregs, bean curd dregs or water grass, instead of assorted feed, and grow fast regardless of water quality are the most likely to be cultured in North Korea, due to the country's deficient feed and poor water purification facilities.

In a bid to help fish farming, special institute are reportedly trying to develop fish feed that is easy to find and promotes growth.

Tropical Catfish

Tropical catfish, North Korea's chief cultured fish, lives in freshwater above 10oC and shows the most rapid growth at the water temperatures at 25o and 28oC.

For additional analytical, business and investment opportunities information,
please contact Global Investment & Business Center, USA
at (202) 546-2103. Fax: (202) 546-3275. E-mail: rusric@erols.com

As unlikely as it seems in cold North Korea, breeding this fish has been extensively promoted and the fish breeding administration used remnant heat from thermoelectric power plants and hot springs to culture it in 2002.

Fries of the catfish hatched in spring are bred at fish farms in the summer and the adult fish winter in hot spring water. Because of this feature, tropical catfish farms are mainly located in South Hwanghae Province, which abounds in hot springs.

North Korea promotes this sector due to the high economic value of the fish, since the polyphagous catfish can be raised to an adult in a short period, feed is easy to get, and the fish is resistant to disease.

North Korea operates tropical catfish farms on the principles of ▲using hot springs, ▲construction of large farms, ▲scientific breeding and ▲self-securing of the land for feed production.

Fries weigh 0.7g but grow to adult weights of 1kg to 1.5kg in five months, and a fish farm with an area of about 1ha can maintain 15,000 catfish, or 300 to 400 tons of product (subject to timely supply of feed and optimum water temperature), according to North Korea.

Regions without hot spring are suggested for "paddy field fish breeding." Hatched fries are put in paddy fields after transplantation or harvesting has been completed. North Korea eagerly recommends raising at least 10,000 tropical catfish in every paddy farm.

[Culture of Other Freshwater Species]

A. Loaches

North Korea recently recommended raising loaches, spreading the remedial effect of the fish. Loaches live naturally throughout the country and are easy to be cultured in large quantities, since they breed on their own appropriate water temperatures and feed on bean curd dregs, soy bean dregs and vegetable chips.

B. Carp Eunjeongeo

This fish was introduced to North Korea in 1994. It is a freshwater fish belonging to the carp family and was reportedly named "eunjeong" (grace) in commemoration of the grace of the North Korean authorities.

Relevant agencies actively recommend culturing this fish, which is similar in shape and size to a Prussian carp, since it can spawn an average 200,000 (maximum 900,000) in just three to four years of culturing. They feed on grass and grow rapidly in any water regardless of quality.

C. Carp Dandubang

This member of the carp family was positively recommended for culturing in 1998 by

North Korea. Fish breeding divisions in Pyoungyang and in hot spring districts have tried to culture this fish.

The government named dandubang as suitable for culturing. Similar to the Prussian carp in shape, it feeds on grass only and spawns about 400,000 eggs in two to three years of culturing.

D. Soft-shelled Turtles

Soft-shelled turtles have been actively recommended for culturing as a source of protein, since they have a relatively long life and great economic value as a high-quality foodstuff, in addition to being easy to culture.

E. Bullfrogs

While South Korea has designated the bullfrog as a principal of ecological devastator and thus to be exterminated, in North Korea, it was selected as a good protein supply and is actively promoted for breeding.

South Hamgyoung Province is most active in bullfrog culturing. Bullfrog farms amount to nearly 27,000ha located in valleys throughout the Province.

[Major Fish Farms]

A. Onjeong-ri, Seongcheon-gun, Pyoungnam

This fish farm, famous for developing the method of winterization and artificial incubation of tropical catfish, has a hatchery of about 160m2 and an outdoor raising pool of over 300m2, which are used as the model for propagating tropical catfish culturing throughout the country.

B. Younggwang Youth Fish Farm

Constructed in 2001 and the largest on the East Coast, this fish farm has 82 raising and hatching pools, and 6 microbe habitats in an area of 300,000ha. Using water from the tiered power plant on the Seongcheon river, enterprise plans to culture 2 million fish, producing hundreds of tons of fish a year.

C. Pyoungyang Fish Farm

Fish farms with an area of 500,000m2 were under construction in the Daedong River basin and the vicinity of Cheondong Reservoir, Sunan District, Sangweoncheon, according to a 1994 release in North Korea.

Annually 1.3 billion freshwater grass carps, including Prussian carp and commemorative fish, will be raised at 300,000m2 of completed fish farms and then released in the Daedong and Botong Rivers, North Korean authorities said.

D. Okryoun Reservoir, Gaeseong

This fish farm, promoted by North Korean authorities at the upper reaches of the Okryoun Reservoir in Gwangdap-ri, Gaepung-gun, Gaeseong, covers 200,000 ha, according to North Korean authorities.

[Seawater Fish Breeding]

General Conditions

North Korea started seawater fish breeding in April 1961. By striving to expand the fish farm area through the 1970s, it managed to expand the total by 110% between 1977 and 1984.

It was in the 1990s, however, that North Korea devoted itself to seawater fish farming. North Korea changed its fishery policy from catching to farming as the catch rapidly decreased in that decade. 1990s. The popularity of marine products as exportable items also motivated the country to promote seawater fish farming.
- Fish catch reached 2.42 million ton in 1985, but decreased every year to December 2000, when it fell to 1 million ton, half of the 1985 figure.

To cope with this difficulty, in parallel with aggressive measures to increase marine production, North Korea established regulations connected with marine resource protection, including the Regulation concerning Promotion, Protection and Control of Marine Resources (July '97), the Law to Prevent Sea Pollution (Dec. '97) and the Law for Fish Farming (Mar. '99).

As the result of these efforts, North Korea managed to have over 5,000 ha of seafish farms by August 2001, and reportedly plans to construct another 24,473 ha.

On the other hand, North Korea attempted to breed lobsters on the West Coast in 1995 and to establish a joint venture with Russian businesses to culture marine products, but KOTRA learned that they failed.

North Korea also tried to construct a land salmon farm near Wonsan, in partnership with a European business, but KOTRA learned the project has not yet started.

[Shellfish Breeding]

A. General Condition

North Korea's shellfish breeding concentrates on exportable items such as black ark shell, bassregi, turban shells, abalone and clams, to acquire foreign exchange. It also promotes breeding fish such as sea bass and sea bream.

In particular, shellfish such as abalone, turban shell and clams are bred in a large scale around Ungjin on the west coast of North Korea.

Marine Animal Research Institute of Western Coast Breeding Project Division developed artificial culturing methods for swellfish and sea cucumbers. It is conducting research on culturing conditions in different geologies and temperatures, in an effort to introduce the artificial culturing method to actual breeding.

B. Breeding Shellfish

Among the many methods, only floating and fixing have been reported in the press, used to culture blue mussels and sea bass. Clams, lobsters, dace and sea bream are cultured in seawater drawn into an artificial pool.

A new hemming method introduced in the South cultures many kinds of fish in a zone enclosed with nets and electric or air bubble curtains, or in a large netted box. Mainly used to culture lobsters, sea bream and flatfish, this method reportedly has good developmental prospects, due to easy management, small feed demand feed and low contamination levels.

In addition, abalone, eel and rainbow trout are intensively cultured in breeding pools in boats made by drawing in seawater, according to North Korean authorities. This method, however, looks experimental, considering the enormous sums needed to operate the boat.

[Seaweed]

A. General Conditions

Major seaweed cultured in North Korea are tangleweed, laver and brown seaweed, to supply subsidiary food to North Koreans.

The production of seaweed by breeding divisions under the jurisdiction of the Marine Products Administration in each province increased by 1.3 to 3 times since last year, thanks to enlargement of seaweed farms throughout the country.

Especially, the tangleweed productivity of per unit area greatly increased last year by enlarging the nutritive area along the eastern and western coasts via dense planting. This method, however, deteriorates the tangleweed quality, South Korean experts insist.

North Korea has constructed major seaweed farms, amounting to over 100 ha, along the eastern coast from Hamheung Gulf to Wonsan Gulf. It has also reportedly constructed seaweed farms of hundreds hectares on the west coast, annually producing hundreds of tons of tangleweed, brown seaweed and clams.

B. Culturing

North Korea's main methods of culturing seaweeds are the bottom, mixed and solid methods, but details are not available due to differences in terminology between the South and the North.

II. Merits, Demerits and Precautions in Promoting Breeding Industry

[Merits and Demerits]

The merits of entering the breeding industry in partnership with North Korea include easy security of available breeding areas (with government permission), lower labor costs than in South Korea and water temperatures appropriate to culturing any seafish and shellfish. However, the low level of quality control, due to the nature of the regime, lack of equipment necessary for culturing (such as management ship) as well as the hardships of feed procuring are demerits to be considered.

[Precautions]

For successful promotion, a project should start small so it can easily be accepted by North Korea, and a method should be discovered to maximize mutual return at minimal investment. Technical cooperation with South Korea as well as investment in facilities should precede the promotion of the project. To minimize investment risk, careful examinations should be conducted on the fishery administration of North Korea, on business feasibility and on location and technical transfer issues.

It should be carefully approached, after deliberate investigation of the actuality of North Korea's fishery industry, including fish breeding, as well as intensive analysis of other cases. Commercial values should be maintained throughout the whole process.

Taeyoung Fishery is a good reference point. An agreement on scallop breeding was signed with a North Korean business, and the firm shipped equipment and materials in two lots to North Korea with permission from the Unification Ministry of South Korea. But the project ended in failure when North Korea refused entry.

Since many cooperative South-North projects have been suspended owing to business conflicts in the South, South Korean businesses that intend to promote breeding in North Korea should also prepare measures to prevent these local conflicts.

NORTH KOREAN ZINC

The following is an edited translation of an article by Abe Keiji, a Japanese historian of North Korean technology, that appeared in Economic Information of East Asia (Feb. 2004, published by East Asia Trade Research Institute).

1. Foreword

Zinc (Zn, atomic number 30 and specific gravity 7.14) is a little lighter than iron or tin. Because of its brisk chemical activity, it is used to form a wide variety of alloys with other metals, and particularly zinc alloyed with iron is widely used in industry.

Zinc production in South Korea increased from 104,000 tons in 1985 to 390,000 tons in 2002, owing to the increased demand for steel plate as the nation's automobile industry developed. However, zinc production, which is closely correlated with the steel and automobile industries, has remained stagnant in North Korea.

The process of refining zinc severely produces pollutants, and North Korea's zinc refining appears to have a connection with its problems of environmental pollution. Nampo Smelting

Works, the leading zinc refinery in North Korea, was reportedly dismantled recently in connection with its pollution problem.

2. Zinc Mines in North Korea

Australia, Canada, the U.S., Peru and China have the largest zinc deposits in the world. In terms of production (as of 1992), Canada leads the list, followed by Australia, China, Peru and the U.S. North Korea is the 14th largest zinc-producing country, after Japan.

Zinc deposits are found in strata belonging to the geologic eras from Pre-Cambrian to Cenozoic, and the geology of Dancheon-gun, North Korea belongs to the Pre-Cambrian period. The main ore produced in Dancheon-gun is zinc ore. Gapdeok Mine, along with Geomdeok among the major mines listed in the North Korea's 1st 7-year Plan, is in Dancheon-gun.

The three largest gold refineries in North Korea under Japanese colonial rule were Jinnampo of Nippon Kogyo, Munpyeong of Sumitomo and Yongampo Refinery of Mitsubishi Kogyo. Gold production began to decline from 1942, when Yongampo Refinery started full operation. From the beginning, gold refineries in North Korea also produced refined zinc, since the element is collected in the process of gold refining.

The production of zinc ground metal increased up to 1.6 times during the 1st 7-year Plan. The major zinc refineries at the time were Nampo, Heungnam, replacing Yongampo of the colonial period, and Munpyeong. In 1965, while the plan was still underway, North Korea shipped 1,489 tons of zinc ground metal to Japan.

In the same year, the country shipped 14,117 tons of zinc ore abroad, and 73,110 tons in 1969, the final year of the 1st 7-year Plan. Considering the fact that the previous year (1968) zinc export was no more than 7,164 tons, the country seems to have used every possible means to achieve the set export target.

In 1992, Japan imported 1.23 million tons of zinc ore from Australia (56.6%), the U.S. (16.5%) and Peru (15.4%). North Korea produced about 120,000 tons of zinc ore that year.

3. Demand for Zinc

Zinc ground metal is used in galvanizing, zinc die-cast alloys, copper alloys and chemical products. Though galvanized iron, a zinc alloys, is the most widely known to the public, the most biggest demand for zinc alloy in industry is for galvanized steel plates, since zinc extends durability by protecting against corrosion.

Fourth in demand among all metals, after iron, aluminum and copper, in the 20th century zinc saw 22 times the consumption of the previous century. The total world demand for zinc fluctuates according to the state of the global economy. For instance, zinc demand decreased during the oil crises of the 1970s, the recessionary period of the 1980s and the collapse of the socialist bloc in the 1990s.

Thus, the economy of North Korea in 1975, 1980-1982 and 1989-1992 when zinc demand saw negative growth, showed sharp negativity, which indicates that the economy of North Korea greatly depends on the world's consumption of non-ferrous metals. This shows, in other words, that North Korea needs to improve the operation of its non-ferrous metal mines and to modernize its refining technology in order to develop its economy.

Unlike copper and lead, which are mostly deposited in underdeveloped countries, the advanced nations of the U. S., Australia and Canada possess more than half of the world's zinc deposits. For this reason, an underdeveloped country which greatly depends on the export of zinc is directly influenced by the economies of these advanced countries. The sudden drop in zinc prices from 1990 through 1991 gravely affected North Korea's 3rd 7-year Plan and caused rumors in Japan that the Collapse of North Korea was near at hand.

A sharp break in zinc prices inevitably strikes a severe blow to the economy of North Korea, especially since it uses zinc ground metal as the a substitution for foreign exchange, which is in short supply.

(Apr. 19, 2004 KOTRA-North Korea Dept., Woo-suk Nam, Tel: 82-2-3460-7413)

NORTH KOREA'S PETROCHEMICAL INDUSTRY[6]

North Korea's chemical industry has been developed with a focus on basic chemistry related to coals, its traditionally abundant natural resources, and those close to them. In the early 1970s, the North attempted to transfer its chemical industry to a series of petrochemical industry, supposedly due to its internal need for oil refineries. South Korea's dazzling success in its heavy and chemical industry is also supposed to have given stimulus to the North's such attempt. Accordingly, the North tried to lay the foundation to gradually shy away from the coal-centered chemical industry led by its major facilities, breaking ground for construction of petrochemical factories in its Anju Industrial Zone.[1] However, the petro-chemistry's share in the entire chemical industry is still insignificant, having failed to live up to the original expectation. Its such poor performance is attributable to the introduction of burdensome foreign loans beyond its capability of repayment for construction of factories, the lack of proper markets and the unstable supply of crude oil.

With completion of the construction of Seungri Chemical Factory in Seonbong in 1973, North Korea came to have the capability of refining and processing 7.23 million bbl. of crude oil, which was increased to 21.69 million bbl. [2]with the completion of Bonghwa Chemical Factory in 1978. Related products are gasoline, naphtha, light oil and lamp oil etc. Naphtha, a raw material for petrochemical products, is produced by Seungri and Bonghwa Chemical Factories and supplied to Namheung Youth Chemical Factory, the North's only petrochemical factory. Namheung Factory's production capability comes to 14,000 tons of propylene and 60,000 tons of ethylene.

1.   Major Petrochemical Factories [3]

North Korea has two oil refineries: Seungri located in the east coast which was built with the aid from the old Soviet Union and Bonghwa located in an area 14km from Shinuiju on the west coast which was built with the aid from China. Namheung Youth Chemical Factory, Bakchon, North Pyongan Province, is producing basic chemical raw materials with naphtha supplied from those two.

Suengri Chemical Factory

The construction of this factory was started in August 1968 as per the North Korea-Soviet Union Agreement for Cooperation on Economy, Science and Technology of March 1967. Upon completion of the first phase of the construction work in 1973, North Korea came to have the capacity of processing 1 million tons of crude oil a year, which was increased to 2 million tons with the completion of the second phase of the construction. Originally, the old Soviet Union guaranteed the supply of 2 million tons of crude oil a year to the North, carrying the crude oil by tankers from Nakhodka to

---

[6] By Won-Joon Jung(North Korea Department ,KOTRA)

Seonbong and planned the construction of pipelines linking the two places, which was not materialized.

The factory is designed based on the crude oil produced in Russia, thus suitable for light-crude oil with the viscosity of 38degrees or higher and not for heavy crude oil and that with high contents of paraffin. [4] Crude oil is supplied to Seonbong either by railroads or tanker vessels. In the case of using tanker vessels, crude oil is delivered to the platform 3.2km away from Seonbong Port and sent to two tanks at the port through the 53cm-diameter undersea pipeline and then to a refinery 6km away. There is a pier (length: 455m, annual cargo handling capacity: 2 million tons) for exclusive use for oil products where two 5,000-ton class vessels can enter at the same time. In addition, there are railroads laid inside the factory where 9 tank lorries for trains can be loaded at the same time and the hourly capacity of loading is 360 tons. The trains leaving here reaches as fare as Tumen, China. It is said that Russian trains can come inside the factory. Power needed for operation of the factory is supplied from the Seonbong Thermal Power Plant. Its industrial water is supplied from nearby streams.

The problem is that Seungri Chemical Factory has not been operating normally since the early 1990s. In the early 1990s, the supply of crude oil from Russia was stopped following the successive collapse of the communist bloc countries. In 1994, the supply of crude oil from Iran or Libya was stopped, too. At the moment, the factory is simply inoperable. In 2002, part of the facility is said to have been operated temporarily with 600,000 tons of crude oil imported from Yemen for commissioned processing of goods.

Bonghwa Chemical Factory

This factory was built with the aid from China in 1975 and located near the border with China in North Pyongan Province to make it convenient to get the supply of crude oil from China. In 1972-1973 the North originally attempted to introduce the refinery facilities with the processing capacity of 4 million tons a year from Japan, France or Italy, to no avail, due to the failure in negotiation for loans. Instead, the construction of the first phase of Bonghwa with annual production capacity of 1 million tons was completed with the aid from China in 1978, which was increased to 1.5 million tons in 1980.

In the early 1990s, the factory was maintaining 70% operating rate, being supplied with 1 million tons of crude oil annually. However, since 2002, the supply of crude oil has been drastically reduced[5] and thus the operating rate has dropped, too. The transportation was carried out by tanker vessels from Dalien, China to Nampo, North Korea. It is assumed that the pipeline linking Tandong, Chian and Bonghwa Chemical Factory was completed in 1976 and has been used since.

The power is supplied from Soopung Power Plant and the industrial water from a nearby stream. The naphtha produced here is assumed to be supplied to Namheung Youth Chemical Factory through the pipeline.

Namheung Youth Chemical Factory

The factory is North Korea's only petrochemical facility and has seven subsidiaries that analyze naphtha and produce ethylene. In 1973, the People's Supreme Council of North Korea announced the plan for construction of a petrochemical complex in North Pyongan Province as part of the 6-year plan. In 1976, the urea fertilizer production facility was completed, followed by oxidized ethylene, EG, NCC, LDPE, PAN facilities in 1979.

Its major products are chemical fertilizers including urea and petrochemical products such as LDPE and AN. Its production capacity is 400,000 tons of urea fertilizers, 270,000 tons of ammonia, 90,000 tons of sodium carbonate, 30,000 tons of paper, 10,000 tons of pasteboard and 40,000 tons of pulp, in addition to petrochemical products such as 60,000 tons of ethylene, 14,000 tons of propylene, 10,000 tons of EO, 10,000 tons of AN, 8,000 tons of EG, 25,000 tons of LDPE, 5,000 tons of PP, and 10,000 tons of acryl thread.

The factory is producing such ethylene-series of products as LDPE, EO,EG etc, using the ethylene as raw material after analyzing the ethylene in the NCC facility from the naphtha supplied from Bonghwha Chemical Factory. Power and industrial water are supplied from the Chongchon Thermal Power Plant and the Chongchon River respectively. Its operating rate is assumed to be low due to the insufficient supply of basic and intermediate raw materials such as crude oil, naphtha and catalyzer and shortage of power supply. It is said that the factory does not have the assembly-line operation process and the facilities are outdated.

2.   Production Capability and Status of Export and Import

North Korea's total capability for refining crude oil stands at a mere figure of 3.5 million tons (2 million tons at Seungri and 1.5 million tons at Bonghwa). The total operating rate of its refinery facilities comes to just 9% with its import of crude oil of 317,000 tons in 2003, compared to South Korea's relevant figures (refinery capacity: 121.4 million tons, amount of crude oil processed: 118.7 million tons and operating rate: 98.1% all as of 2003). Such a drop in capability of refining crude oil is making the problem of deficiency in consumer goods worse, directly affecting the production of chemical fibers or synthetic fibers.

North Korea's Import of Crude Oil

(Unit: 10,000 tons)

Exporter	1991	1992	1993	1994	1995	1996	2002	1998	2003
China	110	110	105	83	102	93.6	50.6	50.3	31.7*
Libya	-	20	10	8	8	-	-	5.3	-
Yemen	-	-	-	-	-	-	60	-	-
Iran	75	22	21	-	-	-	-	-	-

Russia	4	-	-	-	-	-	-	-	-
Syria	-	-	-	-	-	-	-	5.3	-
Total	189	152	136	91	110	93.6	110.6	60.9	31.7

*The figure includes 20,527 tons which was left-over of the 80,000 tons, China's grant in 1998.

It appears that chemical products were the only industrial products of North Korea whose export was increased in 2003. However, in the case of its chemical products, the import always exceeds the export, which is directly related to the reduction in the amount of imported crude oil. As the import of crude oil is reduced, the production of raw materials for production of chemical products is reduced, which requires import of the chemical products to be increased. Though it is essential to increase the import of crude oil to break the link of the vicious cycle, it is not easy to do that under the circumstances.

North Korea's Export & Import of Chemical Products

(Unit: Thousands of Dollars, %)

	1996		2002		1998		2003		
	Amount	Share	Amount	Share	Amount	Share	Amount	Share	Increase/Decrease
Export	55,424	7.6	54,785	6.1	28,312	5.1	39,928	7.8	41.1
Import	138,778	11.1	153,531	12.1	120.440	13.6	147,336	15.3	22.3

Source: "Trend for North Korea's Trade"

----

1) North Korea's industrial zones can be divided into the coastal industrial regions developed from the days of the Japanese imperialists' colonial rule and the inland industrial regions fostered since after the independence from Japan's rule. Anju Industrial Zone belongs to the inland industrial regions located along the Chongchon River. (North Korea's Industry, KOTRA, 1995)

2) North Korea's refinery capability is estimated to be 25.31 million bbl. as of 1990 and it appears that there has been no expansion of facilities since. (North Korea's Industry, KOTRA, 1995)

3) Major contents are extracted from North Korea's Industry, KOTRA, 1995 and North Korea's Industry, the Korea Development Bank, 2000

4) The quality of crude oil is decided as per the API-designated specific gravity: light oil should have the specific gravity of 34 degrees or higher, medium oil of 31-33 degrees and heavy oil of 30 degrees or lower. The specific gravity of crude oil is the lower, the more it contains useful ingredients such as gasoline, naphtha and lamp oil etc.

5) In 1996, North Korea's import of crude oil from China came to 0.936 million tons, which was reduced to 0.506 million tons in 2002. In 2003, it was drastically reduced to 0.317 million tons. (Trend for North Korea's Foreign Trade, p.32, KOTRA, 2003)

By Sang-Hae Chang (North Korea Department, KOTRA)

SHOE INDUSTRY

I. Overview

North Korea's strategy for industrial development has mainly centered around heavy chemical industry while leaving light industry on the sideline. The shoe sector, one of primary products in light industry, barely keeps in balance, meeting the basic local demand. North Korea's shoe industry has developed around two large cities- Pyongyang and Sinuiju; with factories located every metropolitan city to feed the need of each province. An authority body of the Administration Council oversees the overall shoe industry while a research unit of Shoe Control Bureau conducts R&D for raw materials, implements guidelines for standardization and improves shoe-related facilities.

II. Development History of Shoe Industry

1. 1945~1950s
- Rubber shoes were prevalent in 1940&#0;s and leather shoes first produced in tiny volume in 1950&#0;s
- Policies implemented to boost shoe Industry in 1957
- Vinyl chloride used in shoe making

2. 1960s
- Press part was included in the processing of tough fabric shoes or mass production
- Processing modernized to boost productions of leather and synthetic leather shoes
- Factories were set up at Pyongyang and Sunchon.

3. 1970s
- Factories at Sunchon and Hungnam expanded
- Pyongyang factory began to make around 1,500,000 pairs a year
- Vinly chloride-used shoe factories were built at Pyongyang and Haeju.

4. 1980s
- The goal of 100 million pairs output was set as part of the 2nd economic development program designed for 7 years.
- Diverse productions based on gender, function and season
- Quality improvement was emphasized during light industry development campaign

5. 1990s
- Production facility modernized and expanded.
- Such programs as academic presentation and exhibitions were held
- The inter-Korean trade started in the form of processing &#0;on-commission
- Plan for shoe industrial complex at Kaesong and Nampo.

[Production Capacity and Products]

Though North Korea's production capacity has not known exactly, the annual capacity is estimated at 100 million pairs in 1996 base year, and that is compared with South Korea's 195 million pairs. The biggest factory, based in Sinuiju, has capacity to churn out 20 million pairs a year while many other factories are known to have improved their production lines to produce more than 1 million pairs per annum. North Korea use vinyl chloride as material to make vinyl and tough fabric shoes, which are mostly commonly worn by North Koreans. Lack of raw materials such as cloth, rubber, leather and even synthetic leather and aged production equipments are hindering the development in shoe sector. Especially, the scarce of leather and synthetic leather makes leather shoes precious for ordinary people. Even synthetic leather sports shoes, which became common in South Korea in 1980's, are still rare in North Korea in the absence of immature manufacturing technology. Those quality shoes, imported from China, are normally selling at state-operated stores and smuggled at town markets.

[Raw Materials and Technology]

The major raw materials, vinyl chloride and fabric, are mostly domestic sourced, but other materials are imported. Rubber comes from China, Japan and Singapore. In addition to small amounts of leather locally generated from pigs and cows, leather is also imported from the former two countries. But the leather supply considerably falls short of the nation&#0;s need.

North Korea's technology for shoe making appears to have retarded, demonstrating difficulty in producing customized shoes that require complicate processing or designs. Vinyl shoes, which make up more than a half of North Korea's total shoe output, go through a rather simple molding and adhesive processing without upper composition and assembling part. Considering these factors, North Korea's technology seems to match that of South Korea existed between the end of 1960s and early 1970s.

It is noticed that North Korea's product catalogues, aimed at exports, tout leather boots and sandals. That means North Korea is capable of making some high-end shoes that rely on much manual process.

MAJOR FACTORIES

(Unit: ten thousand pairs)

Name of Factory	Location	Production	Major Items

For additional analytical, business and investment opportunities information,
please contact Global Investment & Business Center, USA
at (202) 546-2103. Fax: (202) 546-3275. E-mail: rusric@erols.com

		Capacity	
Pyongyang Shoes	Pyongyang	300	A variety of leather shoes
Pyongyang Shoes	Pyongyang	600	Tough fabric shoes, injection-molded boots
Pyongyang Vinyl Shoes	Pyongyang	700	Women&#0;s netted shoes
Sunkyo Rubber	Pyongyang	300	
Kangseo Shoes	Nampo	100	
Sunchon Shoes	Sunchon	100	A variety of leather shoes
Sunchon Shoes	Sunchon	150	Sports shoes, sneakers
Sinuiju Shoes	Sinuiju	2,000	Sports shoes, handy shoes, working shoes
Sinuiju Shoes	Sinuiju	100	Leather, vinyl, tough fabrtic
Kaesong Shoes	Kaesong	300	Leather and vinyl
Onchon Shoes	Onchon	100	Leather
Haeju Shoes	Haeju	420	Sneakers, sports shoes, padding shoes
Haeju Shoes	Haeju	300	Synthetic leather
Sariwon Shoes	Sariwon	200	Vinyl, padding shoes
Kanggye Shoes	Kanggye	300	A variety of shoes
Hungnam Shoes	Hamhung	300	Synthetic leather
Hamhung Vinyl Shoes	Hamhung	300	Vinyl
Bukchong Shoes	Bukchong	100	
Hoiryung Shoes	Hoiryung	400	Tough fabric, leather
Chongjin Shoes	Chongjin	300	Tough fabric
Chongjin Shoes	Chongjin	100	Synthetic leather
Wonsan Shoes	Wonsan	100	
Hyesan Shoes	Hyesan	100	
Yoowon Shoes	-	-	

Anju Shoes	Anju	-	

[International Trade]

Shoe trade accounts for roughly 1% of North Korea's overall international trade. Most of shoes imported from China, Japan and Hong Kong with the former country being the biggest source. Mediocre manufacturing technology in the shoe industry has linked to sluggish exports of shoes to Europe and Latin America in small individual volume amounted to around $100,000. As major export items coded HS CODE 6403 & 6404 [3], a group of sports & dress shoes, workers, standouts out and indicates that North Korea has been outsourced for process of leather and tough fabric for upper part. In the past three years, Germany has been one of the robust importers of leather shoes, worth $210,000 for the year of 2003,[4] suggesting North Korea is able to command a rather competitive technology for leather shoes than other type of shoes.

Imports by Country

(Unit: $&#0;000)

Country	1996	2002	1998	2003
China	823	947	922	1,727
Japan	143	166	357	247
Hong Kong	1,417	1,710	84	198
Total	2,383	2,823	1,363	2,172

Source: North Korea's International Trade Trend published by KOTRA

[Inter-Korean Trade]

1. The Inter-Korean Trade of shoes

The inter-Korean trade of shoes still remains minuscule, consisting of 1% of the overall inter-Korean trade. South Korea mainly supplies raw materials along with small quantities of finished shoes as supporting items to North Korea to have them processed in North Korea in the form of the processing-on-commission. North Korea in return offers labor needed in processing for either finished or semi-finished products, for which the remaining processes are completed in South Korea. Sometimes, North Korea almost completes processes for uppers, leaving the final part of the process to be done by South Korea.

Inter-Korean Trade History of Shoe

(Unit: $&#0;000)

For additional analytical, business and investment opportunities information,
please contact Global Investment & Business Center, USA
at (202) 546-2103. Fax: (202) 546-3275. E-mail: rusric@erols.com

Category	Output			Input		
	2002	1998	2003	2002	1998	2003
Class of Shoes	146	34	821	1,019	1,216	1,533
Parts	1,035	1,032	980	281	26	152
Total	1,181	1,066	1,801	1,300	1,242	1,685
% of the Inter-Korean Trade	1.0%	0.8%	0.9%	0.7%	1.3%	1.5%

Sourced: South-North Koreas&#0; Relation and Cooperation Trend published by Unification Ministry

2. Trade of Shoe based on Processing-on-Commission

North Korea&#0;s shoes process for South Korea has steadily risen to $3.29 million in 2003 from $177,000 in 1992. South Korea usually supply soles coded HS CODE 6406 and other relevant items in small quantities. Given the fact that sole processing is a key part in making shoes, the sole supply to North Korea still meager, posting $980,000 in 2003. [5]The low level of shoe process, particularly compared with textile process, fails to motivate South Korean shoe manufacturing companies to move their foreign production sites to North Korea from China or East Asian countries, according to analysts in the industry. When the two Koreas first started trading of shoes in 1992, around 22 South Korean shoe makers relied on North Korea&#0;s process but most of these companies have turned away, leaving only three until 2000.[6]

Processing-on-Commission Trade of Shoe between North and South

(Unit: $&#0;000)

Category	Output			Input		
	2002	1998	2003	2002	1998	2003
Class of shoes	-	1	628	1,005	1,216	1,533
Parts	1,013	1,032	980	274	14	152
Total	1,013	1,033	1,608	1,279	1,230	1,685
% of Total inter-Korean Shoe Trade	85.8%	96.9%	89.3%	98.4%	99%	100%

Sourced: ditto

For additional analytical, business and investment opportunities information, please contact Global Investment & Business Center, USA at (202) 546-2103. Fax: (202) 546-3275. E-mail: rusric@erols.com

3. North Korea's Process Ability

Based on the survey conducted for South Korean companies that outsourced process to North Korea, the result shows considerable satisfaction for quality with low defect rate. Nonetheless, analysts cited problems involved in providing manufacturing equipment and technique as main reasons for slow shoe trade with North Korea. It's tough job for South Korean companies to train North Korean people, who are accustomed to manual work, to make them to adapt to complicate automatic processing procedures. By contrast, North Korea labor has proved to be efficient to make shoes that require more manual process. [7]For sports shoes and workers in leather or synthetic leather, North Korea normally produce uppers while South Korea take up such complicate parts of process as fitting measurements, in-sole and out-sole production and final touch.

4. Exports to a Third Party

The prospects of exports of shoes processed by North Korea to a third country vary from country to country in terms of rules on the origin, trade restrictions and tariffs although U.S.A, EU countries and Japan are considered target countries. [8] North Korea's recent effort to improve relations with foreign countries and the growing possibility of U.S.A.'s dropping North Korea off the list of terror-supporting countries will help make the export outlook brighter. Analysts in the industry said the combination of South's solid production technology and cheap and good labor can rekindle the growth in the shoe business to the extent South Korea is able to regain the leading position in the global shoe markets.

5. Others

The labor cost paid to North Korea is accounted for 10% of a total cost incurred for a whole process for shoes, compared with 10 to 30% in case of a textile process. However, high cost incurred by North Korea's poor logistics and storage systems, difficulty imposing speedy progress and inefficiency stemmed from lack of training for manufacturing skills are counted as major problems to be resolved.

1) Sole is made of rubber and upper is done by tough fabric, resembling canvas shoes that were popular in South Korea during 1960-1970.

2) North Korea's International Trade Trend published by KOTRA : North Korea imported rubber (HS CODE 40) worth $1.62 million from China, $1.63 million from Japan and $1.01 million from Singapore.

3) HS CODE 6403 : Out-sole; rubber, plastic, leather or composition leather; upper-leather. Sports shoes, dress shoes and workers belong to this category.

HS CODE 6404 : Out-sole; rubber, plastic, leather or composition leather; upper; textile. Sports shoes, slippers and shoes in fabric belong to this category

4) North Korea's International Trade Trend published by KOTRA : Germany imported leather shoes worth $1.22 million in 2002, $1.23 million in 1998, $210,000 in 2003. No

record tracking inbound of raw materials into North Korea represents the above is genuine exporting not process.

5) Sole (HS CODE 6406), moved to North Korea, totaled $1.04 million in 2002, $1.03 million in 1998 and $980,000 in 2003.

Transfer of Sole (HS CODE 6403) has increased to $550,000 in 2003 thanks to brisk process of sports shoes.

6) Korea Trade Information Service supplied the list of shoe makers which was engaged in shoe process with North Korea.

7) Sports shoes or workers in leather or synthetic leather but dress shoes not included.

8) Article entitled;The prospect of processed products by North Korea; in North Korea News Letter for October described the impact of regulatory conditions such as rule on the origin, trade restriction and tariffs on the export prospect to a third country and analysis. More details are accessible through KOTRA's home page, www.kotra.or.kr/nk.

NORTH KOREA'S IT INDUSTRY[7]

1. Overview

North Korea has not announced any official statistics of its IT (Information & Technology) industry, nor does it in other sectors of industry. Furthermore, North Korea does not announce its basic national information such as the numbers of telephone circuits, telephone sets or distributed PC's, etc. This causes difficulty in grasping actual industrial condition. This is caused not only by the reclusive communist regime but also by its weak communication infrastructure. Consider the fact that information and technology themselves compose high technology industries such as computers and communications that have developed rapidly in recent years. International regulations of COCOM (The Coordinating Committee on Multilateral Export Controls) and the Wassenaar Arrangement, a substitution for COCOM established in 1996, made it difficult for North Korea to introduce new technologies. Accordingly, a huge technological gap has affected North Korea. In addition, economic crises since the mid 90's caused North Korea to lag behind in the general IT industry. Though the infrastructure of computers, hardware and communication in North Korea's IT industry is inferior at present, North Korea ranks relatively high in the field of software and military information technology. In particular, it is reported that some of the game programs of North Korea are world-class and the standards of their manpower are also high. The fact that North Korea is the most frequently visiting country to the U.S. Pentagon reflects its interest in the Internet and information & technology. In addition, the Taepodong missile launch system and Kwangmyongsong satellite development is a sign that North Korea has high level manpower in the areas of information and technology. North Korea is expected to fully recognize the importance of the IT industry to reinforce its information power. We see

---

[7] By Woo-Suk Nam (North Korea Department, KOTRA)

evidence it is putting forth concerted energies to induce communication and Internet projects by the recent South-North Economic Cooperation and Foreign Investment Inducement. Such efforts led to the recent joint software development project between the two Koreas as well as the VOIP (Voice Over IP) technology project to be launched in North Korea by the U.S. StarTAC.

II. Development and status of IT industry in North Korea

1.   Computer Hardware

North Korea started research and development of computer at Kim Chaek University of Science & Technology and Kim Il-sung University since the 60's and made the first generation digital computer of 'Jonjin-5500' at the end of the 60's, which continued to produce the second generation digital computer of 'Yongnamsan 1' at the end of the 70's. In 1982 it launched production of 8-bit computer 'Bongwha 4-1' by assembling components imported from Japan. However, the development efforts did not gained desirable results, affected by insufficient manpower resources and low level of the semiconductor industry, so that North Korea started to send its prominent students to the former Soviet Union and the east European bloc to study computer science from 1985. In 1987 an IC circuit test factory was established in the research institution of technology under the control of the Science Ministry, supported by UNDP, and IC producing factory was launched in Pyongyang along with the establishment of semiconductor factories in Haeju and Tanchon in 1989. In 1989, North Korea constructed Pyongyang Computer Assembly Factory in the areas of the Taedonggang riverin Pyongyang in 1993 [1]

However, deficient development technologies and COCOM's restrictions in high performance products import made North Korea difficult to produce high performance products. It is reported that the Pyongyang Computer Assembly Factory has capacity of producing about 30,000 computers per annum and it seems that North Korea is assembling computers by importing most of the related components from Taiwan, Hong Kong, and China etc. At present, 486DX computers has been represented in North Korea and its catalogue of export products[2] shows IBM compatible products of Pentium level, equipped with Window NT Server OS.

<Table 1> Required specification of programs for export computers of North Korea

Program	Data Transmission and Mail Business Administration	Diagnosis System for Oriental Medicine and Acupuncture
Computer	IBM PC/AT 586 Compatible*2	IBM AT
Main Memory	24MB	640KB
HDD	10MB	3MB

Display		VGA (ega)
OS	-Windows NT server 3.51 -Windows NT work station 3.51 - Windows 95	MS-DOS V 3.3 min.
DB	Oracle 7 Workgroup Server 7.13	

In the meantime, PC hardware for export use is led by AT 386SX-33MHz, AT386DX-40MHz, AT486DX-40 and 66MHz along with 8MB and 16MB memory.

Although North Korea has difficulties in introducing super computer due to COCOM restrictions, high performance computers are being utilized in its military field. For the purpose of developing missiles, North Korea made all efforts to develop necessary computer equipment to regulate missile orbit, collect and decode inductive wave. All of which efforts led to the success of launching the missile Daepodong 1 and Kwangmyongsong 1.

Unlike the excellent utilization of computers in the field of military, its actual private sector usage is merely limited to universities and research institutions centering around the Labor Party and important government organizations. They are using high performance work station computers and some companies are utilizing computers for simple calculation works. However, the Pyongyang Broadcasting on June 22 in 2000 reported that the operation system in small and medium-sized power plants less than 10,000 KW introduced computer systems, showing a gradual expansion of computer usage in its industries. However, it is estimated that the distribution rate of computers over the nation is still extremely low. A recent request of North Korea for 1,000 office usage computers to South Korean government for the dispersed families search and estimation in North Korea shows poor distribution rate of computers.

   2. Software

Unlike deficient hardware, it can be said that North Korea's software industry has been considerably developed. Comparing with the hardware industry, which requires a lot of capital induction, North Korea has been concentrating all its energies to nurture manpower for software industry and establish research institutions since the 80's. The state head Kim Jong-il is encouraging program development by visiting computer-related institutions to award decorations and prizes to researchers since 1993. He also emphasized the necessity of introducing computer technologies from abroad when he made a visit to the Ministry of Science in 1996 and distributed specialized foreign magazines of computer to research centers. [3].

With the enthusiasm for computer program development of the North Korean government, 'National Computer Program Competition and Exhibition' has been held

For additional analytical, business and investment opportunities information,
please contact Global Investment & Business Center, USA
at (202) 546-2103. Fax: (202) 546-3275. E-mail: rusric@erols.com

every year since 1990 to encourage computer development. Also, informatization and program development was planned as its policies and 1991 saw the establishment of 'Long-term Plans to Modernize Science & Technology by 2000'. On the back of these political support of the government, North Korea's software development has been actively launched in various fields including security recognition system, oriental medicine and acupuncture system, word processors, management, air transportation controlling system, and many game software. Some of which software is known to be world class. Even in the world *Paduk* program competition held in Japan in 1998 and 2003, North Korea's 'Eunpaduk' won the first prize and it is reported that its word processor 'Changduk' is at the similar level of South Korea's Hangul word processor.

<Table 2> North Korea's Software Development Diary

Year	Contents	Remark
1983	Reorganized and expanded education courses of electronics and engineering of each university.	
1983	Established 'Computer Science Research Institution' in the Science Ministry and Kim Chaek Univesity of Science & Technology.	
Jul. 1986	Established Pyongyang Information Center.	
Jul. 1990	Established Chosun Computer Center.	
Sep. 1990	Pyongyang Information Center developed a Hangul word processor 'Changduk'.	
Dec. 1990	Held the 1st national computer program competition.	Being held every year.
1991	Established 'Long-term Plans to Modernize Science & Technologies by 2000'. - Contents: Business computerization, management program development, computer network development and construction.	
-	Submit a tender for fingerprint recognition system to Egypt police agency.	
Apr. 1991	Established computer manpower nurturing center in Kim Chaek University of Science & Technology.	
Feb. 1992	Developed science & technology data searching program 'Kwangmyong'.	
1993	Developed Pyongyang Soche program (word processor) 'Seokwang'.	

-	Introduced air transportation controlling system to Pyongyang International Airport.	
1995	Established Eunbyol computer technology trade center.	Specialized development of game S/W.
1996	Developed '2nd version of Changduk' and 'Tangun', a word processing program for window 95.	
Sep. 1996	North Korea's Pyongyang Information Center participated in COMDEX-Asia held in Singapore.	
Feb. 1998	Established 'National Voice Recognition Program Competition and Academic Forum'.	
Aug. 1998	Developed a program 'Chosun Janggi'.	
Sep. 1998	'Eunpaduk' won the first prize in the world computer Paduk competition held in Japan.	Ranked 5th and 4th respectively in the Japan competition and the U.S. competition in 2002.
Jan. 2003	Mathematics research center and others of the Ministry of Science developed voice recognition and fingerprint recognition program.	
Mar. 2003	Chosun computer center participated in <'99 China World Computer Fair> and represented 18 programs.	
Jun. 29 2000	A program research center of Han Duk-su Pyongyang University of Light Industries developed clothes designing program.	To be introduced in all clothes factories in the future.

North Korea is showing its intention to export its programs by representing broad range hardware compatibles like IBM. In the China World Computer Fair in 2003, 'Chosun Computer Center' participated under the name of a Chinese company and represented 18 programs of its development in order to make inroads into overseas markets of software. [4] As a lot of South-North software joint business have been contracted recently, economic results of software developed by North Korea are being visualized.

North Korea's software development institutions include 'Chosun Computer Center', 'Pyongyang Information Center', 'Ministry of Science' and 'Eunbyol Computer Center' and others. Some researches are in progress also in Kim Il-sung University and Kim Chake Industrial University and it has been recently reported that Kim Jong-suk College of Education gained reputation and developed its own programs of education purposes amounting to 2,400 or so for several years. [5] Of these research institutions, 'Chosun Computer Center' can be said to be the mecca of North Korea's computer industry. The company status [6] announced by the CEO shows that Chosun Computer Center possesses about 1,000[7] computer technology manpower at present since the establishment in the Mankyongdae area in Pyongyang in 1990. According to the announcement, the company employs 20-100 students every year by selecting from Kim Il-sung University, Kim Chaek Industrial University, and colleges of science and technologies etc., which employees are distributed to 6 subordinate centers controlling 30 research centers each. It is reported that these research centers possess processing technologies of window 95, NT, and Mac OS, developing about 10 computer programs every year including computer security system, various medical software, management system and others. Other institutions are also actively operated to develop software and <Table 3> to <Table 6) [8] shows software items developed by each institution.

<Table 3> Parts of Items of Programs developed by the National Science Office

Name	English Name	Contents
Bidulgi	DOVE	Electronic conversation collects. Based on about 1,000 sentences for fundamental conversation of Korean-English, English-Korea, Japanese-English, English-Japanese.
Guldongmu	Word-Mate	Software to study Korean and Japanese words. (Korean-Japanese, Japanese-Korean).
Mae	Eagle	Chosun characters automatic recognition program
Mujigae	Rainbow	Computer auxiliary translation system of Japanese-English
Study Tetris	Study Tetris	Studying computer game to learn English words or physical formulas
Business	Business	Professional's system to help write business letters in English
Mangnanigon (Chonggaeguri 1)	Free Ball (Tree-Frog 1)	
Yori-300	Foods-300	Electronics food recipes collection of Korean traditional foods of about 300 kinds

<Table 4> Parts of Items of Programs Developed by Pyongyang Information Center

Name	English Name	Contents
Changduk	Changduk	Document editing program. Possible to edit multi-

For additional analytical, business and investment opportunities information, please contact Global Investment & Business Center, USA at (202) 546-2103. Fax: (202) 546-3275. E-mail: rusric@erols.com

		languages of Korean, English, Japanese, Chinese, and Russian etc.
Tangun	Tangun	Korean language processing program. Possible to input/output Korean language on English window 95.
Electronics Publishing System	DPT	Electronic publishing system of Korean, English, Japanese, and Chinese characters
Insik	Insik	Automatic Korean language recognition system (recognition rate: 95%)
Gohyang	Gohyang	Database management system (DBMS)
Sanak	Sanak	Construction design support system of three dimensions

<Table 5> Parts of Items of Programs Developed by Chosun Computer Center

Name	English Name	Contents
Koryo Chimgu	KORYO Acupuncture	Treatment and education system by acupucture of traditional Koryo period medical system (expert system).
Kumbit Mal	Golden Horse	A system to classify and diagnose physical constitution by fingerprints.
Compex Medical Service System	ISDM	A system utilized for treatment and prescription of diseases by Koryo period's medical system, composed of preliminary medical examination, diagnosis, and Koryo medical system.
Intelligent revenue & expenditure system	Intelligent Salesman	Store sales system. POS (Point of Sales)
Moho-37	MOHO-37	Fuzzy computer controlling system for mineral ore dressing.
Tosong-6	Saturn-6	An air transportation controlling system, composed of radar signal processing, radar data processing, data recording and playing system.
Fingerprint lock	FVS-P	A system to confirm individuals and provide door-opening function by using unique characteristics of

		fingerprints.

<Table 6> Parts of Items of Programs Developed by Eunbyol Computer Technology Research Center

Name	English Name	Contents
Eunbaduk	Silver Baduk	A computer Baduk program developed by artificial intelligence algorithm. Possible to have a match of computer vs. human and human vs. human.
Taekwondo	Taekwondo	Collects basic posture of Taekwondo, basic movement training, physical strength development, special skills and self-protection skills.
Chosun Stamps	Korean Stamps	Collects Chosun stamps of about 3,700 kinds issued from 1945 to 1996. Possible to search by year and topic.

North Korea has developed various and unique software. Utilization of oriental medicine to computer, such as 'Koryo Acupuncture', and martial arts software like 'Taekwondo' shows creativity. Besides, 'Dancing Fountain', which is represented in the export product catalogue, actually connects a real fountain and audio to PC, a very unique program that transforms the streams and changes the colors to melody.

New products are also being developed recently and North Korea is very active to improve the performance of existing products. A recent report [9] says that 'Chosun Computer Center' gained good results and its 'Character Recognition Program' showed character recognition rate of 99.9% printed letters and 95% cursive letters. North Korean Chungang Communication announced that the 'Voice Recognition Program', which records 100 thousand words, exceeded 90% level of word recognition rate. In addition, it said that the mechanical translation program development of English-Korean and Korean-English, suggesting that North Korea has also gained desirable results in the translation program development.

North Korea is also showing great interest in three dimensional graphic technology and Kim Il-sung University's Information Center is reported to intensively study computer graphic technology by utilizing a three dimensional computer image processing software 'Hwangryong 2.0' to imitate an American movie 'Titanic'. [10] It is now launching to establish a research institution developing three dimensional graphic and animation technologies backed up by South Korean companies. [11] Program development of Internet and animation is being enforced as the computer language is transferred to Visual Basic and Java development from the previous Basic, Cobol, and Fortran. From this movement, we can guess that North Korea is making efforts to develop technologies in applied graphic field such as Internet and animation etc.

3. Communication

North Korea's communication industry is very deficient just like its computer hardware industry. Since its communication policies have been limited to only satisfy military demands, private sector communication is extremely deficient. However, It started to launch expansion and modernization of communication facilities in and out of the country with the emphasis of importance in overseas trade in the 80's. Taking the opportunity of preparing the Pyongyang World Youth & Student Festival in 1989 and establishing Rajin-Sonbong Free Trade Zone in 1991, North Korea actively launched to expand and modernize communication facilities home and abroad.

North Korea's international telephone lines only came to about 33 lines in 1984, which are connected through china, the former Soviet Union and Japan, but 1990 saw an expansion of about 50 lines. In 1995, construction of optic-fiber cables between Pyongyang and Hamhung was launched on the back of UNDP and the construction of 300km area was completed in 1995. Also, 530km optic-fiber calbe construction between Hamhung-Chongjin-Rajin-Hunchun was launched in the Rajin-Sonbong area supported by UNDP and Thailand-based Roxely Co., Ltd established a joint venture company of North East Asia Telephone and Telecommunication Co. (NEAT&T), which is providing telephone line, pay phone service, and computer network service, and it is reported that it already secured subscribers for 10,000 telephone lines of the total 15,000 lines built in the nation. In December 2002, North Korea announced that it completed optic-fiber cables in Pyongyang and other 70 cities in the nation along with the automation of toll lines, and completed 400km optic-fiber cable construction between Pyongyang and Shinuiju in early 1998. [12] However, the communication network in other areas, except Rajin-Songbong area, Pyongyang and big cities, on the whole is extremely deficient.

As we look into the realities of North Korea's communication network, total lines amount only to about one million as below, which are mostly concentrated in big cities like Pyongyang. Although North Korea is recently targeting to expand its lines up to two million by introducing used phones and operation sets from Japan, Switzerland and Finland and so on, it is reported that North Korea is still facing difficulties in the project. A close look into the status of communication facilities by areas in North Korea shows that Pyongyang and Hamhung is digital crossbars and the number of operation facilities reach about 240 thousand.

<Table 7> Status of North Korea's Communication Factories

Classification	Factory Name	Major Products
Complex electronic machinery and tools	Nampo Communication Machinery Factory	Radio, TV, audio set, wire broadcasting machinery, wireless telephone etc.

Wire communication machinery and tools	Pyongyang Communication Machinery Repairing Factory	Carrier wave telephone, telephone, PCB (Printed Circuit Board) processed telephone
	Sonchon Honorary Soldier's Communication Machinery Factory	Operation tool, beeping and signaling equipment, telephone, components of operation tool
	May 7 Communication Machinery Factory	Operation tool, telephone
	Kanggae 1st Communication Machinery Factory	Operation tool, telephone
	Pyongyang Communication Machinery Factory	Telephone, automatic operation tool, telephone line, operation facilities
	Pakchon Communication Machinery Factory	Telephone
Wireless Communication Machinery and Tool	Anju Communication Machinery Factory	Medium wave transmitter, wire/wireless communication tool
	Pyongyang Honorary Soldiers' Communication Machinery Repairing Factory	Repair of communication machinery and tool, insulation resistance estimation tool
	Pyongyang Wireless Telephone Repairing Factory	Wireless telephone for ships, TV, wireless phone
	Songgan Communication Machinery Repairing Factory	Wireless military telephone, telephone

Source: November 1995 edition 'North Korea's Industry', Korea Development Bank

<Table 8> Status of Communication Facilities of North Korea by areas

Classification	Number of operation facilities	Classification	Number of operation facilities
Pyongyang	230,800	Haeju	100,600
Hanhung	12,000	Sariwon	102,800
Shinuiju	116,600	Gaesong	65,800
Kanggae	120,700	Wonsan	105,000

For additional analytical, business and investment opportunities information, please contact Global Investment & Business Center, USA at (202) 546-2103. Fax: (202) 546-3275. E-mail: rusric@erols.com

| Nampo | 73,200 | Total | 927,500 |

Source: KOTRA's interior data

<Table 9> Comparison of Status of Communication Facilities in South and North Korea

Classification	Unit	South Korea (A)	North Korea (B)	Comparison (B/A)
Number of telephone lines	1,000 lines	20,223	1,035	0.05
Number of telephone subscribers	1,000 lines	21,510	-	-
Distribution rate (per 100 people)	Unit	37.9	4.3	0.11
Number of international telephone lines	Lines	12,051	215	0.02

Source: KOTRA's interior data

North Korea's international communication network is relatively well-equipped with the former socialist countries so that the wireless network of Pyongang-Peking and Moskow and wire network of Shinuiju-Peking and Chongjin-Bladivostok is currently used. With the western countries, short-wave radio of Pyongyang-Singapore, Pyongyang-Hong Kong, and Pyongyang-Japan and indirect communication network based on the Peking relay station in China is mainly used. [13] IDDD (International Direct Distance Dialing) is currently available between Pyongyang and 170 major cities in the world. As for the U.S., IDDD has been enabled between Pyongyang and Washing, New York, and LA through AT&T, and direct satellite line and international exclusive line was constructed between Japan, where a lot of North Korean residents are living, in November 1990. It seems that Pyongyang only has 2720 public phones at present as of the end of 1996, and mobile telephones and wireless beeping services have been restrictively introduced in the areas of Pyongyang, Rajin-Sonbong free trade zone, and Mt. Kumgang tourist site. [14]

In the meantime, as for the communication network for North Korea's informatization, LAN (Local Area Network) has been established in major institutions including the Office of Science, Kim Il-sung University, and the Central Blue House of the Labor Party in the early 90's. In june 2002, 'Kwangmyong', a remote search system, was established to open the first wide area computer network in North Korea which connects Pyongyang-based LAN and computers in companies. However, as the communication infrastructure has not been established still with provinces, North Korea is recently making every effort to build fundamental Internet infrastructure.

For additional analytical, business and investment opportunities information, please contact Global Investment & Business Center, USA at (202) 546-2103. Fax: (202) 546-3275. E-mail: rusric@erols.com

A recent report [15] of North Korea shows its intention to expand computer network by optic communication by publicizing that it is expanding a nationwide integrated information processing system by connecting individual computers to computer network of institutions on the back of maintenance of optic-fiber telephone communication network, and it is also expanding projects to automatically process management by computers as it develops and operate computer network system by areas and sectors for the people's economy.

III. Conclusion

PROBLEMS OF NORTH KOREA'S INVESTMENT IN ITS IT INDUSTRY

Showing an attitude of participating as a sound member of the international society since the South-North summit talks, North Korea is actively seeking after inducement of foreign investment as it launches omnidirectional diplomacies even to the U.S., Japan, and countries of EU. Although foreign capital inducement, including South Korean capital, is urgent and necessary for North Korea's IT industry development, it has a lot of problems. First, North Korea's hardware infrastructure is extremely deficient. It is prospected that North Korea's own economic realities would not enable to expand communication network, which needs enormous investment in facilities, and the fundamental information infrastructure construction is merely impossible due to the realities of inability to introduce Pentium-level computer. In addition, various restrictions and agreements that make difficult to make an investment in North Korea are still valid so that the closed economic system, which does not secure free business activities, causes difficulties in foreign investment in North Korea. In this vein, foreigner's investment in North Korea is still weak. Recently, North Korea has been aware of these problems and it is making a lot of efforts to change the recognition of foreign investors.

Efforts of North Korea to Promote IT industry

North Korea is showing active efforts to induce investment in its IT industry including computer and information & communication in particular. It is said that North Korea is very friendly to any consultations of investment in its IT industry. Kim Jung-il repeatedly emphasized the state policies of intensively promoting information and technology industry by showing great interest when he looked around Chungkwanchon valley, a so-called silicon valley in China, in his visit to China immediately before the South-North summit talks. The recent announcement of developing 'Shinuiju Valley' and 'Mt. Kumgang Valley' under cooperation with South Korea and plans to establish cutting-edge electronics research complexes show the North Korean leadership's great efforts to promote IT industry. Accordingly, a lot of South Korean companies and several foreign companies are launching IT business cooperation projects with North Korea.

<Table 10> Diary of Major North Korean IT Industry Cooperation Since the South-North Summit Talks.

Year	Contents	Remark

Jun. 13 2000	U.S. based Startec agreed to supply North Korea with its VOIP services.	Contracted and agreement with Choson postal company.
Jun. 16 2000	Herbmedi.com announced import of 'Kumbitmal', North Korea's software of oriental medicine diagnosis of physical constitution.	Developed by Chosun Computer Center.
Jun. 22 2000	Hanabiz Co., Ltd. launched to construct a software complex in Shinuiju under South-North cooperation.	North Korea's People's Economic Union and Chosun Computer Center launched the project.
Jun. 30 2000	Hyundai announced to build high technology IT research complex in the Mt. Kumgang area.	
Aug. 2000	Kira Information & Communication Co., Ltd. Launched to establish a joint investment factory of multi-layer PCBs.	
Aug. 10 2000	Mirae Online Co., Ltd. Launched the business of dual satellited communication in North Korea.	
Aug. 16 2000	Hanaro Telecom imported North Korea's Baduk software and contracted an agreement of establishing a processing manufacturing factory of ADSL signal distributors.	Samchonri imported.
Aug. 24 2000	Union Community Co., Ltd. Launched to establish a factory to produce digital toys in North Korea.	Chetoy.com's MP3 player and memory chip is equipped in the digital toys.
Aug. 28 2000	IMRI Co., Ltd. Developed a product of inputting Korean on Japanese O/S and translating Japanese by using North Korea's S/W, which sells in Japan.	Unicotech is selling
Sep. 20 2000	Lcyber Co., Ltd. Launched to establish a development and research center for 3D contents and animation in North Korea.	Joint cooperation with Kwangmyongsong Co., Ltd
Sep. 21 2000	Unicotech revealed North Korea's multi-language (7 countries) documentation and characters recognizing software 'Sranara'.	

COOPERATIVE BUSINESS OF NORH KOREA'S IT INDUSTRY AND THE PROSPECT

The VOIP service agreement between the U.S.-based communication company and North Korea's Chosun Postal Company was announced at the time of a successful meeting of the summits of South and North summits, which is evaluated to be meaningful as a sign of American company's lauching to North Korea along with the action to alleviate economic restrictions on North Korea. In addition, it is noteworthy that North Korea was confirmed not to evade the ways of being connected to the world any more. North Korea will minimize shocks to communicate with the world through the Internet and actively search for the plans to promote the nation's competitiveness of informatization.

South Korean companies business regarding North Korea's IT industry is led by the cooperation for development of software. It is because they have purposes of gaining actual economic profits by applying excellent software products of North Korea. In addition, it is also because that software industry investment is more convenient to approach than hardware exchanges under the restrictions of Wasenar Agreement and so on or the communication business that requires enormous capital. Besides those companies listed in the table 10, it also seems that a lot of South Korean companies in the field of IT industry are searching for launching businesses toward North Korea [17]. Establishment of various research complexes by utilizing excellent IT manpower of North Korea is already on the way of concrete discussion. Research complexes to create synergy effect by combining South Korea's technology and capital with North Korea's IT manpower are being launched to be established in the areas of Shinuiju and Mt. Kumgang. South Korean persons who met North Korean people engaged in IT industry in the economic cooperation projects all say that they have high level of education and fundamental theories. Daily production of PC produced in North Korea records five per capita, which shows superiority to Chinese manpower of three per capita. [18] Combination of North Korea's basic capacity and cutting-edge technology would secure the best competitive IT manpower. Accordingly, it is prospected that South-North economic cooperation in the field of IT industry will be proceeded in the direction of utilizing North Korea's fundamental technologies and manpower along with the construction of communication infrastructure in North Korea.

Notes:

1. 'Development of North Korea's Computer' has been referred to 'North Korea's Information & Communication Technology Level and Plans for South-North Cooperation' and July 2003 edition of Unification Economy by Prof. Park Chan-mo and KOTRA's 'North Korean Industry' 1995 edition.
2. The catalogue is representing North Korea's export products published by Chosun International Trade Promotion Committee under the Trade Ministry. The name of the catalogue is 'EXPORTERS' and the picture sources of products are registered on http://kotra.or.kr/main/info/nk/business/catal/main.php3.
3. Weekly 'North Korean Trends' No. 448, 2003, Ministry of Unification.
4. 'North Korean Newsletter' July 2003 edition, KOTRA
5. 'Status and Prospect of North Korea's Computer and Information Industry', Lee Yong-jong (http://hri.co.kr/nk/전문가논단/ex2-25.htm)
6. 'North Korean Newsletter' May and July 2003 edition, KOTRA
7. The recent report by this institutions says that about 4,500 software experts are working, led by those in their 20's to 30's. (Electronics Newspaper, Sep. 20. 2000)
8. Table 3 to Table 6 is abstracted from 'North Korea's Technology Level in Information & Technology and Plans for south-North Cooperation, by Prof. Park Chan-mo, from July 2003 edition of Unification Economy.

9. Chosun Chungang Communication, Sep. 19. 2000/12/17
10. 121 page of 'Guide to North Korean Trade Investment' published by unification economy center of Hyundai Economic Research Center.
11. Referred to the contents of Sep. 20. 2000 diary of <Table 10>.
12. Referred to KOTRA's 'North Korean Industry' 1995 and Ministry of Unification's 'Weekly North Korean Trend' No. 375.
13. 'Overall Information on North Korea' 2000, International Information Research Institute
14. 'Status and Policies of North Korea's Information and Communication' by Noh Sung-jun and Park Jong-bong, sources from sysmposium of 'Internet and North Korea' June 23 2000.
15. Chosun Chungang Communication, July 24 2000/12/17
16. 'Shinuiju Valley' and 'Mt. Kumgang Valley' are respectively named by Hanabiz Co., Ltd. And Hyundai as the high technology IT research complexes are to be established on the named regions. Refer to <Table 10>.
17. Of about 180 companies participating in the 'KOTRA South-North Economic Cooperation Explanatory Meeting' (July 5 2000), more than 20 companies related to information and communication industry participated. Considering that most of the companies participating in the explanatory meeting are at the level of mapping out their businesses, it is expected that a lot of IT venture companies will launch businesses in the future.
18. 'Technology Level of North Korea's Information and Communication and Plans for South-North Cooperation's, Unification Economy, July 2003.

NORTH KOREA'S TEXTILE INDUSTRY[8]

Overview

North Korea's textile industry is the country's core industry, and commands a profound importance for foreign trade.

The textile products of North Korea are dominated by chemical fabrics mixed with artificial silk and chemical fiber silk, along with blended fabrics of woolen yarn and cotton yarn. Its textile industry is evaluated to be at a low level in the fields of raw materials, thin silk, and textiles, but is felt to be quite competitive in needlework.

North Korea is backward in its textile industry on the whole, as it failed in the development of competitive raw materials for textiles and therefore fell behind the international industrial stream. As well, it has experienced deficiencies in the speed of its technological development. However, it is making efforts to overcome its economic depression most recently through the processing industry, facilities investment, and cooperation and joint venture investments with both foreign and South Korean companies.

Process of Development

North Korea devised development plans for a textile industry of its own by progressive stages; this process is outlined in the table below.

Process of North Korea's Textile Industry Development

Period	Development measures	Results
Repair & Maintenance (1945~1950)	*Repair and maintenance of existing facilities *Harmonious development of central industries and regional industries *Reinforcment of cotton growing	*Promoted cotton fabrics and silk fabrics. *Actively studied the raw materials produced in various regions.
Postwar Restoration (1954~1957)	*Fundamental groundwork for industrialization *Promotion of industrial crop stock farming	*Restored up to the level of pre-existing facilities. *Constructed farms for state-run industrial crops

---

[8] By Sang-Hae Chang (North Korea Department, KOTRA)

		industrial crops.
		*Reinforced wild raw materials for fabrics.
Production Base Development (1958~1960)	*Expand textile production. *Promote chemical fiber production. *Construct regional factories.	*Constructed and expanded large-scale factories. *Industrialized synthetic fiber production. *Promoted affiliated factories.
Improvement of facilities (1961~1970)	*Replace and expand facilities. *Launch mechanization of handicraft regional industries. *Reinforce and specialize clothing industry.	*Entered into mass production system for chemical fabrics and blended fabrics. *Fully mobilized raw materials. *Introduced advanced technologies with specialization of production kinds.
Production Capacity Expansion (1971~1980)	*Reinforce textile bases (constructed with expansion). *Improve quality of products. *Actively promote knitting industry.	*Launched a modernization and production-efficiency process. *Improved clothing (reinforced research projects). *Constructed knitting factories by provincial (do) level.
Production Capacity Modernization and International Cooperation Reinforcement (1980~1990)	*Modernize textile facilities. *Modernize regional production factories. *Reinforce cooperation in accordance with the joint venture law.	*Started and expanded trade of processed goods with South Korean companies. *South Korean companies increased supply of related facilities.
Reinforcement of Foreign Investment Inducement (1990~)	*Take measures for active economic cooperation between South and North Korea. *Foreign investment inducement law	

For additional analytical, business and investment opportunities information, please contact Global Investment & Business Center, USA at (202) 546-2103. Fax: (202) 546-3275. E-mail: rusric@erols.com

TEXTILE PRODUCTS

1. Textile Yarn

[Natural Fibers]

North Korea encouraged the cultivation of natural fibers such as cotton wool, silk, wool and flax across the nation

Main production area for cotton wool ranges around the lower reaches of the River Daedonggang in Hwanghaenam-*do* and areas in Pyongannam-*do*, where they are currently making efforts to increase production through the impetus of government authorities. Although North Korea controls imports of cotton wool due to a shortage of foreign currency funds, and for the purpose of encouraging the sustainability of cotton complexes, it is facing a chronic shortage of goods in stock because of limitations in climatic conditions and narrow areas for seeding. Accordingly, it depends on the import of a great deal of cotton wool from overseas.

Wool is produced primarily in Hamkyongbuk-do, Yanggangdo, Hamkyongnam-*do*, Jagangdo, and Gangwon-do. However, a great amount of wool is imported from Australia and Russia, as the local stocks are experiencing a shortage due to limitations imposed by conditions of wool breeding.

Silk is mainly produced in Hamkyongnam-*do*, Pyonganbuk-*do*, and Jagangdo, and its production offers high productivity as it is exported to China, Russia, Japan, Italy and many other countries overseas.

[Chemical Fibers]

North Korea made great efforts to produce chemical fibers in order to supplement its shortage of natural fibers. By launching the production of viscose rayon and a PVA-series vinylon in the 50's, acrylic fiber in the 70's and mobilon in the 80's with domestic technology, it tried to establish a self-sufficiency of raw materials of fibers. Although North Korea possessed a production capacity of chemical fibers amounting to 177,000 tons in total as of 2002 (South Korea: 2.5 million tons), actual production remained at just 37,000 tons (South Korea: 2.402 million tons) because of a drop in the operating ratio of factories.

In particular, North Korea takes pride in the production of vinylon (or what they call '*Juche* Fiber'), which is the largest part of its chemical fiber industry. Vinylon is produced by synthetic ammonia process utilizing the raw materials of synthetic resins, synthetic rubber, anthracite coal and limestone. Production of this material was begun in 1951, and was actively expanded in 1961 by the establishment of 2.8 vinylon factories in Hamhung-*shi*. North Korea maintained its policy to establish vinylon as the main raw material for its fiber industry, by completing the first stages of construction on a combined company for vinylon in Sunchon in 1989. However, vinylon fiber has limited prospects for production within North Korea, as it is not at all competitive due to difficulties in the dyeing process and a shrinkage of the fabric during laundry; vinylon is therefore weeded out by a competitive global industry.

In addition to vinylon, one of the main fiber products of North Korea is viscose rayon fiber. In particular, North Korea has a unique production method of extracting natural staple fibers from the reed. This is internationally unprecedented, and it therefore follows that viscose fibers would not be a main production item for their economy, in consideration of the limits to reed production and their insignificant amount of contained cellulose.

As we have examined, North Korea has the disadvantage of producing chemical fibers as the main raw material for its fiber production; these fibers have a low economic value, and they are eventually weeded out in the world fiber industry. This production has occurred for two reasons. One, is that North Korea commercialized their fiber products with a self-developed technology and research of vinylon and viscose fibers, which established an economic independence no matter how unstable. Two, it has been analyzed that North Korea experiences limits on its import of raw materials and is simultaneously unable to produce quality raw materials of fiber. This is due, respectively, to a shortage of foreign currencies and under-developed technologies.

Status and Production Capacity of Chemical Fiber Factories

Factory Name	Place of Business	Production Capacity	Remarks
2.8 Vinylon Combined Company	Hamhung	Vinylon: 50,000 tons mobilon: 10,000 tons	10,000 employees
Chongjin Chemical Fiber Factory	Chongjin	Staple fiber: 30,000 tons Artificial silk: 5000 tons	3,000 employees
Shinuiju Chemical Fiber Factory	Shinuiju	Staple fiber: 20,000 tons	4,000 employees
Namhung Youth Factory (Anju Petrochemical Factory)	Anju, Pyongnam	Acrylic fiber: 10,000 tons	
Sunchon Vinylon Combined Company	Sunchon	Vinylon: 50,000 tons (50,000 tons under construction)	

For additional analytical, business and investment opportunities information,
please contact Global Investment & Business Center, USA
at (202) 546-2103. Fax: (202) 546-3275. E-mail: rusric@erols.com

Hamhung Mobilon Factory	Hamhung	Mobilon: 10,000 tons	

TEXTILE INDUSTRY

North Korea has a special interest in the textile industry, which is dominated by cotton spinning and rayon. The importance of these products has increased within the knitting industry in recent years.

It is estimated that North Korea has facilities of spun yarn production amounting to about 940 thousand plumbs (South Korea: about 2.8 million plumbs) based on the calculation of 1977. Actual current conditions must assume that their general technology level falls far behind that of South Korea, and that their thickness of thread is also inferior to South Korea's (ranging on the whole from a No. 30 to No. 60 yarn count). In addition, spinning machines are mostly composed of low productive ring fine spinning machines that operate at 1,200 rpm/min.

Products are produced by old-fashioned facilities such as low speed spinning machines and weaving machines of small width so that the quality is relatively low. Their under-developed facilities for dyeing and processing and after-treatment also contribute to a coarse product, although the quality of silk spinning (such as raw silk and silk fabrics), is estimated to be high in comparison.

It is estimated that North Korea has about 17,100 weaving machines (South Korea: 76,700 units) with a production capacity of 670 million m^2 as of 2002. However, the actual amount of production only totaled 120 million m^2 (South Korea: 283 million m^2) in 2002, as the weaving machines are old-fashioned and overall productivity is decreasing due to shortages of energy resources, raw materials and machine parts etc.

Status of North Korea's Textile Production

(Unit: 100 million m^2)

Year	1992	1993	1994	2002
Amount of Production	1.7	1.9	1.9	1.2
Production Capacity	6.7	6.7	6.7	6.7

Status of Factories

Name of Factory	Facilities & Number of Employees	Production Capacity & Items	Remarks

For additional analytical, business and investment opportunities information, please contact Global Investment & Business Center, USA at (202) 546-2103. Fax: (202) 546-3275. E-mail: rusric@erols.com

Pyongyang Complex Textile (Pyongyang)	Spinning machines: 200 thousand units Weaving machines: 3 thousand units Employees: 12,000	Textile yarn: 25,000 tons Textile fabric: 138million m^2 Items: cotton yarn, cotton fabrics (cotton cloth, corduroy etc.), silk fabrics, various kinds of underwear, knitted fabrics, socks	Started construction in 1949. Expanded facilities in 1961. Batch production system Operates thermal power station (two stations of 1500kW level).
Ganggae Textile (Ganggae, Jagangdo)	Spinning machines: 210 thousand units Weaving machines: about 4 thousand units Employees: 5,000	Textile yarn: 30,000 tons Textile fabric: 123million m^2 Items: cotton yarn, cotton fabrics, various vinylon products	Completed construction in 1972.
Sariwon Textile (Sariwon, Hwanghae-do)	Spinning machines: 100 thousand units Weaving machines: about 2thousand units Employees: 1,000	Textile yarn: 1,700 tons Textile fabric: 66million m^2 Items: cotton yarn, mixed yarn, cotton fabrics, blend fabrics	Completed construction in 1972. Automated facilities in 1985.
Gaeseong Textile (Gaeseong)	Spinning machine: 7,500 units Weaving machine: about 1,500 units Employees: 3,000	Textile yarn: 3000 tons Textile fabric: 25million m^2 Items: cotton, staple fabric, silk fabric, cotton fabric, various vinylon products	Inaugurated as Gaeseong Textile Cooperative in 1954. Renamed as Gaeseong Textile in 1963. Automated facilities in 1990.
Guseong Textile (Guseong	Spinning machines: 9,000 units	Textile yarn: 1,300 tons	Completed construction in 1954.

For additional analytical, business and investment opportunities information, please contact Global Investment & Business Center, USA at (202) 546-2103. Fax: (202) 546-3275. E-mail: rusric@erols.com

Pyongbuk-*do*)	Weaving machines: about 700 units Employees: 5,000	Textile fabrics: 25million m^2 Items: cotton yarn, mixed yarn, vinylon yarn, cotton fabrics, silk fabrics, blend fabrics	Expanded facilities in 1962. Automated facilities in 1988.
Hamhung Wool & Textile (Hamhung, Hamnam-*do*)	Spinning machines: 50,000 units Weaving machines: about 500 units Employees: 5,000	Cotton fabrics: 0.15m^2 Items: woolen yarn, suit textiles, overcoat textiles, blankets	Completed construction in 1967.
Shinuiju Textile (Shinuiju, Pyongbuk-*do*)	Spinning machines: 112,000 units Weaving machines: about 2,500 units Employees: 3,500	Textile yarn: 1,800 tons Textile fabrics: 0.53m^2	Completed construction in 1947.

Garments

North Korea's garment industry is maintaining a self-reliant production output from its small and medium-sized regional factories, even though production facilities, technologies and product quality are all at a low level. Products are supported by domestic demand, although diversity in the types and designs of products lags far behind global standards.

North Korea considers garments to be an important factor, feeling that they represent national character and cultural level. Therefore they give high priorities to practicality and standardization, and prefer the use of a dark-color dyeing method.

However, North Korea switched over to the age of Western-style dress with the support of government authorities when it announced the 'Clothes Management Regulations' in 1984. In particular, the needle work and processing industries were activated by dint of a law pertaining to cooperation & joint venture investments (with companies affiliated with the Pro-North Korean Resident's League in Japan (*Chochongnyon*)) in the 80's. During this period about 10 companies, including the Moranbong Cooperative Company and Daedong River Clothing Factory, were established through the active factory construction movement of *Chochongnyon*.

With an increase of cooperation with South Korea and overseas companies regarding its processing industry in the 90's (along with enhanced facilities introduction), North

Korea's clothes production technology clothes was improved at the same time as the general garments industry enjoyed a promotional boost.

Status of Cooperation for Garment Industry

Cooperative Company	Production Item	Year of Establishment	Place of Business
Moranbong Cooperative Company	Ready-made clothes, blouses, jeans, jumpers, T-shirts	1987	Dongdaewon area, Pyongyang-*shi*
Daedong River Clothing Cooperative Company	Clothes	1987	Pyongyang-*shi*
Joseon Clothing Cooperative Company	Clothes	1987	-
Nakwon Seongwha Clothing Cooperative Company	Female clothes	1987	-
Neungra Cooperative Company	Ready-made clothes	1987	Pyongyang-*shi*
Bongseonwha Cooperative Company	Clothes	1988	-
Jindallae Cooperative Company	Female clothes	1989	Pyongyang-*shi*
Pyongyang Clothing Joint Venture Company	High quality Western clothes	1992	Pyongyang-*shi*
Pyongyang Cooperative Company	Clothes	1992	Pyongyang-*shi*
Cheongjin Cooperative Company	Clothes, coverings	1992	Cheongjin
Gaeseon Clothing Cooperative Company	Children's clothes	1992	Pyongyang-*shi*
Myonghae Quality	Clothes	1992	-

Ready-made Clothes Factory			
Jeonjin Cooperative Company	Work clothes, shirts, casual pants	1992	Pyongcheon area, Pyongyang-*shi*
Joseon Tripartite United Cooperative Company	Clothes	1992	-
Yeomyong Cooperative Company	Coverings	-	-
Yowon Clothing Cooperative Company	Men's wear, ladies' wear	1990	Junggu area, Pyongyang-*shi*

[Clothes Supply & Changes]

North Korea is supplying clothes basically through a distribution system that is filtered by hierarchical grades of social status. Although the personal consumption of clothes is possible, it seems that common people would rather avoid this economic burden due to high prices and short supplies.

Clothes supply was not sufficient in North Korea by the 70's when the clothing was simple and standardized. By the middle of the 80's, however, they had become greatly interested in clothing and tried to augment the previous standardized clothing culture with western fashions. Slightly before and certainly after this time period, men's wear and Western-style clothes were manufactured according to a generalized pattern, and were available in the three primary colors of green, pink, and orange color (a major shift from the previous dark single color option). In the 90's, North Korean authorities made efforts to develop and change their clothing culture by holding a 'Spring & Autumn Wear Exhibition', 'Ready-made Clothes Exhibition', and 'Dress Fair' etc. These events strove to initiate actual improvements within the nation's clothing culture.

Although North Korea achieved moderate results from its efforts to bring about a revolution in civilian clothing culture, (as initiated by government authorities), actual circumstances find civilians to be still not supplied with sufficient clothing to meet their wants and demands.

Status of Clothes Supply

Object	Frequency	Item & Quantity	Remarks
Workers	1~2 times / year	A suit of working clothes	Free

For additional analytical, business and investment opportunities information,
please contact Global Investment & Business Center, USA
at (202) 546-2103. Fax: (202) 546-3275. E-mail: rusric@erols.com

Students	2 times / year	A suit of a school uniform	At a bargain (government designated price)
Technicians/Teachers	1 time / 3~4 years	Suit material	At a bargain (government designated price)
Over Class level 4	1 time / 2 years	Suit material	Half the price

Trade Status of North Korean Fiber Industry

[Export & Import Status]

North Korea's trade of fiber products in 2003 registered at a US$130 million export and US$127 million import balance through activity with its main trading partners including Japan, China, India, and Hong Kong and others; this was 17% of its total trade amount.

The fiber industry's export balance is still showing a high percentage ratio from North Korea's overall export amount (25.4%). The main export items finished garment products manufactured by processing; North Korea exported fiber-related products to Japan amounting to US$60.18 million in 2003, and 95% (US$57.442 million) of the export amount was comprised of garments. It seems that the high ratio of garment export to Japan is affected by a great deal of quantity re-exported to Japan by cooperative trade of processed goods with Korean Japanese businessmen .

Yearly Export Trade Status of Fiber Products

(Unit: US$1,000)

Year	Export of fiber products	Total export amount	Ratio	Change (%)
1996	210,464	726,676	29.0	-
2002	184,171	904,602	20.4	-12.5
1998	148,097	559,331	26.5	-19.6
2003	130,616	514,962	25.4	-11.8

Yearly Import Trade Status of Fiber Products

(Unit: US$1,000)

Year	Import of fiber products	Total import amount	Ratio	Change (%)
1996	151,670	1,249,617	12.1	-
2002	125,972	1,272,253	9.9	-16.9
1998	88,073	882,863	10.0	-30.1
2003	127,088	964,585	13.2	44.3

About 80% of the total import amount of fiber products was traded with the three countries of Japan, China, and India. Of these products imported, finished products such as garments recorded a low ratio of import, while raw materials including cotton, wool, synthetic fibers in order to produce garments were largely imported. Import of cotton yarn and cotton products, in particular, from India rapidly increased and the brisk trade with Thailand was remarkable. In consideration of the import increase in raw materials for garments, it is judged that the export of fiber products by processing of brought-in materials, which has been in a downward trend since 1994, is expanding at this time of year.

Main Countries for Fiber Products Import & their Trade Status

(Unit: US$1,000, %)

Classification	1998	2003	Change
Japan	41,108	42,485	3.4
China	24,447	22,288	-8.8
India	3,929	35,315	798.8
Taiwan	3,820	8,590	124.9
Thailand	280	5,680	1928.6
Hong Kong	2,390	2,110	-11.7

[South-North Trade Status]

Fiber products registered a high ratio for South-North trade along with agricultural products, metals, and minerals etc. In the early stages of trade between the South and the North, the ratio of products carried out to the North was much higher, but in 1994 fiber products carried out to the North reached US$12.85 million (70% of the total amount brought to the North), while the amount brought in the South hit US$18.5 million

For additional analytical, business and investment opportunities information, please contact Global Investment & Business Center, USA at (202) 546-2103. Fax: (202) 546-3275. E-mail: rusric@erols.com

(10.5% of the total amount brought in). Since then, the ratio of amounts brought into the South has continuously increased with a relatively decreasing ratio of amount carried out to the North. This is largely affected by the fact that South Korean companies are expanding the amount to be brought in by the processing trade of the North.

Brought-ins / Carried-outs of Fiber Products toward North Korea

(Unit: US$1,000, %)

Classification	1996	2002	1998	2003
Brought-ins (compared with the total amount brought into the South)	44,459 (24.4)	47,091 (24.4)	38.794 (42.0)	45,513 (37.4)
Carried-outs (compared with the total amount carried out to the North)	36,339 (52.2)	33,971 (29.5)	28,541 (22.0)	36,286 (17.1)

Souce: 'Status of South-North Trade and Cooperation', Ministry of Unification

Most of the brought-ins and carried outs of fiber products between the two Koreas are traded in the form of processing on commission. Processing trade by South Korean companies toward the North were led by a simple processing of brought-in materials. However, facilities investments for processing are in an upward trend as the regulations for processed goods trade were relaxed thanks to the move to activate economic cooperation between South Korea and North Korea.

Status of South-North Processing Trade of Fiber Products

(Unit: US$1,000, %)

Classification	Carried-outs				Brought-ins			
	1996	2002	1998	2003	1996	2002	1998	2003
Raw materials for fiber products	1,188	489	506	797	-	-	-	-
Textile yarns	2,238	1,282	1,101	1,499	1,373	81	401	128

Textile fabrics	21,664	23,111	15,653	22,569	2	525	86	153
Fiber products	4,162	3,134	4,219	7,135	30,578	37,165	34,551	44,756
Total	29,252	28,016	21,479	32,000	31,953	37,771	35,038	45,037
Ratio of carried-outs/brought-ins of fiber products	80.5	82.5	75.3	88.2	71.9	80.2	90.3	99.0

Source: 'Status of South-North Trade and Cooperation', Ministry of Unification

[Economy of Processing on Commission]

* Processing Price

Processing price is paid under standardized per-piece price regulations to the North, which is estimated to be at a similar level of that paid to China. Though it is a bit flexible, it ranges from 10 to 20% of the export price. In case of products such as men's wear and windbreaker jackets, which need technological treatment, or other products that have a strict requirement, the processing price is relatively high reaching 30 to 40% of the export price. Most of South Korean companies responded that they do not have a good advantage simply from the processing trade compared to that which they enjoy with China. In addition, North Korea has recently demanded an increase to the processing price, which would raise the burden on South Korean companies so that the duty-free advantages gained in accordance with the internal trade authorization might be offset.

Processing Price Structure by Item

(Unit: US$/suit , %)

Item	FOB or amount produced (A)	Processing price (B)	B/A
Men's wear (set)	13~15	5~5.5	35~38
Pants (polyester)	3.6	1	36
Sportswear, parkas, skiwear, waterproof clothes	15~30	N/A	About 30

Sweaters	4~6	0.6~0.7	10~15
Jackets (light)	3~7	0.3~1.0	10~14
Jumpers (casual)	10	1~1.5	10~15
Knitted shirts	5	0.15~0.4	3~5
Overcoats (long coats)	45	7~8	15~18
Duck-down parkas	15	2~3	13~20
Training suits	N/A	N/A	30
Jackets (windbreaker jackets etc.)	5~15	2~6	40

* Logistics & Customs Clearance

Excessive payment for the cost of logistics and distribution and the delay of customs clearance causes duty-free advantages to be ineffective. Although container routes are served for Incheon~Nampo and Busan~Rajin, the high cost of cargo transportation and the instability of route schedules have been suggested as big problems.

* Incidental Expenses

In addition to the cost of processing, incidental expenses for trade with North Korea are incurred so that companies in South Korea feel a minor burden. Types of incidental expenses are as following.

- Oil fuels and tires for vehicles to be provided in case of inland cargo transportation

- Reception expenses (gifts and dinner)
- Excessive cost is demanded when technicians visit or stay in North Korea.
- Consumable expenses (instant noodles (ramyon), food products and appliances etc.)

* Time Limit for Delivery & Claims

To date, there have been few claims arising from time limit for delivery or quality problems. Even if a delivery delay does occur, most cases are caused by logistics and distribution (marine and inland transportation) problems, not by delayed production in North Korea. At any rate, claims upon problems of quality do not have clear and definite regulations for settlement at present, so currently any incurred claims are settled by an offset of the processing price or the bearing of half of the claim damages.

For additional analytical, business and investment opportunities information, please contact Global Investment & Business Center, USA at (202) 546-2103. Fax: (202) 546-3275. E-mail: rusric@erols.com

* Quality & Production Management

The quality of processed fiber products is meeting South Korea's expectation so that the stability of product quality does not pose any significant problems. Although South Korean companies have a slightly different opinion about quality levels, they are satisfied with North Korea's processed products. In particular, those who have directly visited North Korea to instruct on technology, or who have supplemented technological gaps by providing technology instructions to native Korean workers, showed a high level of satisfaction on the whole.

Accordingly, South Korean companies prefer to dispatch their staff to settle maintenance problems from production system failures to simple quality management. However, since it is difficult to dispatch South Korean technicians directly, many companies are send skilled workers from the Han race or Chosun race to North Korea, or provide periodic instruction programs for North Korean workers in China. In addition, work instructions, specifications and VTRs related to work details are sent to North Korea for utilization.

* Supply of Facilities

With the forecast results being attained from plans to activate economic cooperation between the South and the North, facilities investment type processing (as supplied with facilities directly from simple processing work) is gradually showing a brisk increase. As North Korea is relatively well equipped with the fundamental facilities to produce fiber products thanks to a joint investment by the pro-north Korean residents' league in Japan (or *Chochongnyon*) in the 80's, the processing industry in its early stages did not have significant problems. However, estimates project that production capacity has reached the uppermost limit with a recent expanse of the processing industry. Therefore it is necessary to cope with an increase in processed fiber production in the years to come. To this end, government-level supports in league with the industry hope to provide facilities by taking political measures. These are requested in consideration of the risks in facilities supply and processing business as carried out exclusively by small and medium-sized companies.

As for facilities investment type processing-on-commission, plans are in the works to deduct the related prices from the processing price, or to fix the processing price for a certain period of time (more than 5 years) in order to collect the sum gained through profits created by the processing on commission.

* Market

Markets are divided into the South Korean market, where the OEM products of conglomerates are brought in, and third-party countries including Japan and Europe. Market pioneering did not have remarkable problems until now.

It is judged that South Korean companies bringing in whole products from the North to provide their domestic clients with, are showing a relatively stable management status. These products are also gaining better responses from consumers than those with country-of-origin marks from China or other Southeast Asian countries.

For additional analytical, business and investment opportunities information,
please contact Global Investment & Business Center, USA
at (202) 546-2103. Fax: (202) 546-3275. E-mail: rusric@erols.com

Exports to third-party countries are mainly executed through existing buyers, although Europe has had difficulties in securing a quota for export trade, while the high tariffs applied to hostile countries by the U.S. has been a chief obstacle to initiating American export.

* Profitability

Margins range from about 10% to 15% on the whole, and most companies are showing their intention to expand trade - although some companies are gaining profits while others are operating in the red. Considering the various circumstances that dictate factors such as processing on commission, low processing prices, duty-free systems in accordance with the internal trade authorization, and stability of product quality these positive benefits can easily be offset by negative factors such as damages from excessive cost of logistics and distribution and delay of delivery.

Even if logistics costs were reduced and the customs clearance system was improved in the long run, companies may feel a burden from the increase of processing costs and facilities investment capital. In this vein, capital support for facilities supply which is subsidized by the government will enable companies to secure profitability and allow processing business on commission to be activated.

Prospects

North Korea is trying to expand the international span of its fiber industry trade in order to overcome an economic crisis through the continuous inducement of foreign currencies, as well as to reinforce its own fiber industry capacity. Especially, North Korea is showing a great deal of interest in processing business on commission, which leads to an acquisition of foreign currencies by making the most of its excellent and abundant workforce.

Additionally it seems that there are higher possibilities of cooperation between the South and the North that could reduce overall production cost, and considering the present condition of South Korea's fiber industry (it is losing international competitiveness due to a low price attack from developing countries) this could be a viable option. North Korea is hoping to expand its business area by accompanying facilities investment with a break from its present simple processing business. North Korea's fiber industry will further develop on the basis of fundamental changes in its fiber industry, by constructing fiber industrial complexes with South Korea

HOME APPLIANCES IN NORTH KOREA

I. Preface

In North Korea, there is a saying, "Just as the human body is consisted of five organs and six bowels, a household should also be furnished with five furniture and six appliances." According to North Koreans, the five furniture sets include bedclothes closet, wardrobe and three others, while the six appliances are TV set, refrigerator, washing machine, fan, stereo and sewing machine.

North Koreans want to have TVs, refrigerators and washing machines in their homes, but the majority is unable to possess such home appliances due to a short supply resulting from North Korea's underdeveloped electric appliance industry.

North Korea continues to import TV sets, refrigerators and washers from China, Japan and Hong Kong annually, in order to alleviate conditions of short supply.

For South Korean companies, North Korea is very likely to play a role as a production base only in the short-term. However, since it was determined that there is great potential for North Korea to become a new market once North-South economic cooperation is set in full motion, surveying the current status of North Korea's home appliance industry is deemed essential in many aspects.

By studying the status of North Korea's home appliance industry centering on TVs, refrigerators and washing machines, said to be the most representative types of home appliances, we hope this report clarifies issues in the North Korean home appliance industry.

II. Production Status

1. General Status

Not unlike other industries, it's generally known that the North Korean home appliance industry is quite underdeveloped. Among other industrial areas in North Korea, the home appliance industry is in most need of development. This is due to North Korea&#0;s heavy industry-oriented policy that focuses mainly on the machinery industry as well as the country's principle of self-reliance by solving everything with their own resources and technology. The North Korean government's disregard for importing advanced technologies from other foreign countries coupled with stagnation in demand has resulted in insufficient power supply and are the main causes for underdevelopment in the country.

North Korea started home appliance production in the 1960&#0;s. Small factories were set up in different regions, and they began to manufacture refrigerators, electric fans and irons in 1961. It was not until 1969 that they introduced TV sets.

In the early 70s, the North Korean government began to accept electronic technologies from the West. The country first imported a manufacturing facility for washing machines and refrigerators from Japan in 1971, and the facility, with an annual capacity of 50,000 units commenced production in 1972.

Nonetheless, North Korea's electronic industry stagnated after the mid-seventies due to technological setbacks, which ensued due to inactive industries and a troubled economy due to its policy of self-reliance.

A businessman who recently visited North Korea said that it was not easy to find operating factories. It can be deduced that in fact only a small number of TV sets, refrigerators, washing machines and other home appliances are manufactured due to a shortage in materials and electrical power.

Under the policy for improving technological areas to the level of advanced countries within a short time frame, North Korea has been putting more emphasis on the development of its automation and electronic industries since the late 1980s.

2. Production Status

Television sets

■ Production Status

North Korea had an annual TV production capacity of 260,000 units as of 2003. Of the total, both the Daedong-gang and Cheongjin Television Plants have a capacity for producing 100,000 TV sets every year.

North Korea started to manufacture black and while TV sets in the late 60s, and began a small color TV assembly & production system at the end of the 70s. Today, the country manufactures medium and large-sized color TVs.

Of note, North Korea dispatched an economic mission to Yugoslavia in the late 70s in line with its production of color TVs. The North Korean delegation signed a purchase contract with Yugoslavia to take over an old-model vacuum tube TV plant, but the deal turned out to be a great loss for North Korea.

The Yugoslavian counterpart informed the North Korean delegates that currents in the international TV industry were shifting to semiconductor models. Despite the warning, however, North Korea proceeded to import the vacuum tube TV manufacturing plant since it was half the cost of a semiconductor type plant. North Korea completed the Daedong-gang Television Plant three years later, but the plant was inoperative from the outset since parts for the outdated vacuum tube TV sets couldn't be procured.

In addition to the Nampo Communication Equipment Plant located in Pyeongnam, the Daedong-gang Television Plant was completed in 1980. It's the largest television plant in North Korea, and it holds the 'Patriotic Color Television Factory'; which only manufactures color TV&#0;s within its facility.

According to an October 1994 report submitted by the delegation members of the East Asia Association, Germany, upon having visited the Daedong-gang Plant, North Korea imports CRT (cathode-ray tubes) from China to manufacture TV sets for domestic sales. The report disclosed that the manufacturing cost for one TV set is NK\1,300 won (app. US$650) and the retail price is set at NK\2,100 (app. $1,050).

Like other home appliances, North Korean TV sets consist largely of parts that are imported from other countries such as Japan. In fact, cathode-ray tubes and TV cases for 'Jindalle', the most common TV model in North Korea, are imported from Toshiba, Japan for assembly. Also, the large-size TV 'Mokranz'; which North Korea has advertised as being produced domestically, uses vacuum or cathode-ray tubes made by the Japanese company, Sharp. For color TVs, *Samilpo* color TVs are manufactured at the Patriotic Color Television Plant. The model, *Daedong-gang 91* was scheduled to begin production in 1992.

North Korea has currently set its annual color TV production goal at 300,000 units per year and the country is now placing effort in seeking collaboration with foreign companies.

Since such is the case, North Korea's TV manufacturing industry is evaluated to still remain at the first stage among the four stages of electronic industry development: Assembly of finished products, simple part production and assembly of finished products, parts and industrial product development and independent electronic materials development.

NORTH KOREA'S TV PRODUCTION STATUS

(Unit: 1,000)

Year	1995	1996	2002	1998	2003
Production Capacity	260	260	260	260	260

Data source: Korea National Statistical Office, *Comparative economical & social statuses of North & South Korea*

▣ Main Production Plants

【 Daedong-gang Television Plant】

The Daedong-gang Television Plant located at the Daedong-gang District of Pyeong-yang is the biggest television manufacturing company in North Korea with a floor space of 16 acres. It was built after a North Korean economic mission to Yugoslavia for the signing of a purchasing agreement for a vacuum tube TV plant with its Yugoslavian counterpart in the late 70s. This was a move on North Korea's part to start manufacturing color TV sets. However, it was verified that the plant was inoperative from the outset since the parts for outdated vacuum tube TV sets couldn't be procured.

The Daedong-gang Television Plant has an annual assembly capacity of 100,000 TV units, and is furnished with 15 laboratories and a broadcasting station using standard airwaves. It's presumed to have imported a cathode-ray tube manufacturing facility that costed JPY9.1 billion from Toshiba, Japan. The production processes for tuner, rheostat and wires were also supplemented later. The plant now manufactures black and white and color TV sets including parts.

The *Patriotic Color Television Factory* was built within the Daedong Television Plant in 1992 with donation money from the pro-North Korea general association of Korean residents in Japan, and is currently manufacturing 20" color TV sets bearing the trademark,*Samil-pyo*

Nampo Communications Equipment Plant (March 14th Plant)

The Nampo Communications Equipment Plant built on a floor space of 1.5 acres has about 3,000 employees. The plant is one of the largest communications equipment manufacturing facilities in North Korea, and besides televisions, it manufactures radios, wireless and radar equipment . The Nampo plant is geared to a production capacity of 20,000 TV sets per year. It also manufactures radar serviceable for military use, showing clear indications of it being a military factory.

【Sariwon Television Assembly Plant】

The Sariwon Television Assembly plant is located in Sariwon City, Hwanghaebuk-do, and produces television sets and electrolytic condensers.

【Other plants】

Pyongyang Wireless Equipment Repair Factory, Cheongjin Television Plant, Gaeseong Television Assembly Plant, Wonsan Television Assembly Plant, Haeju Television Assembly Plant, etc.

Refrigerators & Washing Machines

◼ Production Status

The scale of refrigerator production in North Korea is considerably small. Only about 50,000 units are produced a year as of 2003, and the country barely began manufacturing refrigerators in 1961.

With this, North Korea's production capacity for refrigerators is unknown due to insufficient data.

In order to increase the production rate for household refrigerators and washing machines, North Korea imported a facility with an annual output of 50,000 refrigerators and washing machines from Japan in 1971 and initiated manufacturing in 1972.

The North Korean government drew up plans to boost production of daily necessities since the late 80;s in an attempt to improve the living standards of its people, but failed to achieve satisfactory results.

Like in the case of TV production, North Korea is capable of making simple and rudimentary parts for refrigerators and washing machines, but imports parts that require intermediate or advanced technical skills from other countries like Japan.

NORTH KOREA'S REFRIGERATORS PRODUCTION STATUS

(Unit: 1,000)

Year	1995	1996	2002	1998	2003
Production Capacity	50	50	50	50	50

Data source: Korea National Statistical Office, *Comparative economical & social statuses of North & South Korea*

▣ Production Plants

There are several production plants for refrigerators and washing machines, but there is no known data pertaining to details of production plants and capacity.

Refrigerator plants:'October 5th''General Automation Plant, Bukjung Refrigerator Plant, Hamheung Household Refrigerator Plant, etc.

Washing machine plants: Dongrim Washing Machine Factory, Liwon Washing Machine Factory, Hamheung Washing Machine Plant, etc.

III. Demand Trends

1. General Status

In North Korea, the social standing and wealth of a person can easily be judged by the number of home appliances that they possess.

For reasons of power shortage and the like, all home appliances in every North Korean household must be registered to the home appliances register at the people's district office. The use of home appliances is strictly controlled in North Korea. When a household is found guilty of using any home appliance without registering it, for example, the government authorities confiscate the appliance(s) and cut the power supply.

At any rate, it's not easy to maintain household appliances, since electrical appliances often break down due to frequent power failures and unstable voltage output and there are considerable difficulties in having them repaired owing to scarce parts.

The people in North Korea generally have four different ways of purchasing home appliances: They can pay for appliances apportioned as gift products on important national holidays at a price designated by the government, or shop from department stores or state-run stores by using a purchase coupon allotted at work. Some people have the privilege of bringing in foreign goods after paying custom duties when they return from their overseas assignments. And there is even a method of purchasing items on the black market.

2. Usage Status by Items

Television Sets

Pyongyang citizens are known to have relatively higher living standards than people in other regions, yet no more than one out of four households has a TV set. In suburban areas, it's estimated that one in thirteen families owns a TV.

Color television was introduced to North Korea earlier than South Korea, but was enjoyed by only high government officials, certain privileged classes and relatives of Jochongryeon members (the pro-North Korea general association of Korean residents in Japan). It is reported that the supply rate of color televisions in North Korea still remains at 10%. Coupled with general underdevelopment in the appliances industry, the main reason for the low TV supply rate is that the cost of a color television equals two years' average salary.

Recently, televisions have been supplied to families living in the border towns between North Korea and China where it's easier for North Koreans to make money dealing with their Chinese counterparts. It is also reported that some of the households in these regions are changing to color TV's.

Even South Korean appliances purchased individually overseas by North Korean citizens, albeit restricted, are allowed in to North Korea. But still, it's surmised that most of the products are used after trademarks have been taken off.

Refrigerators & Washing Machines

Since the production scale of refrigerators and washing machines is much smaller than that of TVs, it is supposed that mainly high government officials residing in Pyongyang use such appliances.

Apparently, refrigerators are practically useless in suburban areas since food items go bad quite fast due to frequent power failures.

IV. Trends in North Korea's Foreign Trade of Home Appliances

1. Foreign Trade Status

Due to outdated facilities, insufficient raw materials and a substandard technological level, North Korea carries out nearly no electronics exports; not even to China or Japan. It's analyzed that North Korea is currently undertaking small scale processing of commissions for some E.U. countries.

North Korea relies largely on imports for TVs, refrigerators and washing machines as it has very few exports. China and Japan are its main routes of import and while the import volume from Japan has recently decreased, the scale of importation from China, Hong Kong and Singapore is steadily increasing. In addition, it is quite extraordinary to note that North Korea is currently extending imports from Austria.

North Korea is known to replace the brand labels of the appliances imported from these countries with a North Korean trademark before distribution.

2. Import & Export Status by Items

TV Set

▣ Export Status

North Korea's main export markets are France and Belgium in the E.U. region. Export to the two countries was nonexistent in 2003 but in 2000, North Korea recorded US$560,000 in actual exports. The results are deemed to be re-exports through the simple processing of commissions when considering the real circumstances of the North Korean economy.

In 2003, North Korea had also achieved US$294,000 in exports to Switzerland and delivered a small amount to Japan as well.

Actual TV Imports by Principal Countries

(Unit: US$1,000)

Countries	&#0;98	&#0;99	2000
Japan	-	58	-
France	-	-	309
Belgium	-	-	268
Switzerland	-	294	-

Data Source: 1.WORLD TRADE ATLAS

2. Report from Korea Trade Center

▣ Income Status

China is the biggest import source for North Korea. The total amount of imports from China in 2000 reached US$5.9 million, which is a 121%

For additional analytical, business and investment opportunities information, please contact Global Investment & Business Center, USA at (202) 546-2103. Fax: (202) 546-3275. E-mail: rusric@erols.com

increase from that of the previous year. Aside from this, North Korea has also bought in a small quantity of goods from Singapore, Japan and Hong Kong. For the most part, black-and-white television sets were procured from China, whereas color TV's came in from other countries.

Imports from Japan and Hong Kong had somewhat decreased in 1998 and 2003. But in 2000, where signs of economic recovery were eminent, color TV imports have picked up again. It is of note that TV sets were mainly imported from Asian countries, and not from E.U. nations to which North Korea exports its processing services.

Actual Imports of TV Sets by Principal Country

(Unit: US$1,000)

Countries	1998	2003	2000
China	2,411	2,665	5,900
Singapore	108	328	564
Japan	243	199	309
Hong Kong	595	194	170

Note: Hong Kong's actual export to North Korea is the amount of re-export

Data source: 1.WORLD TRADE ATLAS

2. Report from Korea Trade Center

Refrigerators

◉ Export Status

Exports to North Korea's long-established trading partners are almost nonexistent, and only a small number were exported to Austria among other E.U. nations in 2003 and 2000.

Actual Exports of Freezers & Refrigerators by Principal Countries

(Unit: US$1000)

For additional analytical, business and investment opportunities information, please contact Global Investment & Business Center, USA at (202) 546-2103. Fax: (202) 546-3275. E-mail: rusric@erols.com

Country	2002	1998	2003	2000
Austria	-	-	1	2

Data Source: 1.WORLD TRADE ATLAS

2. Report from Korea Trade Center

▣ Export Status

In 2000, North Korea imported the most number of refrigerators (including freezers) from China, second from Japan and then Hong Kong. In addition, North Korea procured a small number of appliances from Thailand and Austria. In particular, it was notable that North Korea imported household refrigerators from Austria and other E.U. nations in 2000.

Until 2003, North Korea had imported refrigerators mainly from Japan. Upon entering 2000, however, it not only switched its import routes from Japan to China and Hong Kong but also diversified its lines of import to include Austria. Accordingly, it is noticeable that the amount of imports from Japan is gradually decreasing.

Actual Imports of Refrigerators and Freezers by Principal Countries

(Unit: US$1000)

Countries	1998	2003	2000
China	179	154	390
Hong Kong	44	235	281
Japan	335	293	265
Denmark	41	5	24
Thailand	13	17	11
Austria	-	-	5

Note: Hong Kong's actual export to North Korea is the amount of re-export

Data source: 1.WORLD TRADE ATLAS

2.Report from Korea Trade Center

Washing Machines

◙ **Export Status**

North Korea's actual export to China and Japan is almost nonexistent. It exported US$140,000 of goods to Spain in 2000 and US$27,000 to Austria in 2003, but it is not clear whether its the exports consisted of re-exports through processing trade or were products actually manufactured in North Korea.

Actual Exports of Washing Machines (household & laundry) by Principal Countries

(Unit: US$1000)

Country	1998	2003	2000
Spain	-	-	140
Austria	-	27	-

Data source: 1.WORLD TRADE ATLAS

2. Report from Korea Trade Center

◙ **Export Status**

As in the case of other home appliances, China is the biggest washing machine exporting country for North Korea. In 2000, North Korea set out to import from Spain, Austria and Thailand. And as the scale of imports from Japan consequently decreased, imports from Thailand, Spain and Austria began to increase.

Actual Imports of Washing Machines (household & laundry) by Principal Countries

(Unit: US$1000)

Country	1998	2003	2000
China	11	2	22
Hong Kong	-	8	12
Thailand	-	8	5

Japan	12	4	4
Spain	-	-	4
Austria	-	-	2

Note: Hong Kong's actual export to North Korea is the amount of re-export.

Data source: 1.WORLD TRADE ATLAS

2. Report from Korea Trade Center

Ⅴ. Status of Appliances Processing Trade (Commissioned by S. Korea)

○ Among television sets, refrigerators and washing machines, South Korean companies have commissioned North Korea to process assembly for only televisions. This helps to draw a conclusion that North Korea has nominal technological capabilities in this area.

○ In 2000, the extent of North Korea's processing trade commissioned by South Korean companies reached US$4,164,000, showing a 160% increase from that of the previous year. Such achievement was a result of participation of a South Korean company. The company has been bringing in more television sets from South Korea to be processed in North Korea since 2000.

○ TV processing in North Korea commissioned by South Korean companies is carried out at the Daedong-gang Television Plant, North Korea's representative TV set production facility. Since the plant is located in a special region, the power supply is more stable at this plant than for others located in different parts of the country.

○ Wages for processing trade is either similar or a little lower than what China pays North Korea. Nevertheless, preparation time is required since the current technology of North Korea is determined to be at the same level of South Korea in the 70s.

○ In the processing trade ordered by South Korean companies, television sets are assembled after all parts and equipment are delivered to North Korea from the South. It is understood that there are few outstanding defects in the products since South Korean technicians are dispatched to North Korea when circumstances arise.

○ Several issues have been pointed out. The waiting period between supplying the parts and receiving the finished products is slightly long, and additional expenses other than original costs for commission are generated. In addition, since packing materials and boxes cannot be procured in North Korea due to the unique circumstances of the country, all relevant materials must be forwarded to North Korea. Such aspects lead to a worsening in payability, and pose a hindrance in extending the scope of the processing trade project.

Status of TV Processing Trade (Commissioned by S. Korea)

(Unit: US$1000/%)

Year	Amount	Increase Rate
2002	2,971	75.1
1998	3,147	5.9
2003	1,597	-49.2
2000	4,164	160.7

Data source: KOTIS North-South Trade Statistics

Logistics are said to be the costliest factor in North-South economic interchange. As described in the table below, the current logistics costs for television sets is relatively higher than other logistics costs for cassettes and telephones currently in progress. Since high logistics costs also worsen payability, it seems difficult to extend the scope of processing-on-commission trade in the near future. At the same time, it's determined that the processing-on-commission trade for refrigerators and washing machines is not feasible in the near future since required logistics costs are even higher than for television sets.

Relative Importance of Processing Trade & Logistics Costs against Sales in Electronic Appliances Processing Trade

Items	Cost of Processing Trade	Logistics Cost	Profit & Loss/Total Sales
20" Color TV	4.5%	9.0%	-17.6%
14" Monitor	5.7%	6.1%	-3.0%
Cassette	5.4%	5.9%	-1.9%

For additional analytical, business and investment opportunities information, please contact Global Investment & Business Center, USA at (202) 546-2103. Fax: (202) 546-3275. E-mail: rusric@erols.com

Telephone	4.5%	2.8%	3.8%

Data Source: Samsung Economic Research Institute, "North-South Economic Cooperation Guideline"

VI. Conclusion

○ The technology and production facilities in the North Korean home appliances industry are underdeveloped compared to other industries. The appliances industry can manufacture simple and lower grade products, but North Korea is relying mostly on imports in procuring electrical parts that require an intermediate or advanced degree of technological capacity. In considering the real state of affairs, the North Korean appliances industry is evaluated to be at the same level as South Korea in 70's.

○ Home appliances like TVs, refrigerators and washing machines are in short supply, and it is not easy to purchase them in North Korea. At the same time, the demand is also slight due to power shortages and high prices.

○ In order for North Korea to develop its electronic and home appliances industries as well as to expand the scope of processing trade, common electronic parts must be secured first of all. Significant improvements on the parts manufacturing technology and facilities are called for to realize this end. So North Korea must invite foreign experts in relevant fields and promote technical consultations, while as taking innovative measures to attract foreign capitals and secure technology investments. In addition, North Korea should carry out a policy to trigger the demands within the country so as to accumulate and improve the technological capacity through expanding the scope of supply. To realize such objectives, it's crucial to solve the issues of power shortage and lowering prices for home appliances.

○ In the home appliances processing trade commissioned by South Korea in North Korea, large sized appliances such as washing machines and refrigerators are by no means feasible due to the burden of logistics cost. And it's also determined that the scope of TV processing on commission is not likely to make any substantial improvement.

○ On a short-term basis, if the processing trade is conducted by promoting smaller-sized home appliances, it can minimize the pressure of logistics cost. And when the endeavor is coupled with more constructive collaboration of North Korea, a sufficient leeway will be provided for expanding the business scope of processing on commission.

○ On a long-term basis, however, once the logistics cost drops sharply by the increased quantity of goods transported and the Gyeongeui Railway opens to connect between North and South Korea, the processing trade for small-sized appliances will extend by a great margin and be firmly established. Moreover, it's evaluated that the processing trade for large home appliances, which has relatively higher labor costs, will also be set in motion.

For additional analytical, business and investment opportunities information, please contact Global Investment & Business Center, USA at (202) 546-2103. Fax: (202) 546-3275. E-mail: rusric@erols.com

VINYLON ; NORTH KOREA'S PROUD FIBER MATERIAL[9]

The Vinylon Industry of North Korea

Summary

Vinylon**1)** is a PVA (polyvinyl acetate) fiber made from hard coal or petroleum. It was developed by Lee Seung-gi, a world-renowned scientist of North Korea, in 1939 bearing the title of 'Synthetic Fiber #1';. Research on vinylon had continued with the support of the North Korean government, which attempted to turn the research product into commercial use. After a test product was introduced in 1956, a full-scale mass production system was furnished in 1961 with the establishment of '2.8 Vinylon Factory', a facility with an annual production capacity of 50,000 ton stationed in Hamheung, Pyuongannam-do.

North Korea had extensively advertised vinylon as its principal fiber and unfolded a policy to utilize the new material in improving the people's clothing conditions. In their state of lacking alternative fiber materials such as nylon, vinylon was an important fiber material that can easily be supplied to the North Korean people. The reality is that there are many hardships in clothing the people since North Korea is devoid of crude oil; so producing chemical fibers using petroleum as raw material is very difficult and its cultivated acreage is very limited to produce enough natural fibers such as wool, silk and cotton.

In such situation, it was obvious that North Korea took much interest in vinylon and encouraged its production since the chemical fiber is made from hard coal and limestone abundant in the country. Kim Il-sung, in particular, had shown much interest in the vinylon industry by stressing, "Both the inventor of vinylon and the factory planner are of Joseon (Korean) people. And since it&#0;s based on our abundant raw material, the vinylon industry is wholly our independent industry."

In North Korea, the level of development and utilization of vinylon is still in the rudiment state of being one of the capital goods and advanced materials, while the practical application of vinylon stopped short of mainly using the pure vinylon, unmixed with any other fibers, in making clothes. Still, North Korea's renewed interest in the applicability of vinylon as new material by sloughing off from its customary role and function as the most important fiber material of the people is a change worth of notice.**2)**

Process of Vinylon Production

The process of vinylon production consists of firstly making carbide from coal and limestone, producing acetylene**3)** by adding water, making acetic vinyl by applying acetic acid to the acetylene and finally obtain PVA resin (poval) by converting the acetic vinyl into a wax form. PVA resin becomes yarn concentrate by easily melting in 70~80°C water, and vinylon is produced once the concentrate coagulates in sulfuric solution. The

---

[9] Sang Hae Chang, North Korea Department, KOTRA

For additional analytical, business and investment opportunities information, please contact Global Investment & Business Center, USA at (202) 546-2103. Fax: (202) 546-3275. E-mail: rusric@erols.com

solidified vinylon is then heat-treated for 10 minutes in 215ºC. And once it's acetalized after being digested in formalin, water-resistance vinylon fiber is derived.

In addition, vinylon production consumes much electric power and power has to be evenly supplied in order to produce good quality vinylon. But when the power supply status of North Korea is taken into consideration, their producing high quality vinylon is very difficult.

STRATEGIC INFORMATION AND CONTACTS FOR CONDUCTING BUSINESS

ECONOMIC AND TRADE POLICY

BUILD-UP OF SELF-RELIANT NATIONAL ECONOMY

North Korea¡¯s guidelines for economic policies are build-up of the self-reliant national economy that ¡°can meet the domestic demand on its own and fulfill the needs for technological revolution and material conditions for enlarged reproduction¡± based on the principle of self-reliant rehabilitation. However, recognizing the limitations of the attempts for economic development through purely internal mobilization in the 1980s, it has moved to adopt more pragmatic lines, emphasizing the need for foreign trade and economic cooperation with other nations.

Proclamation of the Rajin-Seonbong Free Economic Zone and enactment of the Law on Attraction of Foreign Investment are the examples in addition to its newly-expressed strong interest in the trade and economic cooperation with the South and the promotion of the Mt. Kumgang Tourism Project. However, it sticks to the time-worn self-reliance in national economic lines, emphasizing ¡°we must stand up against the imperialists¡¯ attempts to make the world economy subordinated to them.

"HEAVY INDUSTRY FIRST" POLICY

North Korea has consistently promoted the economic development policies that places top-priority on heavy industry, trumpeting that heavy industry is the foundation of the development of people¡¯s economy. With unreasonably lop-sided promotion of heavy industry, there has been deepening structural imbalance between industries, which resulted in dilapidation of agriculture and social overhead capital. Nonetheless, the North is still emphasizing the importance of heavy industry as part of its efforts for normalization of the ¡°priority sectors¡± such as power supply, coal mining and metal production which were dealt a severe blow in the structural recession.

PARALLEL DEVELOPMENT OF MILITARY STRENGTH AND ECONOMY

In an effort to pursue the policy of developing the economy and strengthening the military strength at the same time, the North has developed its industries in a military-industry complex type, linking the heavy industry with the munitions industry. Thus, its munitions industry is indistinguishable from the civilian supply industry, as it is deeply linked with the heavy industry centered around the mechanical industry.

People's consumption must be controlled in order to promote the dual goals of strengthening its military strength and developing the economy. As a result, the people are forced to endure the extreme difficulties in shortage of articles of everyday consumption.

For additional analytical, business and investment opportunities information, please contact Global Investment & Business Center, USA at (202) 546-2103. Fax: (202) 546-3275. E-mail: rusric@erols.com

FOREIGN ECONOMIC POLICY OF NORTH KOREA

EVALUATION ON THE LAST YEAR'S FOREIGN ECONOMIC ACTIVITY OF NORTH KOREA

Diplomatic Results

Last year was the year that North Korea's diplomatic activity was very active to the extent that no such history can be found, and that it came closer to the international society, getting out of isolation. The step to make a diplomatic relations with Italy announced on Jan. 3, the very beginning of the year, was a signal telling the beginning of North Korean forward-looking diplomacy, and the normalization of the relations with Great Britain, a closest ally of the US, after the restoration of the ties with Australia and forming a friendly relations with the Philippines, was a very significant development. , .

It is forecast that North Korea will also establish diplomatic relations with more advanced western countries this year. We expect that currently progressing negotiations to make friendly relations with EU nations such as Germany, Spain, the Netherlands and Belgium, and Canada and New Zealand will bear fruitful results during the first half of this year.

The crossing visits between Vice Marshal Jo Myong Rok, No.3 man in North Korea's power system, and US Secretary of State Albright were made, and the relations with the US developed further to the extent that President Clinton's visit to North Korea is reviewed seriously.

We cannot ignore the restoration of the relations with China and Russia, former major diplomatic counterparts. The conclusion of a treaty on 'North Korea-Russia Goodwill, Good Neighbor and Cooperation' in February and Putin's state visit to North Korea in July turned the estranged relations since forming of North Korea-Soviet Union's amity relations into new friendly relations.

With regard to the relations with China, both nations reassured traditional ties and actual cooperative relations through the meeting with President of the presidium of the Supreme People's Commission Kim Yong Nam and Chinese Foreign Minister Tang Jiaxuan in 2003, ensuing unofficial visit to China by Chairman of the National Defense Commission Kim Jong Il before South-North Korea Summit Talks and Foreign Minister Paek Nam Sun and Minister of the Ministry of People's Armed Forces Kim Il Chol's visits to China. Above all, the fact that North Korea is recognized as a cooperative partner, getting out of so called 'bad nation' image in the international society through the Summit Talks between South and North Korea can be evaluated as the most remarkable fruitful result.

RESULTS IN THE AREA OF FOREIGN ECONOMIC COOPERATION

Although there were no visible results in the area of foreign economic cooperation, we could find some signs of change in many areas.

Last June, a measure to ease US economic sanctions against North Korea, announced but postponed continuously, started to take effects. Even though its effects are not visible much, since North Korea was not excluded from the list of terrorism supporting nations, the symbolic significance of the measure was great.

The fact that US Startech Co. agreed with Korean Communications Enterprise of North Korea on the Internet communications business and that Oro Co. agreed with North Korean Magnesia Clinker Co. to cooperate in exporting of North Korean magnesia overseas showed the visible signs of change symbolically. Although it was regretable that the attempted dispatch of a commercial mission to North Korea by US Chamber of Commerce to South Korea was not successful, it became an opportunity to show US enterprises' enhanced interests.

It is also noteworthy that exchanges between North Korea and the nations that made diplomatic ties are expanding. North Korea concluded a pact on investment guarantee, economic cooperation and cultural & scientific cooperation with Italy in last September, and after that, Italian Industry & Trade Minister visited North Korea. It was known that the president of Benetton, as a businessman, tapped a business possibility by visiting North Korea. The visit to North Korea by an economic delegation of Italy is scheduled next year.

Australia also dispatched a market survey delegation of a national foreign trade promotion agency in August, and it was known that an energy related business mission visited North Korea and consulted the cooperative businesses such as maintenance of electric power system. In November, when Australian Foreign Minister visited North Korea, a letter of understanding to promote the cooperation for agricultural technology between the two nations was signed .

It is also remarkable that a jointly ventured multinational corporation between Sweden and Switzerland, Asea Brown Boveri (ABB) made a cooperative agreement with North Korean government. At the end of November, the CEO of ABB visited North Korea himself and agreed to the business of modernizing the nationwide electric power distribution network of North Korea with the Ministry of Metal and Machine-Building Industries and Ministry of Power and Coal Industries. They also agreed to participate in the various electricity & power plant facilities and industrial facilities improvement businesses. The fact that a world-leading multinational corporation started to participate in the development of North Korean social overhead capital area is very significant.

At the same time, the fact that Snowy Mountains Engineering Corp., an Australian engineering consulting company, visited North Korea last July and checked the appropriateness of the project to modernize Pyongyang's water supply and drainage, which receives assistance from a Kuwait fund, is significant in that it is the infrastructure development utilizing a third nation's fund.

As economic situation tuned somewhat favorably, overseas purchase centered on the equipment goods became active. Beginning with dispatching a light-industry-machinery-equipment purchasing mission to Taiwan, the import of cars and buses increased substantially including the importation of 100 cars from Belarus. North Korea imported beer plant facilities from Great Britain and attempted to introduce light airplanes from Poland, which was not successful.

As for inducement of foreign investment, its overall performance is presumed to be minimal, in spite of the reports that some Chinese and Hongkong corporations invested in North Korea. North Korea's investment inducement activity also shrank, since even North Korea's pertinent institutions didn't make much effort in inducing foreign investment, differently from the past, .

Foreign trade promotion activity through international exhibitions has not been activated yet. At the Pyongyang International Exhibition held in May, only 22 companies (Most of them were Chinese and Taiwanese companies.) from 9 countries as overseas businesses participated in the exhibition. It seems that the activity to promote foreign trade didn't reach the full-fledged stage yet, given that the number of hosting of the overseas exhibitions and participations in overseas fairs didn't surpass much the level of 2003.

DIRECTION OF THE FOREIGN ECONOMIC POLICY

It is expected that North Korea will actively pursue foreign economic cooperation this year based on the fruitful diplomatic results achieved last year.

That North Korea pursued forward-looking diplomatic activity last year was an effort to guarantee its system and acquire economic support simultaneously. The effort to acquire economic support through diplomatic activity is forecast to be strengthened more, given that no sign of economic recovery by its own effort has shown and the electric power and energy troubles are getting deeper.

North Korea had evaluated in the commentary of Rodong Sinmun on Dec. 18 last year, "Gradually higher international interests in our country and many countries' intentions to improve the relations with us are becoming an irresistible flow." In the new year's greeting address this year, North Korea also revealed, "We will improve the external relations with any country that respects our sovereign rights and will contribute to the autonomization of the world and the great undertaking of humankind's peace actively." In view of all these, North Korea is likely to solidify foreign relations much more.

The fact that North Korean Finance Minister and Central Bank Governor were changed last October, and in the wake of it, that Foreign Trade Minister was reinforced with a young man in his 40s last December is analyzed as showing North Korean authorities' strong will to pick up the economy through actualization of foreign economic cooperation.

There are, however, some sceptical opinions on the possibility of the western world's actual economic cooperation with North Korea. If economic cooperation with foreign corporations to be in full-swing stage, a certain level of condition requested internationally should be met, but there is no movement of internal reform to do so. Therefore, the opinion, asserting foreign economic cooperation might not expand in spite of the diplomatic performances, is also strong.

For additional analytical, business and investment opportunities information,
please contact Global Investment & Business Center, USA
at (202) 546-2103. Fax: (202) 546-3275. E-mail: rusric@erols.com

The increase of exchanges with the international society can be an opportunity for North Korea to feel the need to change strongly. In the process of discussing economic cooperation, the western world is highly likely to demand North Korean authorities' internal change. The surge of exchanges with the nations that formed new amicable relations with North Korea gives the sense of expectation that the improvement of diplomatic relations can be linked to the economic cooperation and that it also can bring the change of North Korea.

This year's activity for foreign economic cooperation by North Korea is forecast to maintain last year's basic policy. It appears that efforts for the expansion of commercial cooperation with nations that signed diplomatic relations, strengthening of external cooperation to develop social overhead capital and acquirement of economic support to overcome economic hardship will be solidified.

EXPANSION OF THE EXCHANGES FOR COMMERCIAL COOPERATION

It is a general process in which the establishment of diplomatic tie is developed into economic relations as a next step. Accordingly, as more countries form diplomatic relations with North Korea this year, external commercial cooperation also is likely to increase.

Italy that signed an economic agreement guaranteeing investments as well as diplomatic tie last year plans to dispatch an economic mission during the first half of this year to realize the cooperative business in full swing. Sweden and the Netherlands are also scheduled to dispatch economic missions. Taiwan is slated to send a market survey group led by CETRA, its trade promotion agency, and Japan also plans to dispatch a large-scale delegation led by East Asia Trade Research Association to Pyongyang International Exhibition.

The Pyongyang International Exhibition, which had not been much successful until last year, seems to play an important central function in foreign economic cooperation this year. North Korean authorities also try to attract much more participations of foreign companies compared with previous years and the exhibition scale will be extended to 5,000 sq m. It is expected that trade through a fair will be active, since Japan's East Asia Trade Research Association plans to send a large-scale delegation, and many companies of Taiwan, of which 9 companies joined the exhibition last year, are also scheduled to participate in it.

STRENGTHENING OF THE EFFORTS TO DEVELOP THE SOCIAL OVERHEAD CAPITAL FACILITIES

The foreign capital inducement policy as a form of economic special zone development such as intensive investment inducement in Rajin-Sunbong Region seems to be weakening relatively and the cooperation with & investment inducement toward foreign companies to improve social overhead capital (SOC) will be presumably solidified. The signing of an agreement in the electric power area with ABB and the appropriateness investigation of the project to modernize Pyongyang's water supply & drainage by Australian SMEC appear to be a signal to this direction.

Since the loans from the international financial institutions as the source of funds to develop SOC are the most promising, North Korea is forecast to attempt to improve the relations with these institutions. The efforts for the negotiations with the US will be enhanced, because the US representative is supposed to oppose the supply of loans from the international financial institutions, unless North Korea is excluded from the terrorism supporting nations' list.

We cautiously predict that areas of electric power and land transportation such as roads and railways will be developed above all, if once the loans from the international financial institutions are supplied. There is a case in which Vietnam propelled a road construction project by receiving loans from IMF and ADB, when the US withdrew the opposition on the supply of the loans from the international financial institutions before Vietnam established the diplomatic relations with the US.

EFFORTS TO ACQUIRE ECONOMIC SUPPORT FOR OVERCOMING ECONOMIC DIFFICULTIES

North Korea's economy recorded plus growth rate in 2003 and the growth trend is forecast to continue last year as well. This growth trend can be largely attributed to South-North Korean economic cooperation business and foreign countries' support. Especially, in the settlement of food crisis, foreign countries' assistance was crucial.

North Korea received 600,000 tons of food assistance from the US, and 150,000 tons of food and 400,000 tons of coking coal from China through diplomatic negotiations in 2003. Last year, it received the support of 600,000 tons of food from Japan and also from Korea another 600,000 tons of food. (500,000 tons were loan type and 100,000 tons were free.) North Korea received $6.51 million worth of assistance from Australia as well, which made a diplomatic relations with it last year, and other international society such as Food and Agriculture Organization supported it with tens of millions of dollars.

Considering the announcement of North Korean authorities that its food harvest declined 1.4 million tons due to natural disasters in 2000, diplomatic efforts to receive food assistance will be heightened. Especially, assistance requests to the nations under negotiations to open diplomatic relations are predicted. The nations that can support North Korea, however, are limited, therefore, the burden to support North Korea is likely to fall on the hands of China, Japan, America and South Korea in the end.

CHANGE OF THE INTERNAL ECONOMIC SYSTEM

Although, macro-situation progresses in the direction that the economic exchanges between North Korea and the international society expand, there still exists some questions about whether the exchanges can be developed into actual cooperative affairs in terms of micro-perspective.

It is true that external world has strong sceptical views on whether North Korean internal environment can guarantee business activity sufficiently and whether there is profitability in doing business with North Korea, let alone the credibility issue of North Korea.

It is pointed out that there is no change inside of North Korea, although its external negotiations are active. So far, even though many laws were enacted to induce foreign investment, free activity of a company is not guaranteed actually. It's hard to find a remarkable successful case of the advanced businesses to North Korea.

While the World bank raised the problems related to investing in North Korea such as the exchange rate & price system not reflecting actual value, lack of credibility of the statistical data, lack of recognition of business and above all the perceptive differences on the management and labor management as well as the issues of expansion of SOC facilities and law system, the bank stressed the need of education to improve such problems, which can be regarded to have pointed out the matters for North Korea to improve rather precisely.

North Korea needs a long-term strategy to search for a co-existent way that can guarantee profits to the investing foreign corporations as well through the change of its internal system, not just sticking to immediate economic profits, while paying attention to these external views.

WESTERN WORLD'S COOPERATION TO SETTLE THE CHANGE OF NORTH KOREAN SYSTEM

North Korea already admitted that its new targets for economic cooperation should be the advanced western countries as the socialist economic cooperative system collapsed in the beginning of the 1990s. However, it depended on the strategy to settle the issue with military assets such as nuclear bombs and missiles not on the normal economic exchanges, which caused the opportunity to recover economy to be lost and led unsuccessful actual results.

It is very desirable that North Korea set up a policy to expand economic cooperation, from the previous year, through normalization of the relations with the western world, escaping from isolation . Still, the policy is not solid enough yet and there will be many disputable factors inside of North Korea. As the exchanges with the western world expand, the decisive time to reform North Korea's internal system is approaching, and the time could be this year.

The western world's interests in economic cooperation and efforts for it are necessary for North Korea to make a rational decision to get out of economic isolation. At the same time, the attitude urging North Korea to change to be acknowledged as a member of the sound international society is also needed. Because North Korea thinks that it did what it could do so far, some are disappointed at the fact that the foreign investment was not induced as expected, therefore, there will be some internal opposition against the change. If confidence on the maintenance of the system and economic recovery is constructed through the formation of credible relations with the western world, North Korea's open change might settle down as a solid policy.

TRADE POLICY ENVIRONMENT

Korea strongly supports open multilateral trading. In fact, Korea is positioned to benefit tremendously from an open system. The Korean economy has grown rapidly since Korea joined the GATT in 1967. This was made possible by open trade under the GATT/WTO system.

Since its accession to the GATT, Korea has been fully committed to complying with multilateral rules and obligations, and maintaining a free and open market at home. Korea actively participated in the multilateral trade negotiations of the Tokyo and Uruguay Rounds. Since the WTO's inception in 1995, the Korean government has, in cooperation with its trading partners, concluded agreements on trade in information technology products, financial services, and basic telecommunications services. In the past two years, the Korean government has actively participated in discussions on the New Round with the belief that early launching of a comprehensive round is essential to the strengthening of the multilateral trading system.

In December 1996, Korea joined the OECD. As part of its accession commitments, Korea further liberalized the financial sector, in particular, the foreign exchange and capital markets. Through its participation in the various activities of the OECD, including the review of its economic development and regulatory regime, Korea has strengthened its commitment to market openness and stepped up measures to enhance market access.

Despite the serious economic downturn caused by the 2002 financial crisis, Korea has continued to implement its commitments under the WTO agreements. The crisis in fact, prompted Korea to accelerate liberalization. Much progress was made in improving the environment for foreign direct investment (FDI). Korea evinces the fact that continued economic reform and liberalization of markets offer the best possible path to increased prosperity.

In 1998, Korea consolidated the dispersed trade functions of the government under the Ministry of Foreign Affairs and Trade (MOFAT). This institutional change was designed to improve the trade policy-making process and to implement the policies in a consistent manner. As a result, restrictions on trade in Korea are gradually being lifted. Restrictions on many import items have been removed altogether. The remaining restrictive measures apply mostly to basic agricultural products. The Korean government also converted its system of export authorization from one that was positively based to one negatively oriented. It also applies a negative system for import authorization.

Individual imports previously had to receive import authorization from the government, but as of July 1, 1996, the government excluded import licenses (I/L) from the required submission documents for import authorization, streamlining the customs clearance process. In 2003, the government abolished the diversification program of imports (which targeted imports from Japan) and is in the process of implementing measures to simplify and increase the transparency of the import authorization process.

As a member country of the World Trade Organization (WTO), Korea is aggressively lowering tariffs and trade barriers. Regardless of the origin of imports, imported goods are subject to the same tariffs, their value being calculated mostly on the basis of CIF prices.

For additional analytical, business and investment opportunities information,
please contact Global Investment & Business Center, USA
at (202) 546-2103. Fax: (202) 546-3275. E-mail: rusric@erols.com

INVESTMENT ENVIRONMENT IN KOREA

Geographical Location and Market Opportunity

Located in between two giant markets, Japan and China, Korea is the gateway to the East Asian market and is also at the center of a vast Asian market with a total population of 2 billion, including 500 million in the ASEAN countries. In June 2001, China finalized bilateral negotiations with EU and the United States to gain accession to the World Trade Organization (WTO), increasing the likelihood that it will join the WTO within the year. It is anticipated that China will play an active role in the development of world trade. In consideration of the fact that Korea's trade with China is rising rapidly from year to year, it is also expected that Korea will play an important role as a base for making inroads into the growing Chinese market.

Year	Category	Total Trade	Exports	Imports
1996	Amount	19,916	11,377	8,539
	%	20.4	24.2	15.4
2002	Amount	23,689	13,572	10,117
	%	18.9	19.3	18.5
1998	Amount	18,428	11,944	6,484
	%	-22.2	-12.0	-35.9
2003	Amount	22,551	13,684	8,867
	%	22.4	14.6	36.8
2000	Amount	31,252	18,454	12,798
	%	38.5	34.9	44.4

[Source: Korea International Trade Association]

Furthermore, it is expected that Korea will play an essential role in providing large-scale transportation linking East Asia and Europe when North and South Korea succeed in jointly restoring the railway line from Seoul to Euiju. Korea's trade volume as of 2003 was US$241.9 billion, which is the 13th largest in the world and 4th largest in Asia after Japan, China and Hong Kong. In particular, there is active trading activity with the Asian countries that comprise 57% (in 2000) of the country's total trade volume and therefore, Korea is a major exporter in the East Asian region.

As of the end of 2000, Korea had a population of 47.3 million and a GDP level of US$458.6 billion. Korea's GDP is the 4th largest in Asia after Japan, China and India. Following the Asian financial crisis, Korea's GDP plunged -6% but made a quick recovery in 2003 with GDP growing above 10% and recording 9% growth in 2000. This is the best performance among the five Asian countries that were severely affected by the Asian financial crisis, i.e. Korea, Indonesia, Philippines, Malaysia, and Thailand.

For additional analytical, business and investment opportunities information, please contact Global Investment & Business Center, USA at (202) 546-2103. Fax: (202) 546-3275. E-mail: rusric@erols.com

The favorable geographical location, which can be utilized as an export base in the North East Asian region, and the excellent market opportunities offered in the domestic market, was also cited as one of the major reasons for foreign direct investment in Korea according to our interviews with foreign invested companies.

TAX STRUCTURE

North Korea's tax system on foreign investment business enterprise and foreign individual

North Korea established "The law of the DPRK on foreign investment business enterprise and foreign individual" (hereunder ¡°tax law for foreigners¡±) in January 1993 and subsequently consolidated the system of taxation by enacting "Enforcement regulations for foreign-invested business and foreign individual tax law' in February 1994.

Direct Tax	Enterprise Income Tax, Personal Income Tax, Property Tax, Inheritance Tax
Indirect Tax	Turnover Tax
Local Tax	City management Tax, Registration and License Tax, Vehicle Tax

Enterprise Income Tax

Scope of Taxation	* Earnings derived from business activities in North Korea. * Other incomes earned in North Korea, including interest, income from dividends, proceeds from the lease or sale of fixed assets, proceeds from the transfer of assets, royalties on industrial properties and know-how and management fees. * Incomes earned through its branches, agencies or subsidiaries established outside North Korea.
Tax Rate	* For foreign investment-business enterprise in other parts of North Korea : 25% * For foreign investment-business enterprise in the Free Economic and Trade Zone : 14% * For foreign investment-business enterprise in preferential sectors : 10%
	Other incomes such as income from dividends, interest, rent, royalties or other sources in North Korea: • 20% in other parts of North Korea • 10% in the Free Economic abd Trade Zone
Tax Incentive	The enterprise income tax not to be paid or to be reduced in the following cases: When a foreign government or an international financial institute grants credit to the North Korean Government or the state bank, or a foreign bank grants a loan under favourable terms and conditions to a North Korean bank or enterprise

For additional analytical, business and investment opportunities information, please contact Global Investment & Business Center, USA at (202) 546-2103. Fax: (202) 546-3275. E-mail: rusric@erols.com

	incomes from interest payments on such cedit or loans to be exempt from income tax. <ul><li>Foreign investment-business enterprise in a preferential sphere, and in the production sectors in the Free Economic and Trade Zone to be entitled to full exemption from enterprise income for 3 years after the first profit-making year and to a tax reduction of up to 50% for the following two years, provided it is operated for durationof at least 10 years.</li><li>A foreign investment-business enterprise in service sectors to be entitled to full exemption from enterprise income tax for 1 year after the first profit-making year and to reduction of uo to 50% for the following 2 years, provided it is operated for a period of least 10 years.</li><li>A foreign investment-business enterprise engaged in infrastructure development, such as railways and roads, communiction, airports and ports, in the Free Economic and Trade Zone with a total investment fo at least 60 million won to be granted full exemption from enterprise income tax for 4 years after the first profit-making year and a deduction of up 50% for following 3 years.</li></ul>

PERSONAL INCOME TAX

Scope of Taxation	· Income from remuneration for work · Income from dividends · Earnings from industrial property, know-how and copyright · Income from interest payments · Income from lease and other income from rent · Proceedsfrom the sale of assets · Income from gifts · Income from individual enterpris
Tax Rate	* Monthly income which is less than 2,000 won to be exempt from individual income tax * Monthly income which is more than 2,000 won : 4%-20% * Income from dividends, Earnings from industrial property, technical know-how and copyright, Income from interest payments and income from rent : 20% * Income from gifts : 2%-12% * Proceeds from the sale of assets and Income from individual enterpris : 25%

PROPERTY TAX

Scope of Taxation	* Building, vessels ro aircraft owned by a foreign individual in North Korea. * Buildings owned in the Free Economic and Trade Zone to be exempt for 5 years.

For additional analytical, business and investment opportunities information,
please contact Global Investment & Business Center, USA
at (202) 546-2103. Fax: (202) 546-3275. E-mail: rusric@erols.com

| Tax Rate | · Buildings : 1% of registered value
· Ships : 1.4% of registered value
· Aircreft : 1.4% of registered value |

Inheritance Tax

Scope of Taxation	* Property in and outside North Korea inherited by a foreign individual resident. * The remaining value of the property inherited, after all outstanding debts relating to it is settled
Tax Rate	* The value of the property inherited which is less than 200,000 won to be exempt * The value of the property inherited which is more than 200,000 won : 6% - 30%

TURNOVER TAX

Scope of Taxation	· Product sales revenue in production sectors · Goods sales revenues in commercial sectors · Revenues from services in service sectors in transport, banking and tourism
Tax Rate	· Production sector : 1.5-20% of sales revenue, 12-60% on restricted goods such as cigarettes and alchol · Commercial sector : 2% of sales revenue · Service sector : 2-4% of service revenue

LOCAL TAXES

City management tax
Registration and license tax
Vehicle tax

* City management tax to be paid every month for the maintenance and management of public facilities such as parks, roads and waste disposal. * Tax rate : 1% of the total amount of wage and salary payments by an enterprise

* Registration and license tax to be paid for the registration of enterprise, royalties for mining or fishing and other items, and deeds such as technical qualification and lisences.
   a.   Registration of enterprise
      o   Establishment : 500-1,000 won per case
      o   Change in status : 40 won per case

For additional analytical, business and investment opportunities information,
please contact Global Investment & Business Center, USA
at (202) 546-2103. Fax: (202) 546-3275. E-mail: rusric@erols.com

	o	Cancellation : 40 won per case
b.	Registration of royalties for mining	
	o	Initial registration : 1,200 won per mining lot
	o	Change : 10 won per mining lot
	o	Cancellation : 10 won per mining lot
c.	Registration of rpyalties for fishing	
	o	Initial registration : 1,000 won per case
	o	Change : 10 won per case
	o	Cancellation : 10 won per case
d.	Technical lisences and qualification : 20-1,000 won per case	

* Vehicle tax to be paid for the use of a vehicle
* Vehicles to be registered with the financial organization in its area of operation or residence within 30 days of gaining ownership of the vehicle
   · Car : 50 won/ea
   · Bus (up to 12 seats) : 90 won/ea
   · Bus (up to 13-30 seats) : 100 won/ea
   · Bus (over 31 seats) : 120 won/ea
   · Truck : 20 won/tons of loading
   · Special purpose car : 50 won/ea
   · Motorcycle : 20 won/ea

For additional analytical, business and investment opportunities information, please contact Global Investment & Business Center, USA at (202) 546-2103. Fax: (202) 546-3275. E-mail: rusric@erols.com

BASIC TITLES ON KOREA
IMPORTANT!
All publications are updated annually!
Please contact IBP, Inc. at ibpusa3@gmail.com for the latest ISBNs and additional information

Title
Korea North – US Political and Economic Cooperation Handbook
Korea North A "Spy" Guide - Strategic Information and Developments
Korea North A Spy" Guide"
Korea North Air Force Handbook
Korea North Army Weapon Systems Handbook
Korea North Army Weapon Systems Handbook
Korea North Army Weapon Systems Handbook
Korea North Army, National Security and Defense Policy Handbook
Korea North Army, National Security and Defense Policy Handbook
Korea North Banking & Financial Market Handbook
Korea North Banking & Financial Market Handbook
Korea North Business and Investment Opportunities Yearbook
Korea North Business and Investment Opportunities Yearbook
Korea North Business and Investment Opportunities Yearbook Volume 1 Strategic Information and Opportunities
Korea North Business Intelligence Report - Practical Information, Opportunities, Contacts
Korea North Business Intelligence Report - Practical Information, Opportunities, Contacts
Korea North Business Law Handbook - Strategic Information and Basic Laws
Korea North Business Law Handbook - Strategic Information and Basic Laws
Korea North Business Law Handbook - Strategic Information and Basic Laws
Korea North Business Law Handbook - Strategic Information and Basic Laws
Korea North Company Laws and Regulations Handbook
Korea North Country Study Guide - Strategic Information and Developments
Korea North Country Study Guide - Strategic Information and Developments
Korea North Country Study Guide - Strategic Information and Developments Volume 1 Strategic Information and Developments
Korea North Customs, Trade Regulations and Procedures Handbook
Korea North Customs, Trade Regulations and Procedures Handbook
Korea North Diplomatic Handbook - Strategic Information and Developments
Korea North Diplomatic Handbook - Strategic Information and Developments
Korea North Ecology & Nature Protection Handbook
Korea North Ecology & Nature Protection Handbook
Korea North Ecology & Nature Protection Laws and Regulation Handbook
Korea North Economic & Development Strategy Handbook
Korea North Economic & Development Strategy Handbook
Korea North Energy Policy, Laws and Regulation Handbook
Korea North Export-Import Handbook
Korea North Export-Import Trade and Business Directory
Korea North Export-Import Trade and Business Directory
Korea North Foreign Policy and Government Guide
Korea North Foreign Policy and Government Guide
Korea North General Secretary and political System Handbook

For additional analytical, business and investment opportunities information, please contact Global Investment & Business Center, USA at (202) 546-2103. Fax: (202) 546-3275. E-mail: rusric@erols.com

Title
Korea North General Secretary Handbook - Foreign and Domestic Policy
Korea North Industrial and Business Directory
Korea North Industrial and Business Directory
Korea North Industrial and Business Directory Volume 1
Korea North Industrial and Business Directory Volume 2
Korea North Internet and E-Commerce Investment and Business Guide - Strategic and Practical Information: Regulations and Opportunities
Korea North Internet and E-Commerce Investment and Business Guide - Strategic and Practical Information: Regulations and Opportunities
Korea North Investment and Business Guide - Strategic and Practical Information
Korea North Investment and Business Guide - Strategic and Practical Information
Korea North Investment and Business Guide - Strategic and Practical Information
Korea North Investment and Business Guide - Strategic and Practical Information
Korea North Investment and Trade Laws and Regulations Handbook
Korea North Mineral & Mining Sector Investment and Business Guide - Strategic and Practical Information
Korea North Mineral & Mining Sector Investment and Business Guide - Strategic and Practical Information
Korea North Mining Laws and Regulations Handbook
Korea North Recent Economic and Political Developments Yearbook
Korea North Recent Economic and Political Developments Yearbook
Korea North Recent Economic and Political Developments Yearbook
Korea North Starting Business (Incorporating) in....Guide
Korea North Taxation Laws and Regulations Handbook
Korea North Telecom Laws and Regulations Handbook
Korea North Telecommunication Industry Business Opportunities Handbook
Korea North Telecommunication Industry Business Opportunities Handbook
Korea North Transportation Policy and Regulations Handbook
Korea North û US Political and Economic Cooperation Handbook
Korea North Weapons Systems Handbook
Korea South A "Spy" Guide - Strategic Information and Developments
Korea South A Spy" Guide"
Korea South Air Force Handbook
Korea South Air Force Handbook
Korea South Air Force Handbook volt 2
Korea South Army Weapon Systems Handbook
Korea South Army Weapon Systems Handbook
Korea South Army Weapon Systems Handbook
Korea South Army, National Security and Defense Policy Handbook
Korea South Army, National Security and Defense Policy Handbook
Korea South Aviation and Aerospace Industry Handbook
Korea South Aviation and Aerospace Industry Handbook
Korea South Business and Investment Opportunities Yearbook
Korea South Business and Investment Opportunities Yearbook
Korea South Business and Investment Opportunities Yearbook Volume 1 Strategic Information and Opportunities
Korea South Business Intelligence Report - Practical Information, Opportunities, Contacts
Korea South Business Intelligence Report - Practical Information, Opportunities, Contacts
Korea South Business Law Handbook - Strategic Information and Basic Laws
Korea South Business Law Handbook - Strategic Information and Basic Laws
Korea South Business Law Handbook - Strategic Information and Basic Laws

For additional analytical, business and investment opportunities information,
please contact Global Investment & Business Center, USA
at (202) 546-2103. Fax: (202) 546-3275. E-mail: rusric@erols.com

Title
Korea South Business Law Handbook - Strategic Information and Basic Laws
Korea South Clothing & Textile Industry Handbook
Korea South Clothing & Textile Industry Handbook
Korea South Company Laws and Regulations Handbook
Korea South Country Study Guide - Strategic Information and Developments
Korea South Country Study Guide - Strategic Information and Developments
Korea South Country Study Guide - Strategic Information and Developments Volume 1 Strategic Information and Developments
Korea South Customs, Trade Regulations and Procedures Handbook
Korea South Customs, Trade Regulations and Procedures Handbook
Korea South Diplomatic Handbook - Strategic Information and Developments
Korea South Diplomatic Handbook - Strategic Information and Developments
Korea South Direct Foreign Investment Guide: Regulations, Procedures, Contacts
Korea South Ecology & Nature Protection Handbook
Korea South Ecology & Nature Protection Handbook
Korea South Ecology & Nature Protection Laws and Regulation Handbook
Korea South Economic & Development Strategy Handbook
Korea South Economic & Development Strategy Handbook
Korea South Economic and Product Business and Investment Opportunities Yearbook - Strategic and Practical Information
Korea South Education System and Policy Handbook
Korea South Energy Policy, Laws and Regulation Handbook
Korea South Export-Import Trade and Business Directory
Korea South Export-Import Trade and Business Directory
Korea South Foreign Policy and Government Guide
Korea South Foreign Policy and Government Guide
Korea South Government and Business Contacts Handbook
Korea South Government and Business Contacts Handbook
Korea South Industrial and Business Directory
Korea South Industrial and Business Directory
Korea South Industrial and Business Directory
Korea South Industrial and Business Directory
Korea South Intelligence & Security Activities & Operations Handbook
Korea South Intelligence & Security Activities & Operations Handbook
Korea South Intelligence, Security Activities & Operations Handbook
Korea South Intelligence, Security Activities & Operations Handbook
Korea South Internet and E-Commerce Investment and Business Guide - Strategic and Practical Information: Regulations and Opportunities
Korea South Internet and E-Commerce Investment and Business Guide - Strategic and Practical Information: Regulations and Opportunities
Korea South Investment & Business Guide
Korea South Investment & Business Guide
Korea South Investment and Business Guide - Strategic and Practical Information
Korea South Investment and Business Guide - Strategic and Practical Information
Korea South Investment and Trade Laws and Regulations Handbook
Korea South Justice System and National Police Handbook
Korea South Justice System and National Police Handbook
Korea South Land Ownership and Agriculture Laws Handbook
Korea South Medical & Pharmaceutical Industry Handbook

For additional analytical, business and investment opportunities information,
please contact Global Investment & Business Center, USA
at (202) 546-2103. Fax: (202) 546-3275. E-mail: rusric@erols.com

Title
Korea South Medical & Pharmaceutical Industry Handbook
Korea South Mineral & Mining Sector Investment and Business Guide - Strategic and Practical Information
Korea South Mineral & Mining Sector Investment and Business Guide - Strategic and Practical Information
Korea South Mining Laws and Regulations Handbook
Korea South President Handbook
Korea South President Handbook
Korea South Privatization Programs and Regulations Handbook
Korea South Privatization Programs and Regulations Handbook
Korea South Recent Economic and Political Developments Yearbook
Korea South Recent Economic and Political Developments Yearbook
Korea South Recent Economic and Political Developments Yearbook
Korea South Research & Development Policy Handbook
Korea South Research & Development Policy Handbook
Korea South Research & Development Policy Handbook
Korea South Starting Business (Incorporating) in....Guide
Korea South Tax Guide
Korea South Tax Guide
Korea South Taxation Laws and Regulations Handbook
Korea South Telecom Laws and Regulations Handbook
Korea South Telecommunication Industry Business Opportunities Handbook
Korea South Telecommunication Industry Business Opportunities Handbook
Korea South Transportation Policy and Regulations Handbook
Korea Unification Handbook
Korea, North: How to Invest, Start and Run Profitable Business in Korea, North Guide - Practical Information, Opportunities, Contacts
Korea, South: How to Invest, Start and Run Profitable Business in Korea, South Guide - Practical Information, Opportunities, Contacts

GLOBAL WEAPON SYSTEMS HANDBOOK LIBRARY
(PRICE $149.95)

Ultimate handbooks on army, defense policy, intelligence, counterintelligence, national security and related operation, conducted by specific countries. National security and intelligence agencies

Albania Armed Forced Weapon Systems Handbook
Australia Armed Forced Weapon Systems Handbook
Bangladesh Armed Forced Weapon Systems Handbook
Bulgaria Armed Forced Weapon Systems Handbook
Canada Armed Forced Weapon Systems Handbook
China Armed Forced Weapon Systems Handbook
Cuba Armed Forced Weapon Systems Handbook
Czech Republic Armed Forced Weapon Systems Handbook
Estonia Armed Forced Weapon Systems Handbook
Finland Armed Forced Weapon Systems Handbook
France Armed Forced Weapon Systems Handbook
Germany Armed Forced Weapon Systems Handbook
Greece Armed Forced Weapon Systems Handbook
Hungary Armed Forced Weapon Systems Handbook
India Armed Forced Weapon Systems Handbook
Ireland Armed Forced Weapon Systems Handbook
Israel Armed Forced Weapon Systems Handbook
Italy Armed Forced Weapon Systems Handbook
Japan Armed Forced Weapon Systems Handbook
Jordan Armed Forced Weapon Systems Handbook
Korea North Armed Forced Weapon Systems Handbook
Korea South Armed Forced Weapon Systems Handbook
Latvia Armed Forced Weapon Systems Handbook
Lebanon Armed Forced Weapon Systems Handbook
Lithuania Armed Forced Weapon Systems Handbook
Macedonia Armed Forced Weapon Systems Handbook
Malaysia Armed Forced Weapon Systems Handbook
Myanmar Armed Forced Weapon Systems Handbook
New Zealand Armed Forced Weapon Systems Handbook
Norway Armed Forced Weapon Systems Handbook
Pakistan Armed Forced Weapon Systems Handbook
Philippines Armed Forced Weapon Systems Handbook
Poland Armed Forced Weapon Systems Handbook
Portugal Armed Forced Weapon Systems Handbook
Romania Armed Forced Weapon Systems Handbook
Russia Armed Forced Weapon Systems Handbook
Singapore Armed Forced Weapon Systems Handbook
Slovak Republic Armed Forced Weapon Systems Handbook
South Africa Armed Forced Weapon Systems Handbook
Sri Lanka Armed Forced Weapon Systems Handbook
Switzerland Armed Forced Weapon Systems Handbook
Taiwan Armed Forced Weapon Systems Handbook
Thailand Armed Forced Weapon Systems Handbook
Turkey Armed Forced Weapon Systems Handbook
United Kingdom Armed Forced Weapon Systems Handbook

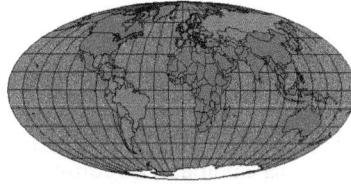

WORLD EXPORT-IMPORT, TRADE AND BUSINESS DIRECTORIES LIBRARY

Price: $149.95 Each
International Business Publications USA
P.O. Box 15343, Washington DC 20003, Email: ibpusa@comcast.net
Phone: 202-546-2103, Fax: 202-546-3275
World Business Information Catalog: http://www.ibpus.com

1.	Albania Export-Import, Trade and Business Directory
2.	Algeria Export-Import, Trade and Business Directory
3.	Andorra Export-Import, Trade and Business Directory
4.	Angola Export-Import, Trade and Business Directory
5.	Antigua & Barbuda Export-Import, Trade and Business Directory
6.	Antilles (Netherlands) Export-Import, Trade and Business Directory
7.	Argentina Export-Import, Trade and Business Directory
8.	Armenia Export-Import, Trade and Business Directory
9.	Australia Export-Import, Trade and Business Directory
10.	Austria Export-Import, Trade and Business Directory
11.	Azerbaijan Export-Import, Trade and Business Directory
12.	Bahamas Export-Import, Trade and Business Directory
13.	Bangladesh Export-Import, Trade and Business Directory
14.	Barbados Export-Import, Trade and Business Directory
15.	Belarus Export-Import, Trade and Business Directory
16.	Belgium Export-Import, Trade and Business Directory
17.	Belize Export-Import, Trade and Business Directory
18.	Bermuda Export-Import, Trade and Business Directory
19.	Bolivia Export-Import, Trade and Business Directory
20.	Bosnia and Herzegovina Export-Import, Trade and Business Directory
21.	Botswana Export-Import, Trade and Business Directory
22.	Brazil Export-Import, Trade and Business Directory
23.	Brunei Export-Import, Trade and Business Directory
24.	Bulgaria Export-Import, Trade and Business Directory
25.	Cambodia Export-Import, Trade and Business Directory
26.	Cameroon Export-Import, Trade and Business Directory
27.	Canada Export-Import, Trade and Business Directory
28.	Cayman Islands Export-Import, Trade and Business Directory
29.	Chile Export-Import, Trade and Business Directory
30.	China Export-Import, Trade and Business Directory
31.	Colombia Export-Import, Trade and Business Directory
32.	Comoros Export-Import, Trade and Business Directory
33.	Cook Islands Export-Import, Trade and Business Directory
34.	Costa Rica Export-Import, Trade and Business Directory

For additional analytical, business and investment opportunities information,
please contact Global Investment & Business Center, USA
at (202) 546-2103. Fax: (202) 546-3275. E-mail: rusric@erols.com

35.	Croatia Export-Import, Trade and Business Directory
36.	Cuba Export-Import, Trade and Business Directory
37.	Cyprus Export-Import, Trade and Business Directory
38.	Czech Republic Export-Import, Trade and Business Directory
39.	Denmark Export-Import, Trade and Business Directory
40.	Dominica Export-Import, Trade and Business Directory
41.	Dominican Republic Export-Import, Trade and Business Directory
42.	Dubai Export-Import, Trade and Business Directory
43.	Ecuador Export-Import, Trade and Business Directory
44.	Egypt Export-Import, Trade and Business Directory
45.	El Salvador Export-Import, Trade and Business Directory
46.	Equatorial Guinea Export-Import, Trade and Business Directory
47.	Estonia Export-Import, Trade and Business Directory
48.	Falkland Islands Export-Import, Trade and Business Directory
49.	Fiji Export-Import, Trade and Business Directory
50.	Finland Export-Import, Trade and Business Directory
51.	France Export-Import, Trade and Business Directory
52.	Georgia Export-Import, Trade and Business Directory
53.	Germany Export-Import, Trade and Business Directory
54.	Gibraltar Export-Import, Trade and Business Directory
55.	Greece Export-Import, Trade and Business Directory
56.	Grenada Export-Import, Trade and Business Directory
57.	Guam Investment & Business Guide
58.	Guatemala Export-Import, Trade and Business Directory
59.	Guernsey Export-Import, Trade and Business Directory
60.	Guyana Export-Import, Trade and Business Directory
61.	Haiti Export-Import, Trade and Business Directory
62.	Honduras Export-Import, Trade and Business Directory
63.	Hungary Export-Import, Trade and Business Directory
64.	Iceland Export-Import, Trade and Business Directory
65.	India Export-Import, Trade and Business Directory
66.	Indonesia Export-Import, Trade and Business Directory
67.	Iran Export-Import, Trade and Business Directory
68.	Iraq Export-Import, Trade and Business Directory
69.	Ireland Export-Import, Trade and Business Directory
70.	Israel Export-Import, Trade and Business Directory
71.	Italy Export-Import, Trade and Business Directory
72.	Jamaica Export-Import, Trade and Business Directory
73.	Japan Export-Import, Trade and Business Directory
74.	Jersey Export-Import, Trade and Business Directory
75.	Jordan Export-Import, Trade and Business Directory
76.	Kazakhstan Export-Import, Trade and Business Directory
77.	Kenya Export-Import, Trade and Business Directory
78.	Kiribati Export-Import, Trade and Business Directory

For additional analytical, business and investment opportunities information,
please contact Global Investment & Business Center, USA
at (202) 546-2103. Fax: (202) 546-3275. E-mail: rusric@erols.com

79. Korea, North Export-Import, Trade and Business Directory
80. Korea, South Export-Import, Trade and Business Directory
81. Kuwait Export-Import, Trade and Business Directory
82. Kyrgyzstan Export-Import, Trade and Business Directory
83. Laos Export-Import, Trade and Business Directory
84. Latvia Export-Import, Trade and Business Directory
85. Lebanon Export-Import, Trade and Business Directory
86. Libya Export-Import, Trade and Business Directory
87. Liechtenstein Export-Import, Trade and Business Directory
88. Lithuania Export-Import, Trade and Business Directory
89. Luxemburg Export-Import, Trade and Business Directory
90. Macao Export-Import, Trade and Business Directory
91. Macedonia, Republic Export-Import, Trade and Business Directory
92. Madagascar Export-Import, Trade and Business Directory
93. Malaysia Export-Import, Trade and Business Directory
94. Malta Export-Import, Trade and Business Directory
95. Man Export-Import, Trade and Business Directory
96. Mauritius Export-Import, Trade and Business Directory
97. Mauritius Export-Import, Trade and Business Directory
98. Mexico Export-Import, Trade and Business Directory
99. Micronesia Export-Import, Trade and Business Directory
100. Moldova Export-Import, Trade and Business Directory
101. Monaco Export-Import, Trade and Business Directory
102. Mongolia Export-Import, Trade and Business Directory
103. Morocco Export-Import, Trade and Business Directory
104. Myanmar Export-Import, Trade and Business Directory
105. Namibia Export-Import, Trade and Business Directory
106. Netherlands Export-Import, Trade and Business Directory
107. New Caledonia Export-Import, Trade and Business Directory
108. New Zealand Export-Import, Trade and Business Directory
109. Nicaragua Export-Import, Trade and Business Directory
110. Nigeria Export-Import, Trade and Business Directory
111. Northern Mariana Islands Export-Import, Trade and Business Directory
112. Norway Export-Import, Trade and Business Directory
113. Pakistan Export-Import, Trade and Business Directory
114. Panama Export-Import, Trade and Business Directory
115. Peru Export-Import, Trade and Business Directory
116. Philippines Export-Import, Trade and Business Directory
117. Poland Export-Import, Trade and Business Directory
118. Portugal Export-Import, Trade and Business Directory
119. Romania Export-Import, Trade and Business Directory
120. Russia Export-Import, Trade and Business Directory
121. Samoa (American) Investment & Business Guide
122. Samoa (Western) Export-Import, Trade and Business Directory

123. Saudi Arabia Export-Import, Trade and Business Directory
124. Scotland Export-Import, Trade and Business Directory
125. Singapore Export-Import, Trade and Business Directory
126. Slovakia Export-Import, Trade and Business Directory
127. Slovenia Export-Import, Trade and Business Directory
128. South Africa Export-Import, Trade and Business Directory
129. Spain Export-Import, Trade and Business Directory
130. Sri Lanka Export-Import, Trade and Business Directory
131. St. Helena Export-Import, Trade and Business Directory
132. Sudan Export-Import, Trade and Business Directory
133. Suriname Export-Import, Trade and Business Directory
134. Sweden Export-Import, Trade and Business Directory
135. Switzerland Export-Import, Trade and Business Directory
136. Syria Export Import & Business Directory
137. Taiwan Export-Import, Trade and Business Directory
138. Tajikistan Export-Import, Trade and Business Directory
139. Thailand Export-Import, Trade and Business Directory
140. Tunisia Export-Import, Trade and Business Directory
141. Turkey Export-Import, Trade and Business Directory
142. Turkmenistan Export-Import, Trade and Business Directory
143. Uganda Export-Import, Trade and Business Directory
144. Ukraine Export-Import, Trade and Business Directory
145. United Arab Emirates Export-Import, Trade and Business Directory
146. United Kingdom Export-Import, Trade and Business Directory
147. United States Export-Import, Trade and Business Directory
148. Uruguay Export-Import, Trade and Business Directory
149. US Export-Import, Trade and Business Directory
150. Uzbekistan Export-Import, Trade and Business Directory
151. Venezuela Export-Import, Trade and Business Directory
152. Vietnam Export-Import, Trade and Business Directory
153. Yugoslavia Export-Import, Trade and Business Directory

For additional analytical, business and investment opportunities information,
please contact Global Investment & Business Center, USA
at (202) 546-2103. Fax: (202) 546-3275. E-mail: rusric@erols.com

INVESTMENT, TRADE STRATEGY AND AGREEMENTS HANDBOOK
STRATEGIC INFORMATION AND BASIC AGREEMENTSLIBRARY

Price: $99.95 Each
World Business Information Catalog: http://www.ibpus.com

TITLE
Afghanistan Investment, Trade Strategy and Agreements Handbook - Strategic Information and Basic Agreements
Albania Investment, Trade Strategy and Agreements Handbook - Strategic Information and Basic Agreements
Algeria Investment, Trade Strategy and Agreements Handbook - Strategic Information and Basic Agreements
Angola Investment, Trade Strategy and Agreements Handbook - Strategic Information and Basic Agreements
Antigua and Barbuda Investment, Trade Strategy and Agreements Handbook - Strategic Information and Basic Agreements
Argentina Investment, Trade Strategy and Agreements Handbook - Strategic Information and Basic Agreements
Armenia Investment, Trade Strategy and Agreements Handbook - Strategic Information and Basic Agreements
Australia Investment, Trade Strategy and Agreements Handbook - Strategic Information and Basic Agreements
Austria Investment, Trade Strategy and Agreements Handbook - Strategic Information and Basic Agreements
Azerbaijan Investment, Trade Strategy and Agreements Handbook - Strategic Information and Basic Agreements
Bahamas Investment, Trade Strategy and Agreements Handbook - Strategic Information and Basic Agreements
Bahrain Investment, Trade Strategy and Agreements Handbook - Strategic Information and Basic Agreements
Bangladesh Investment, Trade Strategy and Agreements Handbook - Strategic Information and Basic Agreements
Barbados Investment, Trade Strategy and Agreements Handbook - Strategic Information and Basic Agreements
Belarus Investment, Trade Strategy and Agreements Handbook - Strategic Information and Basic Agreements
Belgium Investment, Trade Strategy and Agreements Handbook - Strategic Information and Basic Agreements
Belize Investment, Trade Strategy and Agreements Handbook - Strategic Information and Basic Agreements
Benin Investment, Trade Strategy and Agreements Handbook - Strategic Information and Basic Agreements
Bolivia Investment, Trade Strategy and Agreements Handbook - Strategic Information and Basic Agreements
Bosnia and Herzegovina Investment, Trade Strategy and Agreements Handbook - Strategic Information and Basic Agreements
Botswana Investment, Trade Strategy and Agreements Handbook - Strategic Information and Basic Agreements
Brazil Investment, Trade Strategy and Agreements Handbook - Strategic Information and Basic Agreements
Brunei Darussalam Investment, Trade Strategy and Agreements Handbook - Strategic Information and Basic Agreements
Bulgaria Investment, Trade Strategy and Agreements Handbook - Strategic Information and Basic Agreements
Burkina Faso Investment, Trade Strategy and Agreements Handbook - Strategic Information and Basic Agreements
Burundi Investment, Trade Strategy and Agreements Handbook - Strategic Information and Basic Agreements
Cambodia Investment, Trade Strategy and Agreements Handbook - Strategic Information and Basic Agreements
Cameroon Investment, Trade Strategy and Agreements Handbook - Strategic Information and Basic Agreements
Canada Investment, Trade Strategy and Agreements Handbook - Strategic Information and Basic Agreements
Cape Verde Investment, Trade Strategy and Agreements Handbook - Strategic Information and Basic Agreements
Central African Republic Investment, Trade Strategy and Agreements Handbook - Strategic Information and Basic Agreements
Chad Investment, Trade Strategy and Agreements Handbook - Strategic Information and Basic Agreements
Chile Investment, Trade Strategy and Agreements Handbook - Strategic Information and Basic Agreements
China Investment, Trade Strategy and Agreements Handbook - Strategic Information and Basic Agreements
Colombia Investment, Trade Strategy and Agreements Handbook - Strategic Information and Basic Agreements
Comoros Investment, Trade Strategy and Agreements Handbook - Strategic Information and Basic Agreements
Congo Investment, Trade Strategy and Agreements Handbook - Strategic Information and Basic Agreements

TITLE
Congo, Democratic Republic of the Investment, Trade Strategy and Agreements Handbook - Strategic Information and Basic Agreements
Costa Rica Investment, Trade Strategy and Agreements Handbook - Strategic Information and Basic Agreements
Côte d'Ivoire Investment, Trade Strategy and Agreements Handbook - Strategic Information and Basic Agreements
Croatia Investment, Trade Strategy and Agreements Handbook - Strategic Information and Basic Agreements
Cuba Investment, Trade Strategy and Agreements Handbook - Strategic Information and Basic Agreements
Cyprus Investment, Trade Strategy and Agreements Handbook - Strategic Information and Basic Agreements
Czech Republic Investment, Trade Strategy and Agreements Handbook - Strategic Information and Basic Agreements
Denmark Investment, Trade Strategy and Agreements Handbook - Strategic Information and Basic Agreements
Djibouti Investment, Trade Strategy and Agreements Handbook - Strategic Information and Basic Agreements
Dominica Investment, Trade Strategy and Agreements Handbook - Strategic Information and Basic Agreements
Dominican Republic Investment, Trade Strategy and Agreements Handbook - Strategic Information and Basic Agreements
Ecuador Investment, Trade Strategy and Agreements Handbook - Strategic Information and Basic Agreements
Egypt Investment, Trade Strategy and Agreements Handbook - Strategic Information and Basic Agreements
El Salvador Investment, Trade Strategy and Agreements Handbook - Strategic Information and Basic Agreements
Equatorial Guinea Investment, Trade Strategy and Agreements Handbook - Strategic Information and Basic Agreements
Eritrea Investment, Trade Strategy and Agreements Handbook - Strategic Information and Basic Agreements
Estonia Investment, Trade Strategy and Agreements Handbook - Strategic Information and Basic Agreements
Ethiopia Investment, Trade Strategy and Agreements Handbook - Strategic Information and Basic Agreements
Finland Investment, Trade Strategy and Agreements Handbook - Strategic Information and Basic Agreements
France Investment, Trade Strategy and Agreements Handbook - Strategic Information and Basic Agreements
Gabon Investment, Trade Strategy and Agreements Handbook - Strategic Information and Basic Agreements
Gambia Investment, Trade Strategy and Agreements Handbook - Strategic Information and Basic Agreements
Georgia Investment, Trade Strategy and Agreements Handbook - Strategic Information and Basic Agreements
Germany Investment, Trade Strategy and Agreements Handbook - Strategic Information and Basic Agreements
Ghana Investment, Trade Strategy and Agreements Handbook - Strategic Information and Basic Agreements
Greece Investment, Trade Strategy and Agreements Handbook - Strategic Information and Basic Agreements
Grenada Investment, Trade Strategy and Agreements Handbook - Strategic Information and Basic Agreements
Guatemala Investment, Trade Strategy and Agreements Handbook - Strategic Information and Basic Agreements
Guinea Investment, Trade Strategy and Agreements Handbook - Strategic Information and Basic Agreements
Guinea-Bissau Investment, Trade Strategy and Agreements Handbook - Strategic Information and Basic Agreements
Guyana Investment, Trade Strategy and Agreements Handbook - Strategic Information and Basic Agreements
Haiti Investment, Trade Strategy and Agreements Handbook - Strategic Information and Basic Agreements
Honduras Investment, Trade Strategy and Agreements Handbook - Strategic Information and Basic Agreements
Hong Kong, China SAR Investment, Trade Strategy and Agreements Handbook - Strategic Information and Basic Agreements
Hungary Investment, Trade Strategy and Agreements Handbook - Strategic Information and Basic Agreements
Iceland Investment, Trade Strategy and Agreements Handbook - Strategic Information and Basic Agreements
India Investment, Trade Strategy and Agreements Handbook - Strategic Information and Basic Agreements
Indonesia Investment, Trade Strategy and Agreements Handbook - Strategic Information and Basic Agreements
Iran, Islamic Republic of Investment, Trade Strategy and Agreements Handbook - Strategic Information and Basic Agreements
Iraq Investment, Trade Strategy and Agreements Handbook - Strategic Information and Basic Agreements
Israel Investment, Trade Strategy and Agreements Handbook - Strategic Information and Basic Agreements
Italy Investment, Trade Strategy and Agreements Handbook - Strategic Information and Basic Agreements
Jamaica Investment, Trade Strategy and Agreements Handbook - Strategic Information and Basic Agreements
Japan Investment, Trade Strategy and Agreements Handbook - Strategic Information and Basic Agreements
Jordan Investment, Trade Strategy and Agreements Handbook - Strategic Information and Basic Agreements
Kazakhstan Investment, Trade Strategy and Agreements Handbook - Strategic Information and Basic Agreements
Kenya Investment, Trade Strategy and Agreements Handbook - Strategic Information and Basic Agreements
Korea, Dem. People's Rep. of Investment, Trade Strategy and Agreements Handbook - Strategic Information and Basic Agreements
Korea, Republic of Investment, Trade Strategy and Agreements Handbook - Strategic Information and Basic Agreements

TITLE
Kuwait Investment, Trade Strategy and Agreements Handbook - Strategic Information and Basic Agreements
Kyrgyzstan Investment, Trade Strategy and Agreements Handbook - Strategic Information and Basic Agreements
Lao People's Democratic Republic Investment, Trade Strategy and Agreements Handbook - Strategic Information and Basic Agreements
Latvia Investment, Trade Strategy and Agreements Handbook - Strategic Information and Basic Agreements
Lebanon Investment, Trade Strategy and Agreements Handbook - Strategic Information and Basic Agreements
Lesotho Investment, Trade Strategy and Agreements Handbook - Strategic Information and Basic Agreements
Liberia Investment, Trade Strategy and Agreements Handbook - Strategic Information and Basic Agreements
Libya Investment, Trade Strategy and Agreements Handbook - Strategic Information and Basic Agreements
Lithuania Investment, Trade Strategy and Agreements Handbook - Strategic Information and Basic Agreements
Luxembourg Investment, Trade Strategy and Agreements Handbook - Strategic Information and Basic Agreements
Macao, China SAR Investment, Trade Strategy and Agreements Handbook - Strategic Information and Basic Agreements
Macedonia, The former Yugoslav Republic of Investment, Trade Strategy and Agreements Handbook - Strategic Information and Basic Agreements
Madagascar Investment, Trade Strategy and Agreements Handbook - Strategic Information and Basic Agreements
Malawi Investment, Trade Strategy and Agreements Handbook - Strategic Information and Basic Agreements
Malaysia Investment, Trade Strategy and Agreements Handbook - Strategic Information and Basic Agreements
Mali Investment, Trade Strategy and Agreements Handbook - Strategic Information and Basic Agreements
Malta Investment, Trade Strategy and Agreements Handbook - Strategic Information and Basic Agreements
Marshall Islands Investment, Trade Strategy and Agreements Handbook - Strategic Information and Basic Agreements
Mauritania Investment, Trade Strategy and Agreements Handbook - Strategic Information and Basic Agreements
Mauritius Investment, Trade Strategy and Agreements Handbook - Strategic Information and Basic Agreements
Mexico Investment, Trade Strategy and Agreements Handbook - Strategic Information and Basic Agreements
Moldova, Republic of Investment, Trade Strategy and Agreements Handbook - Strategic Information and Basic Agreements
Mongolia Investment, Trade Strategy and Agreements Handbook - Strategic Information and Basic Agreements
Montenegro Investment, Trade Strategy and Agreements Handbook - Strategic Information and Basic Agreements
Morocco Investment, Trade Strategy and Agreements Handbook - Strategic Information and Basic Agreements
Mozambique Investment, Trade Strategy and Agreements Handbook - Strategic Information and Basic Agreements
Myanmar Investment, Trade Strategy and Agreements Handbook - Strategic Information and Basic Agreements
Namibia Investment, Trade Strategy and Agreements Handbook - Strategic Information and Basic Agreements
Nepal Investment, Trade Strategy and Agreements Handbook - Strategic Information and Basic Agreements
Netherlands Investment, Trade Strategy and Agreements Handbook - Strategic Information and Basic Agreements
New Zealand Investment, Trade Strategy and Agreements Handbook - Strategic Information and Basic Agreements
Nicaragua Investment, Trade Strategy and Agreements Handbook - Strategic Information and Basic Agreements
Niger Investment, Trade Strategy and Agreements Handbook - Strategic Information and Basic Agreements
Nigeria Investment, Trade Strategy and Agreements Handbook - Strategic Information and Basic Agreements
Norway Investment, Trade Strategy and Agreements Handbook - Strategic Information and Basic Agreements
Occupied Palestinian territory Investment, Trade Strategy and Agreements Handbook - Strategic Information and Basic Agreements
Oman Investment, Trade Strategy and Agreements Handbook - Strategic Information and Basic Agreements
Pakistan Investment, Trade Strategy and Agreements Handbook - Strategic Information and Basic Agreements
Panama Investment, Trade Strategy and Agreements Handbook - Strategic Information and Basic Agreements
Papua New Guinea Investment, Trade Strategy and Agreements Handbook - Strategic Information and Basic Agreements
Paraguay Investment, Trade Strategy and Agreements Handbook - Strategic Information and Basic Agreements
Peru Investment, Trade Strategy and Agreements Handbook - Strategic Information and Basic Agreements
Philippines Investment, Trade Strategy and Agreements Handbook - Strategic Information and Basic Agreements
Poland Investment, Trade Strategy and Agreements Handbook - Strategic Information and Basic Agreements
Portugal Investment, Trade Strategy and Agreements Handbook - Strategic Information and Basic Agreements
Qatar Investment, Trade Strategy and Agreements Handbook - Strategic Information and Basic Agreements
Romania Investment, Trade Strategy and Agreements Handbook - Strategic Information and Basic Agreements
Russian Federation Investment, Trade Strategy and Agreements Handbook - Strategic Information and Basic Agreements
Rwanda Investment, Trade Strategy and Agreements Handbook - Strategic Information and Basic Agreements
Saint Lucia Investment, Trade Strategy and Agreements Handbook - Strategic Information and Basic Agreements

TITLE
Saint Vincent and the Grenadines Investment, Trade Strategy and Agreements Handbook - Strategic Information and Basic Agreements
San Marino Investment, Trade Strategy and Agreements Handbook - Strategic Information and Basic Agreements
Sao Tome and Principe Investment, Trade Strategy and Agreements Handbook - Strategic Information and Basic Agreements
Saudi Arabia Investment, Trade Strategy and Agreements Handbook - Strategic Information and Basic Agreements
Senegal Investment, Trade Strategy and Agreements Handbook - Strategic Information and Basic Agreements
Serbia Investment, Trade Strategy and Agreements Handbook - Strategic Information and Basic Agreements
Seychelles Investment, Trade Strategy and Agreements Handbook - Strategic Information and Basic Agreements
Sierra Leone Investment, Trade Strategy and Agreements Handbook - Strategic Information and Basic Agreements
Singapore Investment, Trade Strategy and Agreements Handbook - Strategic Information and Basic Agreements
Slovakia Investment, Trade Strategy and Agreements Handbook - Strategic Information and Basic Agreements
Slovenia Investment, Trade Strategy and Agreements Handbook - Strategic Information and Basic Agreements
Somalia Investment, Trade Strategy and Agreements Handbook - Strategic Information and Basic Agreements
South Africa Investment, Trade Strategy and Agreements Handbook - Strategic Information and Basic Agreements
Spain Investment, Trade Strategy and Agreements Handbook - Strategic Information and Basic Agreements
Sri Lanka Investment, Trade Strategy and Agreements Handbook - Strategic Information and Basic Agreements
Sudan Investment, Trade Strategy and Agreements Handbook - Strategic Information and Basic Agreements
Suriname Investment, Trade Strategy and Agreements Handbook - Strategic Information and Basic Agreements
Swaziland Investment, Trade Strategy and Agreements Handbook - Strategic Information and Basic Agreements
Sweden Investment, Trade Strategy and Agreements Handbook - Strategic Information and Basic Agreements
Switzerland Investment, Trade Strategy and Agreements Handbook - Strategic Information and Basic Agreements
Syrian Arab Republic Investment, Trade Strategy and Agreements Handbook - Strategic Information and Basic Agreements
Taiwan Province of China Investment, Trade Strategy and Agreements Handbook - Strategic Information and Basic Agreements
Tajikistan Investment, Trade Strategy and Agreements Handbook - Strategic Information and Basic Agreements
Tanzania, United Republic of Investment, Trade Strategy and Agreements Handbook - Strategic Information and Basic Agreements
Thailand Investment, Trade Strategy and Agreements Handbook - Strategic Information and Basic Agreements
Timor-Leste Investment, Trade Strategy and Agreements Handbook - Strategic Information and Basic Agreements
Togo Investment, Trade Strategy and Agreements Handbook - Strategic Information and Basic Agreements
Tonga Investment, Trade Strategy and Agreements Handbook - Strategic Information and Basic Agreements
Trinidad and Tobago Investment, Trade Strategy and Agreements Handbook - Strategic Information and Basic Agreements
Tunisia Investment, Trade Strategy and Agreements Handbook - Strategic Information and Basic Agreements
Turkey Investment, Trade Strategy and Agreements Handbook - Strategic Information and Basic Agreements
Turkmenistan Investment, Trade Strategy and Agreements Handbook - Strategic Information and Basic Agreements
Uganda Investment, Trade Strategy and Agreements Handbook - Strategic Information and Basic Agreements
Ukraine Investment, Trade Strategy and Agreements Handbook - Strategic Information and Basic Agreements
United Arab Emirates Investment, Trade Strategy and Agreements Handbook - Strategic Information and Basic Agreements
United Kingdom Investment, Trade Strategy and Agreements Handbook - Strategic Information and Basic Agreements
United States of America Investment, Trade Strategy and Agreements Handbook - Strategic Information and Basic Agreements
Uruguay Investment, Trade Strategy and Agreements Handbook - Strategic Information and Basic Agreements
Uzbekistan Investment, Trade Strategy and Agreements Handbook - Strategic Information and Basic Agreements
Vanuatu Investment, Trade Strategy and Agreements Handbook - Strategic Information and Basic Agreements
Venezuela, Bolivarian Republic of Investment, Trade Strategy and Agreements Handbook - Strategic Information and Basic Agreements
Viet Nam Investment, Trade Strategy and Agreements Handbook - Strategic Information and Basic Agreements
Yemen Investment, Trade Strategy and Agreements Handbook - Strategic Information and Basic Agreements
Zambia Investment, Trade Strategy and Agreements Handbook - Strategic Information and Basic Agreements
Zimbabwe Investment, Trade Strategy and Agreements Handbook - Strategic Information and Basic Agreements
ACP (African, Caribbean and Pacific Group of States) Trade and Investment Agreements Handbook - Strategic

**For additional analytical, business and investment opportunities information,
please contact Global Investment & Business Center, USA
at (202) 546-2103. Fax: (202) 546-3275. E-mail: ibpusa3@gmail.com**

TITLE
Information and Basic Agreements
ANCOM (Andean Community) Trade and Investment Agreements Handbook - Strategic Information and Basic Agreements
ASEAN (Association of South-East Asian Nations) Trade and Investment Agreements Handbook - Strategic Information and Basic Agreements
AU (African Union) Trade and Investment Agreements Handbook - Strategic Information and Basic Agreements
BIMSTEC (Bay of Bengal Initiative for Multi-Sector Technical and Economic Cooperation) Trade and Investment Agreements Handbook - Strategic Information and Basic Agreements
BLEU (Belgium-Luxembourg Economic Union) Trade and Investment Agreements Handbook - Strategic Information and Basic Agreements
CACM (Central American Common Market) Trade and Investment Agreements Handbook - Strategic Information and Basic Agreements
CARICOM (Caribbean Community) Trade and Investment Agreements Handbook - Strategic Information and Basic Agreements
CEFTA (Central European Free Trade Agreement) Trade and Investment Agreements Handbook - Strategic Information and Basic Agreements
CEMAC (Economic and Monetary Community of Central Africa) Trade and Investment Agreements Handbook - Strategic Information and Basic Agreements
CEPGL (Economic Community of the Great Lakes Countries) Trade and Investment Agreements Handbook - Strategic Information and Basic Agreements
COMESA (Common Market for Eastern and Southern Africa) Trade and Investment Agreements Handbook - Strategic Information and Basic Agreements
EAC (East African Community) Trade and Investment Agreements Handbook - Strategic Information and Basic Agreements
ECCAS (Economic Community of Central African States) Trade and Investment Agreements Handbook - Strategic Information and Basic Agreements
ECO (Economic Cooperation Organization) Trade and Investment Agreements Handbook - Strategic Information and Basic Agreements
ECOWAS (Economic Community of West African States) Trade and Investment Agreements Handbook - Strategic Information and Basic Agreements
EFTA (European Free Trade Association) Trade and Investment Agreements Handbook - Strategic Information and Basic Agreements
Energy Charter Treaty members Trade and Investment Agreements Handbook - Strategic Information and Basic Agreements
ESA (Eastern and Southern Africa) Trade and Investment Agreements Handbook - Strategic Information and Basic Agreements
EU (European Union) Trade and Investment Agreements Handbook - Strategic Information and Basic Agreements
Eurasian Economic Union Trade and Investment Agreements Handbook - Strategic Information and Basic Agreements
Gulf Cooperation Council Trade and Investment Agreements Handbook - Strategic Information and Basic Agreements
Latin American Integration Association Trade and Investment Agreements Handbook - Strategic Information and Basic Agreements
League of Arab States Trade and Investment Agreements Handbook - Strategic Information and Basic Agreements
Mercado Común Sudamericano (MERCOSUR - Economic Community Consisting of Argentina, Brazil, Paraguay, and Urugua) Trade and Investment Agreements Handbook - Strategic Information and Basic Agreements
OCT (Overseas Countries and Territories) Trade and Investment Agreements Handbook - Strategic Information and Basic Agreements
Organization of the Islamic Conference Trade and Investment Agreements Handbook - Strategic Information and Basic Agreements
Southern African Customs Union Trade and Investment Agreements Handbook - Strategic Information and Basic Agreements
Southern African Development Community Trade and Investment Agreements Handbook - Strategic Information and Basic Agreements
South Asian Free Trade Area Accord Trade and Investment Agreements Handbook - Strategic Information and Basic Agreements
South Pacific Regional Trade and Economic Cooperation Agreement Trade and Investment Agreements Handbook - Strategic Information and Basic Agreements
Arab Maghreb Union Trade and Investment Agreements Handbook - Strategic Information and Basic Agreements
West African Economic and Monetary Union Trade and Investment Agreements Handbook - Strategic Information and

For additional analytical, business and investment opportunities information, please contact Global Investment & Business Center, USA at (202) 546-2103. Fax: (202) 546-3275. E-mail: ibpusa3@gmail.com

TITLE
Basic Agreements

www.ingramcontent.com/pod-product-compliance
Lightning Source LLC
Chambersburg PA
CBHW061354210326

41598CB00035B/5978